Teaching and Learning in Higher Education

Linda Evans and Ian Abbott

CASSELL
London and New York

Cassell

Wellington House	370 Lexington Avenue
125 Strand	New York
London WC2R 0BB	NY 10017-6550

www.cassell.co.uk

First published 1998

British Library Cataloguing-in-Publication Data
A catalogue record for this book is available from the British Library.

ISBN   0-304-70102-5 (paperback)

Typeset by BookEns Ltd, Royston, Herts.
Printed and bound in Great Britain by Redwood Books, Trowbridge, Wilts

TEACHING AND LEARNING
IN HIGHER EDUCATION

Related titles from Cassell:

Dennis Child: *Psychology and the Teacher, 6th edition*
L. B. Curzon: *Teaching in Further Education, 5th edition*
Roland Meighan and Iram Siraj-Blatchford: *A Sociology of Educating*
Robert Phillips: *History Teaching: Nationhood and the State*

Contents

Acknowledgements

We would like to thank our colleague, Ann Lewis, for her very helpful comments on earlier drafts of some of the material in this book. Thanks also to Sandra Dowse and Glyn Evans for the parts they have played in helping to put the manuscript together.

This book is dedicated to the late Dr Graham Stiles

Introduction

This book is set within the context of the changing face of higher education in the United Kingdom. It is a book about compromise: about making changes, moving forward and adapting to unfamiliar climates in ways which incorporate consideration of different perspectives. It develops ideas for improvement out of an understanding of the day-to-day realities of the environment which is its focus.

As higher education has shifted to centre stage in the wider arena of educational reform in the UK, teaching and learning have come under the spotlight. 'Innovation' has become the byword and there is a growing movement towards radical change in the ways in which knowledge, understanding and skills are passed on to students. There is no shortage of literature offering higher education teachers ideas for developing new approaches to course delivery, for enhancing students' learning experiences or for improving attainment. Redefinition of what teaching in higher education involves has become a key constituent of the reshaping process from which will emerge the new-look, post-Dearing university of the twenty-first century. It is against this background that our book is placed.

Yet our book is not simply another prescriptive text promoting innovatory teaching approaches. Indeed, we have misgivings about many of these books, and about the innovation bandwagon which both underlies them and is perpetuated by them. Our misgivings arise out of what are, essentially, epistemological concerns. The promotion of innovatory teaching in higher education does not, for the most part, appear to be supported by a sound academic rationale: a weakness resulting from the tendency for most of the specific examples of alternative methods to reflect imaginative ideas, personal preferences or prejudiced views about the best ways to teach higher education students, rather than empirical evidence of what students really want, and what they consider to be their main learning needs. Furthermore, many teaching suggestions are flawed because they fail to incorporate consideration of tutors' needs, particularly those arising out of the demands and pressures of their jobs in their entirety. They are, therefore, based on incomplete and, as a result, inaccurate knowledge of the context in which they are placed.

Our criticism of the innovative teaching bandwagon does not reflect disapproval of the kinds of teaching approaches which it promotes – as far as these are made explicit. We are by no means unreceptive to new ideas. Our concern is that they should be properly justified. We are, for example, perfectly comfortable with a rationale for the promotion of distance learning, or tutor-independent study methods, based on a need to cope with larger student–teacher ratios. What has often occurred, though, is that innovative approaches have been promoted, and adopted, with insufficient attention having been paid not merely to the rationale for them but to the underlying issues.

This book represents an attempt to present a more realistic, and realizable, picture of teaching and learning in twenty-first-century higher education in the UK. Based upon a qualitative study carried out in 1993–94, involving over fifty research interviews with higher education tutors and students, it highlights the needs both of the teachers and of the taught, and examines ways in which higher education might develop in order to meet these needs. Whilst accepting the impossibility of obtaining, even through research, an accurate contextual picture, we have tried, at least, to represent in our book and, in particular, to inject into our analyses something of the day-to-day reality of the business of teaching and learning in higher education.

The current agenda for change in higher education focuses on teaching quality. There is much talk of excellence in teaching, without, in most cases, any clearly justified explanations of precisely what this involves, and why. In the absence of agreed criteria for excellence, innovatory practice has been given prominence as the best way forward but, again, precisely what constitutes innovation is not always made explicit.

We believe that excellence in teaching involves achieving and maximizing effective teaching. Yet here, too, there is a problem because there is no consensus about what effective teaching in higher education involves. It may be argued that teaching in higher education is already effective, since most students successfully complete their courses, but this argument is dismissed by those who are keen to promote more 'deep' learning, which research has revealed to be under-represented as an approach to study, or by those who predict that current teaching will be ill-equipped for accommodating the diverse learning needs of the widening student population. Clearly, interpretations of effective teaching depend upon criteria for effectiveness which, in turn, will reflect conceptions of higher education and its purpose. However, it is not enough simply to argue that teaching methods need to become more effective, or to talk of excellence in teaching, without defining key terms or at least explaining what they mean. Too often references are made to 'effective' teaching which fail to make clear how 'effective' is to be interpreted: effective for whom, and at what? Yet, without proper analysis and clarification, it is impossible to make any serious attempt at addressing the really important issues underlying the debate about teaching and learning in higher education, such as: what are the criteria for effective teaching? how can these be met? what, if anything, needs to change? and, what is the best way of achieving any requisite change?

This book represents a rational examination of teaching and learning in higher education, both how it is and how it ought to be if it is to accommodate the needs and interests of students and their teachers. Reflecting our concern that prescribed policy and teaching methods should be formulated out of an analysis of what is needed, rather than being based on assumptions that change and innovation are long overdue, our empirical evidence calls into question the need for radically different approaches to be applied across the system as a whole, without reference to their purpose.

At a general level we adopt a wide interpretation of 'teaching and learning', employing it to refer to everything which is involved in the respective 'jobs' of being either a tutor or a student: to what Martin Trow (1997) identifies as 'the private life' of higher education – 'the life that is experienced in lecture hall and seminar, in a teacher's room or office, in libraries and laboratories'. We present images of this 'private life' in the chapters which follow. This is fundamentally a book of students and tutors talking, and it is this talking which provides the basis of the rationality underlying our examination.

Part I of the book presents the context within which are set the key issues being examined. Chapter 1 traces the background of reform within higher education which has put teaching and learning under the spotlight, and Chapter 2 provides details of the research upon which the book is based.

Part II presents the perspective of the students involved in our study. Chapter 3 examines students' views on the comparative usefulness and effectiveness of the different modes of course delivery which they most commonly experience, and Chapter 4 is concerned with their levels of involvement in, and commitment to, their courses, and the factors which influence these. Chapter 5 draws out students' study-related needs, as they themselves perceive them, and develops a model of study-related needs and preferences and course-related influences on their satisfaction.

Part III is tutor-focused. The nature of higher education tutors' work is described in Chapter 6, which also analyses the literature on what influences academics' attitudes to their work: in particular, their job satisfaction and morale, and what this reveals about their job-related needs. Chapter 7 looks at what the academics in our study want from their work, and why, and examines the extent to which they achieve what they want, what prevents them from, and assists them in, achieving it and what they need in order to enhance their job satisfaction. It reveals what aspects of their work tutors find fulfilling, and what are identified as sources of dissatisfaction. Chapter 8 focuses more narrowly on tutors' roles as teachers, describing different attitudes towards, and levels of commitment to, this component of their work and how these attitudes are reflected in preferred teaching methods. Chapter 9 consolidates the material in the preceding three chapters. It highlights academics' needs through the model of the job-fulfilment process which is presented, and which was developed from our research findings.

Chapter 10 is the only chapter in Part IV. Here, the focus is on the implications of our research findings for policy development and practical application. This final chapter discusses various ways in which teaching and learning in higher education may be developed in order to represent compromise, by contributing towards meeting the needs of students and of tutors. It suggests specific policy and ideas which are likely to be acceptable to both parties. It sketches out images of teaching and learning in higher education which offer something for everyone.

Part I

Background

Chapter 1

Teaching and Learning in Higher Education: The Context

INTRODUCTION

In common with all sectors of education in the United Kingdom during the 1990s, higher education has undergone a period of rapid change. Many of these changes have been the result of central government policies designed to increase student numbers, obtain better value for money and improve accountability through the imposition of a range of quality-control mechanisms.

The entire system was radically reformed by the removal in 1992 of the binary divide between universities and polytechnics, by an unprecedented growth in student numbers, by changes to the funding mechanism and by an obsession with quality control measured by external assessors. As a consequence, the tranquil world of higher education has been forced to embrace characteristics of a market philosophy which has been accepted by both of the main political parties and become a feature of British society in the late twentieth century. Acceptance of these changes has been universal because central government has retained and strengthened control of the funding mechanism. The adoption of a more explicit market ethos has come to dominate working conditions, academic activities and the very character of higher education. Resistance to these changes has been limited and largely unsuccessful. This implementation of wide-ranging reform in higher education has had a profound impact on life in the universities.

A significant feature of this reform has been the increasing importance placed on the development of high-quality and innovative teaching and learning strategies. Tutors are being encouraged to review their approaches to teaching and to adopt a range of methods designed to increase student motivation and participation, and improve learning. In the chapters which follow we consider the views of our sample of students and tutors on the range and impact of the teaching methods of which they have experience, and in the final chapter we suggest a number of policies aimed at satisfying the needs of both parties. However, before we begin that process we need to look at the wider context in which universities operate and at the nature of the reforms which have taken place. This will foster a greater understanding of the policies which have already been implemented and of the impact they have had on students' and tutors' working lives. The purpose of this chapter, therefore, is to consider the background, development and substance of the reforms which have taken place and their impact on teaching in universities, on tutors' work and on the particular university in our study.

REFORM OF THE SYSTEM

The Dearing Review, culminating in the Dearing Report (NCIHE, 1997), has undertaken the most far-reaching examination of the purpose, organization, control and funding of higher education for thirty-five years, since the Robbins Report of 1963. The recommendations of the 1997 report are likely to increase the pace of change and lead to fundamental developments in a number of areas. However, the policies which had already been implemented, prior to Dearing, have impacted upon all aspects of university life. Griffin (1997) sums up the nature of the changes effected by the earlier reforms, describing a picture which is familiar to members of the academic community:

> Higher education in the United Kingdom is in crisis. Few would disagree, although different voices would identify different crises. The crisis in funding resulting from the provision of a mass system to meet demand for access is self-evident, as the government reduces its financial support to higher education. A Robbins-style committee of inquiry into the future of higher education under the chairmanship of Sir Ron Dearing is currently reporting on its 'shape, structure, size and funding' to meet the needs of the next twenty years.
>
> Then, more students with increasingly varied backgrounds and attainments, have precipitated a crisis in how the teaching and learning process should be both conceived and managed, mass enrolment having coincided with both a reduction in staff and a heavier teaching and administrative workload for academics. At the same time the latter on tighter, less often permanent contracts are pressured to publish scholarly work regularly, so that their institutions may gain high ratings in the cynical national research assessment exercises. To these escalating pressures have to be added the widespread perception of higher education staff that the academic community is itself under threat in that collegiality is being lost as institutions are more firmly managed along business lines. Universities have become organisations adopting a more explicit market ethos which dominates working conditions, academic activities and the very character of higher education. (Griffin, 1997, pp. 2–3)

At the core of these changes has been the government's wish to increase the take-up of university education by people representing a broad spectrum of the population. This upsurge in demand for university places has had a dramatic effect on all aspects of higher education.

Increasing student numbers

The origins of the attempts by central government to increase the opportunities for people to obtain a university education can be traced back to the major reforms introduced as a result of the Robbins Report (1963). This report paved the way for the mass expansion of higher education with the granting of university status to a number of Colleges of Advanced Technology and the opening of new universities. This process was continued by the announcement by Anthony Crosland in 1965 of the continued expansion of polytechnics and colleges offering vocational and practical courses under local education authority control and the creation of the Open University in 1969. The major aim of these policy initiatives was to increase the number of young people attending university. In the prewar period approximately 3 per cent of the eligible age group attended Oxbridge or the metropolitan universities which had been established in the nineteenth century. By the time of the publication of the Robbins Report this figure had increased to 7 per cent. The postwar baby boom, rising living standards and a growing middle class further increased the demand for higher-education places. Yet, despite a steady growth in student numbers, only a small minority of the population actually obtained places at university, and by the end of the 1970s the number of full and part-time students was still only 12.7 per cent of the relevant age group, drawn predominately from the middle class (Ainley, 1994, p. 12).

Despite the growth in the number of higher-education institutions and the subsequent rise in student numbers, by the end of the 1970s the system continued to retain many of the features of the pre-Robbins era. In particular, funding continued at relatively generous levels with little external control. Universities were still allowed a huge amount of autonomy, through their Royal Charters, to control their internal affairs with minimal outside interference and they were able to set their own standards, against which they judged their own quality. Academic tenure provided staff with a safety-net which enabled them to operate with a great deal of independence. However, the election of a Conservative government in 1979 was eventually to bring about massive changes in higher education.

Initially, higher education was not identified as a major priority area of the Thatcher government. Despite a recognition of the need to increase greatly the participation rates of 18-year-olds in higher education, the figure had risen only to 15 per cent by 1988 (Alderman, 1996, p. 183). Numbers actually fell at one point in the early 1980s owing to financial cutbacks, yet the late 1980s saw a realization by the government of the need for increased entry into higher education. Underpinning this process has been the belief that an increase in the number of young people entering higher education would lead to a more educated workforce and, ultimately, to greater prosperity for the nation through improved economic performance. As a consequence, there was a commitment to a target of approximately one-third of the relevant age group obtaining university places, and this effected a rapid growth of student numbers (see Table 1.1). Participation rates rose accordingly, and higher

Table 1.1   Full- and part-time students in higher education institutions in the UK

	1988	1992	1996
Postgraduate	134,000	211,600	352,079
Undergraduate	502,600	769,200	1,346,203
Total	636,600	980,800	1,698,282

Source: 1988 and 1992 figures: Parry (1997); 1996 figures: HESA (1997)

education in the United Kingdom shifted from being restricted to an elite to being accessible to a much larger segment of the population.

In a relatively short period the government had created a system of mass university education. Not only have student numbers now increased but the background of entrants to higher education has also radically altered. A greater proportion of mature students and people with a range of alternative qualifications and experience are now entering degree programmes. Nevertheless, only 10 per cent of young people whose parents are unskilled and on low incomes actually enter higher education, compared to 80 per cent from a professional background (Carvel, 1997, p. 4). This overall growth is all the more remarkable, given the pressure to force down costs and given the greater financial constraints which had been imposed on universities. The large-scale increase of student numbers was an integral part of the desire to create the conditions necessary for increased flexibility in higher education. Allowing student intakes to rise at a time of severe financial constraint would inevitably impact upon the culture within higher education institutions, and, in particular, impose changes to ways of working and to teaching methods. At the same time, increased emphasis has been placed on quality assurance as universities have been forced to become more accountable to the government through their funding bodies. As a direct result of these pressures, much greater attention is being directed at the teaching and learning methods employed in higher education and at the function and purpose of the research carried out. 'Quality' and 'standards' have become the key words in higher education in the UK as universities have begun to face up, however reluctantly, to the realities of reform.

Centralization and quality control

The problems created for institutions by rising student intakes and greater accountability were exacerbated by the drive for greater central control of the university system which had been incorporated in the 1988 Education Reform Act and, more significantly, in the 1992 Further and Higher Education Act, which established the Higher Education Funding Councils for England (HEFCE), Scotland (SHEFC) and Wales (HEFCW). The creation of these funding councils linked central government funding to student numbers and was a major factor in the continued growth of participation rates. Other aspects of the imposition of greater central control and accountability, which were features of this period, included the abolition of tenure for academic staff in 1988, the establishment of 'inspections' by the funding councils and the removal of the binary divide between polytechnics and universities.

At the same time as increased central control was being imposed, the government was putting pressure on the universities 'to treat university education as a marketable product' (Johnson, 1994, p. 375) by encouraging competition between institutions and greater choice for students, who were represented in more clearly defined 'consumer' roles. The polytechnics, for example, had long campaigned for university status, believing that the creation of a 'level playing-field' would enable them to compete more effectively in the education market-place. However, in some cases, existing distinctions between universities were exaggerated by the removal of the binary divide, as some of the former polytechnics were still perceived as being second-class institutions because of their relatively poor research record. The apparent paradox of creating market conditions at the same time as imposing greater centralized control was evident in other aspects of education policy and was part of a concerted campaign by the government to change radically the entire system.

The marketization of university education, allied to the movement from an elite to a mass system, has led to continued government pressure on universities to maintain quality. The introduction of mechanisms designed to measure standards across all higher-education institutions in areas such as teaching and research has ensured that the government has put in place a number of external controls. As a consequence, more emphasis was placed on applied research, collegiality was reduced and pressure to raise standards was linked to funding. Quality control was at the heart of these developments and a range of procedures was introduced in an attempt to measure quality.

Before the abolition of the binary divide the polytechnics had a well-developed system of quality control through the standards imposed by the Council of National Academic Awards (CNAA) and a system of inspection through Her Majesty's Inspectorate (HMI). The old universities were allowed to operate independently without outside interference, controlled by their senates. Granting university status to the polytechnics provided the opportunity for the establishment of a centralized funding and control body. The conditions necessary for imposing an external system of quality control were now in place. The Higher Education Funding Councils established teams of inspectors who would visit institutions, carry out inspections on the quality of teaching and award grades. The grades awarded would be linked to future funding arrangements. Considering the new universities' former quality control mechanisms, which had been in place for a number of years, it is surprising that the old universities outperformed their newer counterparts in the formal assessment of teaching quality. Despite a national average of only one department in five being awarded an excellent grading, the old university upon which our study focuses, for example, had by June 1997 achieved excellent ratings in eleven out of the thirteen departments assessed.

A similar process was initiated with regard to research. The research selectivity exercises again linked perceived performance to a grading system which determined the funding received by the department. The process involves external assessors looking at the overall research profile of the department. The research carried out by individual members of staff is an integral part of this process, and increased pressure has been placed on academics to obtain external funding and to increase their published output, since higher ratings for individual departments result in additional funding. Considering the more established research reputations of the majority of staff in the old universities it is not surprising that their departments have received higher ratings, on average, than those obtained by the new universities. The higher funding levels which they achieved as a consequence have enabled them to retain their relative superiority, in relation to research, over the former polytechnics.

Towards a 'learning society'

The process of reform of higher education in the UK has culminated in the establishment of the National Committee of Inquiry into Higher Education (NCIHE), generally referred to as the 'Dearing Review'. The Committee's Report contains significant proposals for the transformation of all aspects of higher education including funding, management and student access (NCIHE, 1997). Its specific recommendations are, to a large extent, a continuation and extension of the major features of reform which we have identified. In particular, emphasis was placed on quality, standards and increasing student participation rates in higher education:

> Over the next 20 years, we see higher education gaining in strength through the pursuit of quality and a commitment to standards. Central to our vision of the future is a judgement that the United Kingdom (UK) will need to develop as a learning society. In that learning society, higher education will make a distinctive contribution through teaching at its highest level, the pursuit of scholarship and research, and increasingly through its contribution to lifelong learning. National need and demand from students will require a resumed expansion of student numbers, young and mature, full-time and part-time. But over the next decade, higher education will face challenges as well as opportunities. The effectiveness of its responses to these, and its commitment to quality and standards, will shape its future. (NCIHE, 1997, p. 7, para. 1.3)

Weaving together the two main strands of policy development which run through the higher-education reform programme – increased participation rates and improving quality of provision – the Dearing Report recommends the provision of opportunities for lifelong learning through the development of a learning society. The focus on developing a learning society reflects a stakeholder economy ideology and is ostensibly a fundamental shift from the economic imperative for a more skilled workforce which was the driving force behind the expansion of higher education in the 1980s. However, we believe that the rhetoric relating to creating a learning society is likely to be much more impressive than the reality of its implementation. In practice, economic considerations seem certain to continue to have a profound impact on the way in which higher education develops in the twenty-first century and, whilst the terminology employed to justify the continued expansion in higher education may be increasingly more palatable, the underlying economic rationale will remain unchanged, allowing pressures on academic staff to increase.

THE IMPACT OF THE REFORMS ON ACADEMICS' WORK

The ranking of universities according to their research records, to which we referred earlier, is bound to have an impact on their overall profiles. Those enjoying a high ranking will find it easier to attract leading researchers on to their staff and may devote more of their resources to research across a wide spectrum. At the other extreme, some universities may find themselves concentrating on teaching, with research being squeezed to the margins and based specifically around curriculum areas. These developments are likely to have a profound effect on academic staff's attitudes to their work, and will impact upon the nature of their jobs.

However, it has long been widely – though by no means universally – accepted in British higher education that there is a link between teaching and research, and great emphasis has been placed, within individual institutions, not only on the need to raise the institution's research profile, as reflected by its research rating, but also to maintain and improve teaching quality. As we illustrate in Chapter 6, academic staff are, certainly for the present, expected to be researchers, teachers and administrators. Yet the possibility cannot be ruled out that, as the quality-control mechanisms impose greater pressures on universities and their staff, jobs may be redefined. It is not too difficult to imagine a situation in which a new university with a low research rating might give up the unequal struggle and concentrate solely on teaching.

The loss of research opportunities for individuals, departments and even, in extreme cases, entire institutions is one possible outcome of the introduction of the various quality-control mechanisms. These external pressures have also seriously undermined academic professional autonomy. Their potential impact has not been restricted to the new universities, and anecdotal evidence suggests that they are greatly resented by many academics, especially in the old universities, for reasons which Johnson (1994) summarizes:

> What is not possible without irreparable damage to the relationships at stake in a good university education (and the same is true also of schools) is the general application of bureaucratic procedures which purport to shape and measure how all the individuals concerned teach and engage in the pursuit of knowledge. Yet it is a model of this kind that inspires the stream of 'assessment' procedures with which universities are now afflicted, all of which add to the 'red tape' cutting in on time available for the real work of academics. It no longer matters how well an academic teaches and whether he or she sometimes inspires their pupils; it is far more important that they have produced plans of their courses, bibliographies, outlines of this, that and the other, in short all the paraphernalia of futile bureaucratization, required for assessors who come from on high like emissaries from Kafka's castle. (Johnson, 1994, p. 379)

External constraints focusing on measurement of performance and greater accountability and the rapid expansion of the number of entrants into undergraduate programmes have imposed severe pressures on academics, who have seen a major alteration of their working lives and conditions of service. The most significant work on the effects on academics' working lives of the evolution of higher education has been carried out by Halsey, who in three major studies has chronicled the changing face of academia (Halsey and Trow, 1971; Halsey, 1979; Halsey, 1995). He identifies the evolving nature of higher education and, in particular, the financial constraints imposed by central government which have had significant consequences for academic staff:

> First, and never to be forgotten, we have at last seen the emergence of the basis for a genuine mass higher education system. Thus is an ancient educational dream realized. But, in the same process, and under the pressure of the two trends, we have seen the introduction of powerful managerial pressures from the centre as the two sides of the divide have converged. Pressure from above, of course, always meets cultural resistance. The commitment of academic professions to what Martin Trow has always called a private life of teaching and research is more stubbornly resistant than the public shape of the system, i.e. its formal governance and relations to government.
>
> What is perhaps least appreciated (and did not for me fully emerge until I had read hundreds of comments from the respondents to the 1989 survey) was that the rhetoric of business models and market relations – the language of customers, competition, efficiency gains, 'value for money', etc. – could be so totally substituted for relations of trust. To put it bluntly, academics were invited to believe that an impoverishment of the staff–student ratio could be counted as an efficiency gain: and some, like Douglas Hague, believed it. Others of us remain or indeed become increasingly sceptical of the capacity of the government through the Funding Council either to measure teaching or research efficiency or to do substantive justice through centralized control of the minutiae of the private teaching and research life of universities, their faculties, and their departments. (Halsey, 1995, p. 305)

The reforms designed to increase quality and accountability and the creation of a mass system of higher education have imposed heavier workloads on individual members of staff. A survey by the Association of University Teachers (AUT) has claimed that the average hours worked per week by British academics have increased from 40.5 in 1962 to 54.8 in 1994 (Court, 1996, p. 255). The overall quality and quantity of teaching and research have come under external scrutiny through the operation of the Funding Councils, and there has been an increase in academics' accountability. This, and the greater external control exercised, indirectly, on their working lives has resulted in what is often described as the proletarianization of the profession. Ramsden (1992) outlines the nature of the changes to academics' work:

> It is little exaggeration to say that these changes, taken together, mean that the average university or polytechnic teacher is now expected to be an excellent teacher: a man or woman who can expertly redesign courses and methods of teaching to suit different groups of students, deal with large mixed-ability classes, and juggle new administrative demands, while at the same time carrying a heavy research responsibility and showing

accountability to a variety of masters as both a teacher and a scholar. How are we to adapt to this changed environment? (Ramsden, 1992, p. 2)

One way in which many universities have decided to tackle the challenges posed by this changed environment is to initiate mechanisms for developing the skills and expertise of their staff in ways which equip them better to undertake the demands of new roles and ways of working. The reforms to the higher-education system which we have outlined above were, therefore, followed by a steady growth in the provision of institutional staff development.

STAFF DEVELOPMENT IN HIGHER EDUCATION

Most institutions have taken on board the need for staff development and have established dedicated units. There is now, in higher education, a large industry involving an increasing number of full-time staff trainers who have responsibility for improving tutors' performance in various areas of their work. In particular, emphasis has been placed on developing and promoting new teaching approaches.

Developing teaching

Developments in teaching in higher education have reflected the need to address three specific features of the post-reform system: more students, greater diversity amongst students and increased demands on tutors' time.

Rising student numbers at a time of financial constraint have prompted institutions to reconsider how particular courses are staffed and delivered. Between 1976 and 1997 funding levels per student have fallen by 40 per cent (Carvel, 1997, p. 4). In this financial climate employing additional staff to cope with extra students was generally not a viable option for university managers. The impact of more students entering the system has therefore tended to manifest itself as a deterioration of circumstances, either in increases to teaching group sizes or in heavier teaching loads for tutors.

In addition, the backgrounds and entry qualifications of the students who are entering higher education are changing. There has been, for example, in recent years, a larger proportion of mature students and an upsurge in the number of applicants with General National Vocational Qualifications (GNVQs) rather than A levels. Generally, students who enter higher education through this route have different expectations about the type of teaching and support they will receive. Within GNVQ courses much greater emphasis is being placed on active learning approaches, with teachers providing individual assistance to students (Abbott, 1997; Further Education Development Agency, 1997, pp. 27–9). Tutors in higher education are, therefore, having not only to teach larger groups but also to cater for diverse backgrounds, expectations and ability and attainment levels.

Moreover, the increasing demands have not been compensated for by a reduction in other aspects of tutors' work. Indeed, as we have identified earlier in this chapter, expectations in relation to individuals' research output have risen and administrative burdens have become heavier. From the tutors' perspective, then, the main problems which have been created as a result of the reforms of the higher-education system are how to cope with increased, and often changed, responsibilities, with no more and, in some cases, less time available to do so, whilst also sustaining or developing a respectable research output. These problems are exacerbated by the fact that, in most cases, academic staff are appointed to lecturing posts with little or no training in teaching methods, although there is growing pressure for mandatory training qualifications (Utley, 1997a). The response of many universities has been to jump onto the staff development bandwagon; in the absence of any standard qualifications structure, many individual institutions have devised their own training programmes. Most recently, the Dearing Report has recommended the establishment of an Institute for Learning and Teaching in Higher Education to 'accredit programmes of training for higher education teachers; to commission research and development in learning and teaching practices; and to stimulate innovation' (NCIHE, 1997, p. 371).

Another aspect of the post-reform staff development industry has been the proliferation of training and self-help books and manuals, prescribing ways of improving teaching. Much of this published material is designed to improve the skills of tutors in specific areas such as lecturing, small-group work, assessment methods and teaching large groups (see, for example, Gibbs and Jenkins, 1992; Gibbs, 1992a; Drew and Bingham, 1997). Many of these publications convey a pervasive message which is imbued with a strong bias towards active-learning approaches at the expense of the more traditional methods found in higher education and especially manifested in lectures (see, for example, Gibbs, 1995a; Ashcroft and Foreman-Peck, 1994). The most popular 'buzz' words and key terms are: 'active-learning', 'student-centred', 'experiential' and 'tutor-independent'.

Innovation in teaching and learning: seeking a rationale

The greater prominence now being given to staff development in higher education can, in part, be attributed to increased scrutiny of teaching by the respective funding bodies. Institutions have been concerned about improving their teaching rating, and it is difficult to imagine that the level of resources devoted to this area would have been made available without some external pressure. As a consequence, staff development units have become an integral part of many universities' drive to raise teaching standards.

The promotion of innovative teaching methods has been a key component in this process. In some instances, though, there has been no clear justification for the adoption of alternative teaching strategies, and there often appears to be an element of informed guesswork underlying the methods proposed and the conclusions reached. In these circumstances it is difficult to disagree with the view put forward by Ramsden (1992, p. 11) that many newly introduced teaching and learning strategies have been 'based on naive theories of learning and ignore the down-to-earth reality of good teaching'. However, there are exceptions to this. Some work, for example, has been based on the need to foster 'deep' approaches to learning, which are characterized by approaching a task for its own sake so that an optimum amount of understanding is obtained, as opposed to a 'surface' approach in which no real understanding has taken place and the learner creates an impression of learning to complete a particular task (see, for example, Gibbs, 1995a; Chalmers and Fuller, 1996).

The failure to develop a clear rationale for the introduction of alternative approaches to teaching and learning in higher education can be partly explained by recognizing that a significant amount of the published material in this area has not been based upon the findings of empirical research. As a consequence, any interpretation of the needs of students and tutors is relegated to the status of being anecdotal and/or impressionistic. In addition, the emphasis on what it is believed students want, or need, from higher education has meant that many of the teaching materials do not fully take account of what tutors' needs may be, and, in particular, of their changed circumstances. In the current climate of pressure and accountability there is a need to accommodate both parties' needs, and staff development programmes have to give tutors guidance in developing teaching strategies which are time-saving, cost-effective and of high quality, as well as providing the means to improve student learning, participation and motivation. Developed from analysis of our research findings, specific suggestions for staff development in universities are included in the final chapter of this book.

A WIDER PERSPECTIVE

As we have outlined throughout this chapter, the structure and culture of higher education have been dramatically altered by imposed reforms. Greater external control and accountability are now recognized by academic staff as an integral part of university life. As a consequence, the pressure on academics to fulfil a variety of functions has increased, and their research, teaching and administrative loads have all altered accordingly. At the core of these changes is the impact of the reform of higher education on the conditions under which teaching and learning take place. Yet, despite this impact, teaching and learning in higher education have remained fairly resistant to the changing conditions. As Utley (1997b) points out:

> Many lecturers are refusing to budge in the face of pressure to step down from the podium and embrace innovative teaching methods that hand authority back to the student.

There appears to be widespread acceptance of the need for them to change, but a lack of agreement about the form that any change should take:

> Nearly everyone from the medievalists to the medics agrees that university teaching methods have got to change. Rapidly and Radically.

But there the consensus ends. Should the lecture be abandoned? Is technology really a substitute for talking? How is real learning best achieved? And how can lecturers find out whether what they do every day actually works? (Utley, 1997c)

This book, through coherent analysis of the findings of pertinent research and of the key issues involved, makes a contribution towards reaching agreement about the form that developments in teaching and learning in higher education should take.

Chapter 2

The Research

INTRODUCTION

The research upon which this book is based originated from recognition of the need to explore different ways in which universities can provide high-quality teaching which is cost-effective, not only in financial terms, but in relation to tutors' time and consideration of factors which may influence their job satisfaction. That such teaching should also be acceptable to students is implicit in our describing it as 'high-quality'.

To the best of our knowledge, which is based upon an extensive literature review, no other research in this field incorporates the perspectives of both tutors and students. There is no shortage of literature on the subject of teaching in higher education which is prescriptive in nature, identifying criteria for and characteristics of teaching which is considered effective in maximizing student learning and achievement. However, the extent to which this has drawn upon pertinent research is not always explicit, and many texts seem to be based upon opinion informed by first-hand experience, rather than empirical study. As experienced and successful higher-education teachers we, too, had many ideas upon which prescriptions for academically effective and cost-effective teaching could be based, but we wanted to have a rather more certain (to the extent that this is achievable) than speculative basis for our suggestions. We wanted empirical evidence, and our research was the means of obtaining it. This chapter presents an outline of our research design.

THE RESEARCH DESIGN

Specific aims and objectives

The main aim of our study was: to acquire greater understanding of how teaching in higher education may be effective in meeting what both students and tutors perceive as their needs. Within this main aim we identified four specific objectives:

1.   to identify students' perceptions of course content, assessment and teaching; to compare their realistic expectations with perceived experiences; to solicit their views on ways in which course delivery might, if at all, be better matched to their requirements
2.   to identify tutors' perceptions of the appropriateness of course content, assessment and teaching methods in terms of meeting students' needs
3.   to identify tutors' perceptions of the appropriateness of the expenditure of time which their teaching requires; the extent to which it constrains or enables them in relation to meeting the requirements of other aspects of their work
4.   to identify the degree of congruence between tutors' and students' perceptions of effective teaching and to develop strategies for improvement.

Conceptual framework

The conceptual basis of our study was the fulfilment of individuals' personal needs as a crucial determinant of their perceptions, attitudes and behaviour: we examine this in more depth when presenting our findings in Chapters 5 and 9. Elaborated and contextualized, this conceptual basis translated into a conceptual framework which incorporates identifying, first, tutors' personal job-related needs and students' personal study-related needs, and, second, the degree of congruence between both sets of needs.

The organizational strategies which tutors apply to their teaching, for example, are devised and selected with a view to fulfilling their personal, job-related needs. These needs, in turn, reflect values held and will, therefore, vary from individual to individual; but they will incorporate perspectives on issues such as student needs, course requirements, institutional/departmental requirements, career ambitions, and role conflict and ambiguity. These may be variously constraining or enabling in terms of the fulfilment of personal needs. Moreover, individuals' personal needs will not necessarily remain static, but will alter as their priorities change and as different constraints present themselves, are dealt with or are overcome. Similarly, students' perceptions of the teaching which they receive will be influenced by individual personal needs, reflecting values held and incorporating consideration of issues such as course requirements, their own expectations, future career ambitions and interpersonal relations. Within this conceptual framework, the key to identifying university teaching which is effective in meeting both tutors' and students' needs lies in exploring the degree of congruence between tutors' and students' perceptions.

Research questions

Our study was designed to seek answers to the following research questions, which emerged out of the conceptual framework:

1.   What are (*a*) students' and (*b*) tutors' perceptions of students' needs, requirements and preferences in relation to their courses, and how effectively do they consider that these are being met or satisfied?
2.   What are (*a*) students' and (*b*) tutors' perceptions of the implications of perceived course effectiveness, and what, if any, remedial measures do they suggest?
3.   What degree of congruence exists between students' and tutors' perceptions of effective teaching?
4.   What range of organizational strategies in relation to their teaching do tutors employ? What factors influence their choice? To what extent do these enable or constrain them in their work? How does this affect their job satisfaction and morale?
5.   In relation to 1, 2, 3 and 4, what differences, if any, are identifiable between (*a*) subject departments, (*b*) the student sample, (*c*) the tutor sample, and what factors account for these differences?
6.   Is it possible to identify features of teaching which contribute towards making it effective for both students and tutors?

Methodology

The study sought answers to the research questions listed above by means of semi-structured interviews with twenty tutors and thirty-six students from an old university which is recognized for its strong research focus.

Sampling

Our sample of tutors and students represents four different degree courses: English and American studies, physics, law and education. By this sampling, an arts course, a science course and two courses which, to different degrees, may be considered to be vocational were represented. Within these four different subjects sample sizes were broadly proportionate to the numbers of tutors and students who were involved in the second-year course and were, specifically, as shown in Table 2.1.

Table 2.1   Composition of sample

	Tutors			Students		
	Male	*Female*	*Total*	*Male*	*Female*	*Total*
English and American studies	1	2	3	1	6	7
Physics	3	1	4	7	2	9
Law	3	2	5	3	7	10
Education	3	5	8	3	7	10

PROCEDURES FOR OBTAINING STUDENT SAMPLE

The student sample was confined to second-year students, since they would have sufficient experience of being students and of their institution, their departments and their courses to make informed evaluative comments. They were also unconstrained by the pressures of final-year assessment and were therefore likely to be more available for, and amenable to, interview. Our sampling of students was based upon that employed by Ramsden and Entwistle (1981), whose study involved second-year students of six different subjects.

Access was requested first from the university's administration and then from the heads of the four departments who ran the degree courses upon which our study focused. We were then, in the case of each department, referred to a tutor whom the head of department nominated to liaise with us. Our nominated link tutors suggested appropriate means of contacting student interviewees. These differed between the four departments. Law students were approached by means of letters in their pigeonholes (see Appendix for a copy of the letter and attached pro-forma). An initial trawl of letters to students selected randomly from a course list yielded quite a good response, but second and third trawls, to different students, were required before we achieved the required sample. In the cases of the other three courses we were granted five-minute slots at the beginning or end of group teaching sessions to outline the nature of our research and to appeal for interviewee volunteers. We felt that this approach would have personal appeal and would serve to introduce ourselves to students to whom we were not known and, thus, might yield a good response. This was not the case, however, and the small number of students who came forward in response to our personal appeal had to be augmented, in all three subject samples, by intervention in the form of follow-up pleas from the course tutors.

Clearly this method of sample selection is far from ideal, and the methodological weaknesses which emanate from it constitute significant limitations, which we acknowledge. The sample of students was largely confined to those who ranged from being reasonably to very conscientious and reasonably to very motivated. Many of the students whose participation we were eventually able to procure suggested that the lack of success of our earlier attempts to secure volunteers did not reflect students' hostility to, or even lack of interest in, our research, but resulted from assumptions that others would volunteer. The more disaffected, unenthusiastic or uninterested student minority was not represented because such students are unlikely to bother responding to requests to participate. We tried to ensure propor-tionate representativeness in relation to gender and ethnicity, and accept that a more representative sample could probably have been achieved by paying students for their participation; but, though ours was a funded study, its budget was inadequate for incorporating such measures.

PROCEDURES FOR OBTAINING TUTOR SAMPLE
In the case of the tutor sample, we tried to ensure proportionate representativeness in relation to seniority and length of service at this university and in relation to reputed research or teaching orientation. Tutors were selected by us, based upon discussions with, and suggestions from, their departmental colleagues with whom we liaised over our research. All whom

we approached agreed to participate. Though it does not necessarily reflect proportionately the distribution amongst the full group which the sample represented, we were also anxious for our sample to include representatives of minority sub-groups such as professors, women professors, women physics tutors and part-time bought-in staff. Sample breakdown details in relation to gender and seniority are provided in Table 2.2.

Table 2.2 Tutor sample breakdown

	Female			
	Lecturer	*Senior lecturer*	*Reader*	*Professor*
English and American studies		1		
Physics	1			
Law	1			1
Education	4*	1		

	Male			
	Lecturer	*Senior lecturer*	*Reader*	*Professor*
English and American studies	2			
Physics	1	2		
Law	2	1		
Education	2*			1

* The sub-sample of education tutors includes two bought-in, part-time tutors. Bought-in tutors represented a sizeable minority of the education teaching staff. They were, typically, seconded, early retired or part-time schoolteachers or LEA advisory teachers who were bought in to teach on one or two courses, and/or to undertake students' school practice supervision. Usually they provided study leave cover.

Data collection

Our choice of semi-structured interviews as our method of data collection was based upon our concern to uncover, and enhance our understanding of, the complexities of personal needs fulfilment, as outlined in the conceptual framework presented above. We therefore needed to gather data which were, for the most part, qualitative rather than quantitative. We were aware that much of our data collection would be both exploratory and opportunistic, in the sense that we could not always be certain in which direction we would be taken, and that there might be opportunities to be seized by pursuing emergent topics which we had not anticipated. These considerations led us towards interviewing as an appropriate method, since it facilitated two-way exchange between researcher and research subjects which would allow us to probe, rather than simply accept responses, and which, in this respect, was superior to questionnaires, even though its time-consuming nature would restrict our sample size. We rejected alternative or supplementary methods, such as diaries, which place the onus of responsibility for data collection upon research subjects, since we considered these to be too demanding of subjects' time, too dependent upon their sustained goodwill and commitment, and too susceptible to neglect. Observation was also rejected as an alternative or supplementary method for several reasons. First, it might have been interpreted as judgemental and/or intrusive. Second, two of the departments upon which our study focused had at the time of the study recently been, or were about to be, involved in external assessments which involved observation, and we felt that further observation on our part would be untimely and unwelcome. Third, observation is susceptible to encouraging atypically superlative behaviour on the part of those being observed, which distorts the data and reduces reliability. Whilst this effect is likely to diminish over time, our period of observation would have been too short to benefit from the effect. Fourth, since we were principally concerned with soliciting research subjects' own views about teaching effectiveness, rather than with formulating our own objective evaluations, we considered observation to be a less appropriate method of data collection than interviewing.

Although we wanted to encourage interviewee-initiated conversation, we designed an interview schedule of key topics and core questions. This was intended to ensure that answers to the research questions were sought and that data on certain common topics might provide the basis for comparison within, and between, the sub-samples. The commonality was particularly important since the study involved two interviewers. For the most part, we were successful in ensuring this degree of commonality, but on a few occasions specific core questions were not able to be included because of interviewee-imposed time restraints. All interviews were tape-recorded, with the interviewees' permission. Interviewees were guaranteed anonymity and we have used fictitious names throughout in presenting our findings. The average duration of interviews was forty-five minutes.

Interview schedules

Two interview schedules were prepared: one for use with the student sample and one for use with the tutor sample.

INTERVIEW SCHEDULE: STUDENTS

The students' schedule included the following key topics and, within these, core questions, allowing for probing, requests for elucidation or greater specificity, etc., at the interviewer's discretion:

> *Background and biographical outline*
> Age band
> Home/family background
> Type of education
> Reasons for choices of: university, course, career (if appropriate), personal/career aspirations and achievements, attitude to study – extent and nature of motivation (extrinsic/intrinsic).

University-education-related expectations and aspirations
Personal objectives:
  simply to pass, or to excel?
  targeted degree class?
  relative importance of social life and study?
  importance of career preparation?
Discuss reasons behind answers given.

Course-specific expectations and preferences
A thorough, comprehensive knowledge of the subject, or assessment-focused limitations?
Vocational relevance?

Expectations relating to course delivery – criteria for effectiveness:
  group size?
  quality of tutor?
  availability of tutor?
  method(s) of delivery?
  what makes a good lecture/seminar, etc.?
  what makes a good lecturer/tutor?
  what makes for unsatisfactory delivery?

Evaluations of the course and its delivery
How satisfied are you, in general, with your course?
Do you regret choosing it/parts of it? Would you recommend it to others?
Discuss specific components of it, e.g. options, lab work, etc.
Discuss different kinds of teaching received.
Describe a typical ... (seminar/lecture/examples class). What usually happens?
Can you recall the most useful session you've ever had? Would you say this has been the most memorable? Why? What distinguished it?
Would you like more of these?
Can you explain precisely why it was so successful for you? Did others share your views?
What about particularly unsuccessful sessions?
Level(s) of typical: student–student interaction, student–tutor interaction, student-led input?

Views or preferences in relation to:
  student participation
  group sizes
  vocational preparation (if applicable)
  student autonomy in relation to study habits
  preparation for/feedback on assignments
  individual help
  tutor availability
  innovative teaching
  tutors' research priorities
  resources availability

Acceptable alternative approaches
Views on:
  larger groups
  less frequent meetings
  more tutor-independent learning approaches

INTERVIEW SCHEDULE: TUTORS
The tutors' schedule included the following key topics and, within these, core questions, allowing for probing, requests for elucidation, greater specificity, etc., at the interviewer's discretion:

Biographical outline
Qualifications
Length of service
Previous experience/jobs
Responsibilities within the department/university

Identifying the 'ideal' job
What would your 'ideal' job here at _____ University involve? Describe it to me.
What aspects of the job make you feel good?
What aspects of the job give you a 'kick' or a 'buzz'?
Describe a good day. What sort of things could happen to make a day good for you?
Describe a bad day. What could happen to make a day bad for you?
What aspects of the job would you get rid of, if you could?
Generally, what components of the job do you prefer? e.g. teaching, research and publication, administration, consultancy, a combination ... ?

Job values, leading to job-related 'needs'
Building on this picture that you've built up of your 'ideal' job, can we move on to try to identify more specific things that you value about the job, to give some idea of job-related 'needs'? (Distinguish between what interviewee values about her or his actual job, and what s/he would value if s/he had it – i.e. 'real' and 'hypothetical' job values.)
Why do you/would you value these specific things that you've mentioned? What's underlying them?

Why do you value ...? (Go through list, one by one. Prompt if required.) Is it the peer recognition, or approval from students, or sense of personal achievement, or feeling that you're earning your salary ... etc. that you value? (Discuss and reach interviewee-verified consensus about identification of job-related values and needs.)

Extent to which job-related needs are being met
Identify constraints and enabling factors – what would remove some of these constraints? Less teaching? team teaching? larger groups? more decisional participation? less administration? ... etc.

Focus on implications for teaching and teaching methods
Can you think of any realistic ways in which your teaching could be altered to 'enable' you more; to help meet more of your overall job-related needs?

Attitude and approach to teaching
Importance of teaching component of job
Views on students' needs and preferences
Views on the tutor's role in relation to students – (Discuss accessibility, didacticism versus tutor-independent learning, accountability.)
Views on teaching methods, course content, course design appropriateness and effectiveness
Examples of teaching methods which s/he typically uses, and discuss rationale for them
Any atypical, or particularly memorable, teaching sessions to describe? What made it memorable? Students' reactions?

Comments on, and, if applicable, evaluations of, staff development programmes; formal and informal support?

ANALYSIS OF DATA

Interviews were transcribed, and transcriptions used as the basis for analysis. Data reduction was an incrementally reductive process, involving several levels of coding, focusing increasingly narrowly on categories of increased specificity. Data were analysed, in the first instance, by categorization in relation to the research questions, presented above. This first-level coding sorted data into broad categories, such as: tutors' perceptions of students' needs, tutors' task preferences, students' attitudes to study, etc. Thereafter, coding involved a breakdown of more specific determinants of these descriptive codes. For example, tutors' perceptions of their own needs were coded according to determinants of their needs, such as peer recognition, meeting challenges, making a contribution, etc. Patterns emerging out of the coding process revealed evidence of what may be broadly categorized as 'typologies', such as: intrinsically motivated students, strategically motivated students, tutors who are resistant to change, etc. For the most part, these 'typologies', which were often unclearly defined and with blurred distinctions, are not highlighted in the findings presented in the book. Their most useful purpose was to reveal, and heighten our awareness of, underlying commonalities, from which models were developed to illustrate what we refer to as the 'lowest common factor': that is, the most fundamental, universally applicable, factor(s) in relation to the issue in question. Elucidation of these 'lowest common factors' represents the final analysis/analyses and is important since it facilitates and informs practical application of the findings and policy-making. Identifying and illustrating sub-group diversity, variations in patterns and individual differences is an important analytical stage which elucidates contextual 'reality'. However, the key to understanding what underlies that 'reality', in order to make manageable the practical application of research findings and also to apply inter-contextual transferences, lies in discovering the 'lowest common factor'.

LIMITATIONS

We are aware of, and acknowledge throughout this book, several limitations of our study, the most significant of which concern its scale, the sampling and the implications of these for the generalizability and wider applicability of the findings. Clearly, there is scope for larger-scale follow-up studies of different types of higher-education institutions, with different organizational cultures, traditions and priorities, and using samples drawn from a wider range of subject disciplines. Such studies will have much to contribute towards presenting a fuller picture of teaching and learning in higher education in the UK.

Part II

The Student Perspective

Chapter 3

The Knowledge

INTRODUCTION

This chapter focuses upon the key element of university education: the acquisition of knowledge. It examines students' perceptions and evaluations of the various teaching contexts in which information is imparted to them, skills are taught, and experiences offered, with the purpose of adding to their store of knowledge and enhancing their understanding of concepts which are pertinent to their courses.

Our research did not examine the ways in which students learn, nor did it evaluate the effectiveness of specific teaching approaches in facilitating learning. This chapter does not, therefore, include cognitive or psychological considerations. It simply presents and examines students' views about the extent to which specific modes of delivering course-related information were successful in satisfying their own needs and preferences as they perceived them, since this fulfilment of needs is the main criterion for effectiveness of teaching and learning which we apply to our study. As we point out in Chapter 5, the need to obtain pertinent information was the basic study-related need identified by our students, and was common to all of them. All of our students identified getting a degree as the essential purpose of their being at university, and all of their study-related needs contributed to and fed into this overriding purpose.

There was a common approach to the transfer of knowledge across three of the courses, English and American studies, education and law. The basic format employed by these courses consisted of large-scale lectures, smaller seminar groups and a limited amount of one-to-one interaction, which was usually associated with the assessment process. In the physics course lectures were the predominant teaching method and these were supported by small-group examples classes, where students' prepared answers to specified problems were discussed. Students were also expected to carry out practical experiments and to discuss the results with tutors, often on a one-to-one basis.

This chapter examines students' explanations of which teaching approaches seem to work best for them, in relation to the acquisition of knowledge and skills, and why they work. It presents their assessments of the advantages and disadvantages of three methods of delivering course-related information: lectures, small-group teaching and one-to-one interaction, revealing study-related preferences in relation to each.

LECTURES

The most common form of providing knowledge to students in British higher education is through a lecture programme. All of the four degree courses upon which our study focused utilized this teaching method to a lesser or greater extent. Student audience sizes ranged from 20 to 220. The general format was one in which the student adopted a passive role as the recipient of information. The basic function of the lecturer was to present this information.

There is, amongst those who write on the topic of teaching methods in higher education, a widespread belief that lectures have limited effectiveness as a mode of teaching. Gibbs (1995a), for example, suggests that 'lecturing is a relatively poor teaching method' (p. 21) and many practical books aimed at a readership of teachers in higher education advocate the development of alternative methods to lecturing (see, for example, Ashcroft and Foreman-Peck, 1994; Raaheim *et al.*, 1991). The basis of the criticism levelled at lecturing as a teaching method is research which has demonstrated that students learn less effectively through this approach. Moreover, there is evidence that lectures encourage only 'surface' learning, which involves acquiring facts and memorizing them, rather than 'deep' learning, which involves greater understanding (Saljo, 1984). Bligh (1972), for example, carried out a survey of twenty-three research studies which compared lecturing with other teaching methods. In eighteen of the studies lecturing was considered worse than the other alternatives, and in the other five studies there was no significant difference in terms of developing students' ability to acquire problem-solving skills, analyse information and synthesize data.

However, as we point out in the Introduction to this book, our research was primarily concerned not with investigating the various ways in which students learn but with their perceptions of their study-related needs. It was, therefore, in relation to the capacity for satisfying their perceived need for course-related information that the students in our sample evaluated lectures as a teaching method. On this basis, supporting Gibbs's and Habeshaw's (1989, p. 47) assessment of them as 'effective at conveying factual information', lectures were considered to be, for the most part, an effective teaching method.

The efficiency potential of lectures was highlighted by one of the law students in our sample:

> Instead of giving us fifty or sixty pages of background handouts you can talk about it in the lecture in five minutes. (Hakan, law student)

This comment reflects the consensual approval for lectures, in principle, amongst our sample. However, whilst, for the most part, they all generally supported the principle of lectures as a potentially effective teaching method, students' evaluations of specific lectures which they had attended were wide-ranging. Analysis of our findings revealed these evaluations to be influenced by specific considerations reflecting precisely what students want from lectures, in relation to the information which is imparted. Four evaluative features of lectures were identified: *recordability of information, comprehensibility of information, usefulness of information* and *interestingness of content and delivery*. We examine each of these features in turn.

Recordability of information

Our students attached great importance to the accumulation of a set of notes, taken during lectures, which would give them a firm basis of information which they perceived as necessary for success in assessed coursework and examinations. Unanimity that the basic purpose of lectures was to convey information is illustrated by the following representative comments:

> I've always regarded lectures as the sort of way you listen and learn ... Lectures are there to provide information. (Colin, education student)

> I like taking down the notes. I feel I learn better being lectured to as opposed to discussing. I seem to take in much more knowledge by being lectured. (Oliver, education student)

> I think, from the lectures, you need to know what the law is, and yet to be able to talk about it as well. On some of the courses you get too much talking around it, without having decent notes about what the law is. (Angie, law student)

Much criticism was directed at badly structured, poorly presented and incoherent lectures which failed to provide students with the opportunity to acquire a set of notes which they considered to be sufficiently detailed for the purpose of exam revision:

> I don't like the way the lectures are done here. I hate it when you get lecturers who write random words on the board. There are two who actually write sentences so that your notes read like a textbook, but lots just scribble random words. I don't like that at all and I find it difficult to revise from. (Greg, physics student)

> One person who lectures, he knows what he's talking about ... He can start off saying one thing, and you're dutifully writing it down, and listening, and he'll break off, mid-sentence, or reverse himself, or go to another point, and then come back to the bit he's done. So you're all over your page, and you've arrows showing how this bit goes here and this bit, there ... and, like, it's just silly. And everyone ... people just look at each other, throw down their pens and just sit back, and, like, just try and take in what he's saying, rather than waste time writing it down. Because, if they write it down they know that it's just going to go over their head because they're just spending so much time trying to concentrate on putting the right stuff in the right place. And, in the end, things

just go from bad to worse and you end up just sitting there, and then your mind wanders and then it's all over for the day. (Alan, law student)

And, so, like, the lecture's incoherent and it's illogically arranged and, it's very confusing, and very difficult to make notes from. (Felicity, education student)

By the same token, lectures in which students were able to acquire a comprehensive set of notes were, predictably, deemed to be effective:

Lectures are really good – some of them are *really* good. Some of the lecturers give us guidelines. They say, you know, 'This is the structure I'm following during the lecture'. So, you know, it's easy to follow the lecturer and that gives us the time to take some notes. (Hakan, law student)

Lecture handouts, summarizing the content, were considered equally effective as a lecture structure which facilitated note-taking, since they fulfilled the same purpose: that of acquiring information which would be useful for exam revision:

I think it's very good when they give you outlays and that sort of thing – they actually give you something on paper that you can work from, and some of the lecturers give you a handout which they'll base their lecture around. And they'll stick to it – which is very good, so you know where you're at. But you get other lecturers that'll not give you anything. They'll start the lecture – sometimes they won't even say what they're talking about and will just go straight into it. And it's very difficult, especially for revision, to come back to it and say, 'Oh, yes, this is about this'. (Dorothy, law student)

I like it when they give you a printed sheet and it's very carefully structured – I think that's really important. Because I don't think there's any point in just scribbling down every thing they say, I think there needs to be a structure. (Deborah, law student)

One person . . . he actually brought in a lecture sheet one week and it was the best lecture he had given all term because he just followed it. (Alan, law student)

Whilst a concern to record the information imparted was a general pervasive feature of students' evaluations of lectures, it was particularly evident amongst physics students. Of all four student sub-samples, the physics students were distinct with respect to the emphasis which they placed on the acquisition of pertinent information. Indeed, their comments suggested a general acceptance of the adequacy of rote learning for meeting their assessment-focused study-related needs, and the measure of success in accommodating these needs which was afforded to any one lecture was its facilitation of comprehensive note-taking. Evidence of this distinction between physics and the other three sub-samples of students became even more pronounced in relation to their attitudes towards the comprehensibility of information imparted in lectures.

Comprehensibility of information

Although the acquisition of information seemed to take precedence amongst physics students, as a study-related need, over understanding of the information which was imparted, this prioritization was not evident to the same extent amongst the other three sub-samples. Most of the education, law and English and American studies students included comprehensibility of information as an important criterion for effectiveness in lectures:

> It doesn't matter how hard it is – if he's structured and if he's expressing himself well and then you can understand what he is talking about – that's it. It doesn't have to be easy. And I think that's what makes a good lecture. (Hakan, law student)

> The lectures stood out because every lecture was set out pretty clearly. And the way they were set out and taught made it easy to understand it ... It sank in more clearly than anything else. (Clive, law student)

Reflecting this prioritization, the English and American studies, law and education students were evidently more expectant than were the physics students that the information conveyed to them during lectures should make sense. Whilst the physics students seemed to accept the main purpose of lectures as being the imparting and receiving of information, and comprehensibility of information an added bonus, for the other three sub-samples comprehensibility was evidently an essential requirement. They expected it; they usually, rather than sometimes, received it; and they were, accordingly, less tolerant and more indignantly critical than were the physics students when it did not feature. This discrepancy is, we feel, due to the distinct nature of science subjects, in relation to arts and social science subjects. First-degree course syllabuses in the physical sciences tend to include more information than opinion, focusing on proven facts and theories, on 'objective' reality, rather than the subjectivity of alternative views. In the physical sciences there is an accumulated body of knowledge which students need to acquire. Ideally, they will also understand the information imparted, but the acquisition of the knowledge is essential and integral to study of the subject. This distinction between subject disciplines is recognized by Tait, Speth and Entwistle (1995, p. 324), who, referring to deep, surface and strategic approaches to study, point out:

> These approaches are more usefully seen as conceptual categories than as descriptions of individual students, and the importance of them to different disciplines varies to some extent. High deep and strategic approaches are generally associated with good performance, while high surface approaches are less likely to be so. However, in science-based subjects in particular, high surface approach combined with high deep or high strategic approaches is commonly seen in successful students because of the nature of the discipline they are studying.

Moreover, Meyer and Scrivener (1995), referring to their study of changes in the learning behaviour of students on a science-based degree course, highlight, as a typical study-related problem, the suggestion that 'They [students] don't really know how to take notes and tend to focus on the minutiae of legibility and delivery of lectures, resulting in improvidence' (p. 49).

Particularly interesting is the broad similarity between our impression of a general trend amongst most of our physics students towards mechanical learning arising out of lectures and specific features of learning behaviour manifested by some of Meyer's and Scrivener's (1995, pp. 51–2) problematic science students:

> They appeared to have little, if any, grasp of the basis of 'scientific method' and, when questioned, could recall little (if any) material delivered in lectures only hours previously. Both students, however, managed to scrape along by transferring segments of information from lecture notes and text books into laboratory write-ups with sufficient editorial skill to obtain adequate marks ... Students who were clearly weak, and who were observed to be having difficulty in understanding things at a conceptual level ... were able to provide good answers to questions of a type previously encountered, and performed comparatively well ... in the examination.
>
> ... This student was interviewed ... in order to establish how some of the essential course concepts were being understood. The interview data clearly indicated that this student had developed a successful coping strategy. The basis of this strategy rested on an almost perfect ability to recall key definitions and explanations given in lectures. However, when questioned further about the meaning of some of these, the student commented along the lines of 'You don't want to try and understand things too deeply or you will just get confused; some things should just be accepted without question.'

Many of our physics student interviewees indicated that comprehensibility of lectures took low priority amongst their study-related needs and preferences. Although it was welcomed when it occurred, it was evidently not considered to be an essential requirement, and there was a general acceptance that the main aim of attending lectures was to record, rather than to understand, information:

> The purpose of lectures is merely to pass information across – simply to write down the information ... I've been to so many lectures now, on so many courses, and there's so much information to digest, I don't believe I'd remember any particular lecture. (Frank, physics student)

> I think a lecture should be for the lecturer to convey all the information to us. (Fiona, physics student)

> All it is, really, is working through methods, theories ... and lecturers will do that on the board at the front, and it's just, sort of, copied into notebooks and, depending on the lecturer – some will just, sort of, stand at the front and write out boards and boards full of notes and stuff that no one, at the time, really understands ... (Graham, physics student)

Indeed, one physics student suggested that, because of what he perceived as the course's emphasis on rote learning and regurgitation of information, at the expense of understanding and application, it would be conceivable for non-physics specialists to pass a physics degree course examination, having digested the appropriate information. Another student even provided anecdotal evidence that a lack of concern for comprehensibility of information conveyed in lectures extended to the tutors. He spoke of one tutor:

> He's not a very good lecturer ... and we found out from some people who have him as a personal tutor that he'd got *some* information, copied it directly from a book, and didn't understand it himself! (Edward, physics student)

Clearly, students' expectations, preferences and needs in relation to course content and delivery will be determined by subject-specific culture and norms, which, in turn, are perpetuated by prevailing trends in teaching methods. Entwistle (1995, p. 39) suggests that 'Effective teaching, particularly in higher education, depends critically on the content and traditions of the individual discipline or profession.' His examples (Entwistle, 1995, p. 43) of comments made by the Scottish Higher Education Funding Council's (SHEFC) assessors on teaching methods in university physics departments rated as 'excellent' provide further evidence that the priority which our physics students afforded to information acquisition, and their acceptance of a mechanical approach to learning, reflect teaching and learning traditions in science subjects:

Ancient University A
'Lectures observed were well delivered using mainly traditional methods ... there was, in general, little interaction with the students.'

Ancient University B
'... A mainly conventional approach to lecturing was adopted with use of blackboard and overhead projector the chief means of delivery ... There were also interesting teaching development projects in hand, but not yet implemented.'

Ancient University C
'The lectures were all clearly delivered, though occasionally in a rather mundane manner, and more student participation would have been desirable. There were a few notable exceptions in which interesting lecture demonstrations were observed.'

1960s University D
'Lectures tended to be traditional: there was scope for more variety in presentation and activity ... [as] in some cases [they] were not particularly imaginative ... little student participation was evident.'

Setting them apart from the physics students, the other three sub-samples generally manifested a greater concern to understand, as well as to record, the content of lectures. Some students clearly felt that one of the purposes of lectures was to provide mental challenges, to get the audience thinking about controversial issues. They expected to participate in lectures, not orally but mentally, and, by this process, to extend their knowledge and understanding of their subject:

As far as a useful lecture goes, I think anything that gives a different slant, er, because a lot of time when you read a book you've got the gist, you understand, but it's challenging your perspectives and making you think about the text as a whole that I find most useful. (Valerie, English and American studies student)

The lecturers take it in turns ... and have different ideas, and contradict each other ... I mean, some tutors love poets and others hate them. There's one poet, ... and ... one tutor loved him and then, the next week, another tutor came and just ripped him to pieces! It's quite interesting, seeing both sides of the input. Also, we're encouraged to look at criticisms, which is conflicting opinions, and you learn to just pick out the best bits of each one, and make it your own. (Jane, English and American studies student)

I find the format of lectures – you know, being able to sit there for an hour and ... listen to somebody talking about a subject – very accessible. I like to be able to hear somebody's informed views and then take them away with me and think about it and relate it to what I've thought about the subject and what I know about it. (Tina, English and American studies student)

All students, including physics students, preferred to be able to understand, as well as record, the content of lectures; the distinctions arose in relation to the priority which they afforded comprehensibility of information. There was evidence of some subject-discipline-related patterns which undoubtedly reflect the nature and content of the subjects and traditions in course delivery. Most notably, and reflecting the interpretative, rather than purely informative, model of their course's content and delivery, it was the English and American studies sub-sample which, on the whole, placed the greatest emphasis on getting to grips with the views and ideas presented in lectures.

The law, education and physics samples represented a broader spectrum of preferences in relation to comprehensibility of lectures. Some students' comments indicated a preference for receiving facts and information, whilst others seemed to prefer being encouraged to reflect, analyse and thoroughly understand. For this latter category, structure and delivery style were considered to be important influences on comprehensibility. Badly structured lectures in which information was presented in a confusing way made understanding more difficult. Similarly, too much information, presented too quickly, resulted in students' attention being directed at copious recording, leaving them with insufficient time to assimilate and comprehend the ideas being presented. Much was attributed to tutors' capacity for presenting material at a level which undergraduates were able to understand, and in a way which makes it easy to follow what is being said:

> The lecturers talk too fast ... so you're always scribbling down stuff ... some of them know their stuff so well that they can't explain it. (Doris, law student)

> Some of the lectures – the lecturer likes to explain things to you, and some of them – they don't really explain it and, basically, you're just copying down what's on the board, and just hoping you can understand it when you come to read it through. (Daniel, physics student)

> He's brilliant! But I, and a lot of other students, find he can't ... er ... get across his enthusiasm for the subject and direct it at a level which we will understand. He's up there in the clouds somewhere! And although everything he's saying is right ... everything he's saying is fabulous ... for somebody who knows very little about the subject – and trying to make notes is *impossible*! I mean, I've been to so many of his lectures and I've just started my notes, and I've put my pen down half-way through and just ... given up. (Cathy, law student)

> I don't know ... I mean ... I've thought – I don't know quite what it is ... whether it's that I'm not putting enough time into it, but some lecturers just don't seem to ... communicate – they don't seem to ... they, sometimes ... you look at the notes – the note structures are very poor ... the diagrams on the board are very ... abstract ... they seem to fly off at tangents ... they don't seem to keep the essence of what's going on ... and so it just becomes a load of information; it doesn't become a concept, or an idea, which, of course, is incredibly important in physics. (Harold, physics student)

> For me, er ... I need a very clear, concise, to-the-point, sort of, lecture style. Er ... with a beginning, middle, and end, as it were. But this particular lecturer, sort of, starts off on one point, goes off on a tangent, ... then you begin to think, 'Well, what's she on about?' Then she comes back to what she's talking about ... Although she knows exactly what she's on about; she knows her stuff ... she just can't put it across. (Grace, education student)

> I think there's a problem with lectures where tutors are saying things, and they speak in a very, very ... elevated language – maybe it's *my* weakness, I don't know – but, sometimes you have to stop and think, 'Are they saying what I *think* they're saying?' ... and it goes on, and on, ... and you can't decide exactly what point is really being made. (Jenny, English and American studies student)

Usefulness of information

Lectures serve students' study-related needs only if the information which they communicate is useful to them. Two main categories of usefulness were identified by our students: assessment-related and vocation-related.

Information which was useful for course assessment was that which constituted the course syllabus and which, directly or indirectly, potentially informed or featured in coursework or examination answers. It was distinct from background, peripheral information which, out of strategic considerations, many students dismissed as superfluous.

There is much overlap between recordability and usefulness of information, since the rationale for students' focus on recording is that the information recorded is useful for assessment. Whilst most of our student interviewees, as we point out in the next chapter, tended to be strategically focused upon acquiring information which had assessment-related usefulness and placed comparatively little value on background, supplementary information, there was a minority of students who considered this kind of information useful. Appreciation of background, peripheral information was particularly noticeable amongst the English and American studies students, to which sub-sample belonged most of our minority of very conscientious, intrinsically motivated students (see Chapter 4). Many English and American studies student interviewees spoke of their enthusiasm for their subject, of their desire to become 'well read', and of one of their purposes in coming to university being to learn for the sake of learning. It is not surprising, therefore, that to such students all information which was imparted to them on their courses was considered useful. This wider interpretation of usefulness, in relation to information, is reflected in the representative comments of one of the students in this category:

> The lectures are normally good – quite informative – and they'll direct you to pursue other areas ... link up with other things ... The best thing with this course has been ... er ... knowing that I'm quite well read now ... being able to say, 'Yeah, I know that. I know where this fits into this' – that sort of thing ... A good lecture is ... where the lecturer gives you the background of ... er ... the novel, or the poet, or whatever, and ... er ... maybe some historical context, and ... er ... tells you what happens in it, or some of the major themes. (Karen, English and American studies student)

Vocation-related usefulness of information was important to two of our student sub-samples, law and education, but particularly so to education students. Most of the education students intended becoming teachers and, since the degree for which they were studying incorporated Qualified Teacher Status, they expected the course to include extensive vocational training, which they typically referred to as the 'practical' components of the course. Most accepted the need for their course to include the theory, as well as the practice, of education, and accepted that practical relevance was not the only criterion for usefulness of lecture material. They did not, therefore, expect all lectures to focus upon practical issues, nor did they consider more theoretically focused lectures to be ineffective, provided that they conveyed information which had assessment-related usefulness. On the other hand, lectures which included much vocationally relevant information, especially 'tips for teachers', were rated particularly highly.

The law students did not value vocation-related usefulness to the same extent as did the education students. It was a minority of the law students' sub-sample who identified vocational relevance of information as an issue, and very few of this minority seemed to consider it particularly important. This discrepancy between the two sub-samples reflects their subjects' different statuses as vocational courses. There is no unanimity amongst the law community over whether or not, and to what extent, law degree courses should be categorized as vocational, and the general view amongst non-specialists is probably one which considers semi-vocational status appropriate. A key distinction between the education course upon which our study focused and the law degree course is that the one incorporates a vocational qualification and entitlement to entry into a profession and the other does not.

It is interesting that, whilst, on the one hand, students' criteria for usefulness, in relation to information conveyed through their courses, are essentially assessment-related, reflecting their relatively short-term, degree-focused goals, on the other hand their concern for vocational relevance reflects more long-term considerations. The benefits of many aspects of students' higher education which are recognized and promoted by tutors and are often implicit in course aims have long-term, general vocational relevance. Academic study potentially develops many interdisciplinary skills which will often enhance professional competence. It is these aspects of learning which underpin the 'deep' approach that tutors typically encourage, and which O'Neil (1995, p. 117) describes generally as 'the essence of academic life as I understand it', referring to them more specifically: 'Enhancing student qualities such as self-reliance, intellectual capabilities and intrinsic interest in learning are important aims of higher education' (O'Neil, 1995, p. 118).

Our evidence reveals students, for the most part, to afford little value to such potential benefits, either through ignorance or through strategic expediency. Yet, those to whom they are applicable value more tangible, profession-specific course elements to which higher-education tutors generally attach less importance. Our explanation, which we base upon our research findings, for this apparently inconsistent value system is that it is underpinned by students' conceptions of specific professions, which tend to be under-developed and formulated out of impressionistic constructs and restricted professionality perspectives. Moreover, since these conceptions often persist well into, and sometimes throughout, professional life-spans, permeating occupational cultures, they tend to be reinforced and perpetuated by work experience. Students therefore carry with them long-held conceptions of what their chosen profession entails on a day-to-day, pragmatic basis, which focuses on immediate, functional concerns at the expense of long-term, underlying, developmental issues. Those following non-vocational degree courses, and who have no clear idea of what career they intend to follow, are the least likely to be interested in acquiring and developing skills, no matter how useful to professional life they are considered to be, which have no relevance to course assessment. Yet our evidence suggests that even those with clearly defined career plans and intentions, and whose degree course incorporates preparation for their chosen profession, are similarly unconcerned with developing skills which do not fit into their impressionistically determined schemata of professional competence. Essentially, if students have, for example, acquired the notion that one of the most important skills utilized in the teaching profession is the management of pupils' behaviour, they will value any input in their education degree course which contributes to their developing this skill, but will dismiss as irrelevant course provision for developing analytical skills, since, as a non-visible aspect of teaching, analysis has not been incorporated into their conception of what the job involves.

Interestingness of content and delivery

In the next chapter we examine the importance of tutors' delivery styles in engaging students' interest in their courses and fostering their motivation. In this section we focus on the contribution which interesting lecture content and delivery make to students' learning – to their understanding and their knowledge and skills acquisition.

Without necessarily referring to effects on their knowledge or understanding, a small number of students included reference to interestingness of content and delivery in their responses to our asking them what makes a good, and a bad, lecture:

> If the lecturer comes across in a way that inspires you to go away and learn something for yourself, or, if you want to teach in that particular way, then that's been a good session. (Yvonne, education student)

> Some [lecturers] perform in the lecture, and hold your interest, and others are just reading off a sheet ... like, they're delivering a paper – and that's a lecture! ... Humour is always something to wake everybody up. You can make the material interesting ... you can pick out some funny bits ... er, some tutors include biographical details ... that get you interested. (Jane, English and American studies student)

> Last term we had a really good subject – we were doing the philosophy of education – and it was really interesting. But the lectures we had were *horrendous* because you ... firstly, it sounds like really obvious stuff – but, you couldn't *hear* the guy properly. He spoke on the same level, and it was very monotone ... very boring ... and you really had to concentrate to listen and pick out the exciting things in what he was saying. Whereas, if somebody'd had a bit of enthusiasm about it, and a bit of 'oomph', it would've automatically brought all that across to us. (Ruth, education student)

> I recently went through a lecture course with a guy called Ivan _____, and he was one of the best lecturers I've every had ... He was inspiring ... he was interesting ... he really, sort of, grabbed you and said, 'Hey, look!' ... And, of course, too many times, particular

lecturers open a book each week, copy out two pages, read it to you, almost … and … you could go and get the book out of the library and find the bit they used, and it's exactly the same. And there's no re-capping, so, if you … one day … completely didn't get it, you'd go into the next lecture, and there's no re-cap, and you've lost the lecture from then on – from then on, the lecture's dead for you … Ivan *spoke* to you … he communicated with you, individually … and, also, he used very good analogies as well – well, 'analogy' is probably the wrong word, but, in the case of when electrons make power down a cable … the higher the frequency of the electricity, the more loss you get, due to wastage, … and he mentioned that … er … that was because, the higher the frequency of the electricity, the more it travels on the outer surface of the wire, that's why they use very thin strands of wire, because there's a greater surface area. And I remember thinking, 'Wow! *really*? That just makes so much sense!' (Harold, physics student)

We were surprised, however, at the comparatively few references to interestingness in students' evaluative comments amongst the sample as a whole. Much greater importance had been attached to assessment-related usefulness and recordability of information as lecture features which contributed towards satisfying study-related needs. Interestingness appeared, by comparison, to represent preferences rather than core needs, and, in this respect, it was ranked more on a par with comprehensibility. Our impression was that, in general, students would, given the choice, prefer uninspiring, lack-lustre delivery of information which is useful to them for course assessment to entertaining delivery of what they consider to be peripheral, irrelevant information.

SMALL-GROUP TEACHING

Predictably, much of what students valued about, and wanted from, lectures was also what they valued about, and wanted from, small-group teaching. All of the four desirable features of lectures identified in the previous section – recordability of information, comprehensibility of information, usefulness of information and interestingness of content and delivery – were also applied to students' evaluations of small-group teaching. Indeed, students' evaluative comments often failed to distinguish between these two different modes of course delivery, and included illustrations which involved their flitting to and fro between references to lecture and small-group teaching examples.

A distinction emerged, however, in relation to students' ranking of the specific features of the teaching. Whereas the most important features of lectures were generally considered to be usefulness and recordability of information, with, depending on the subject discipline, comprehensibility and interesting-ness being afforded lower priority, recordability of information conveyed through small-group teaching was relegated to the lowest priority level. This shift of emphasis reflects students' views on the distinct functions of lectures and small-group teaching, illustrated by one student's comment:

I've always regarded lectures as the, sort of, where you listen and learn, and the seminars as where you discuss and chat. (Colin, education student)

The participatory, discursive nature of small-group teaching gave rise to specific expectations in relation to the knowledge, skills and understanding to be acquired through this mode of course delivery. From these expectations there emerged a fifth feature which students valued and which they applied to small-group teaching. This is probably best labelled broadly as clarification of information. More specifically, clarification of information included the confirmation of the validity of students' own emergent ideas and analyses through verificatory discourse. It also included tutors' expansion on points introduced in lectures which, in some cases, might involve the articulation of alternative perspectives and views which conflicted with those presented by other academics.

For the most part, our students greatly valued the opportunities which small-group teaching provided for following up topics introduced in lectures. Many considered lectures and seminars to go hand-in-hand, as a complete learning package, which, together, first imparted a large amount of information and then, second, expanded upon that information, whilst also analysing it in finer detail. Consequently, one of the criteria for a good seminar was that it consolidated lecture-generated knowledge and understanding:

> There's one lady who's always had structure in her course. Er ... and the seminars, because she structures them quite well, relate to the lectures. Er ... and instead of, sort of, as with other lecturers, dumping you with ... well, sort of, 'There's your lecture notes. Solve all these problems' ... she gives you your lecture notes ... the seminars are, sort of, structured to complement the lecture notes ... and that, I find, is more helpful than just, sort of, giving you a load of questions and leaving you to it, and in your own time ... And I attend most of her seminars. (Clive, law student)

> Er ... that system's great when it ... follows on and you've got a sequential thing, and when there's a matter to discuss. What I've found, occasionally, is that you go into a lecture, you listen for an hour ... and – this happened last year in a lecture on gender ... and people came out of the lecture feeling quite strongly about it, and we went to the seminar group and the tutor didn't want to do anything on it, because it'd been offensive, so he changed the subject entirely ... Now, that's frustrating! (Colin, education student)

Nevertheless, despite general approval for a coherent link between lectures and seminars, students varied in their assessments of the potential of small-group teaching for facilitating learning and enhancing knowledge and understanding. There was also diversity in the reasons underlying these varied assessments. Those who valued other students' ideas as much as those of tutors clearly found small-group discussions a useful vehicle for the exchange of views:

> *Interviewer: Do you feel that you're getting 'value for money' from student-led seminars where the tutor isn't there?*
> Yes, because you're still using the other students and increasing your own understanding. And, like, if they don't understand something you can explain it to them, and that helps. (Angie, law student)

> You can feed as much off students as you can off lecturers. (Alan, law student)

> Last year we had a lot of student-led seminars, which was where we didn't actually have a seminar tutor in the room. And you'd sit down and you could talk it through with

them – with everybody else in the room – and get a good answer out of it, because everybody was contributing. (Doris, law student)

I think seminars where somebody *does* turn them into a mini lecture are, sort of, frustrating for the students ... I, sort of, always suspect that there's not as much exchange of ideas and information amongst the students in seminars as the seminar tutors would like, and as much as would be beneficial for the students. So, I think, again, it's like, the process of ... the business of having to, sort of, arrive at conclusions through speech that's very effective in seminars, really. (Tina, English and American studies student)

Some, however, were less enthusiastic about seminars, considering them either too directive in the learning approach that they fostered or too prone to be insufficiently focused on pertinent issues to be of use:

I would find it a lot easier if they ... if I went into a seminar and they said, 'This is the reading that you've got to do', you know, 'if you've got any problems come and see me and we'll talk about your problems', rather than there being so much contact time, and you're just sat there with everybody else ... I feel like it would be just as easy for me to go away and do the reading myself, and I'd get more done. (Poppy, education student)

What happens in student-led seminars is, sometimes the lecturer's there as an observer, without any intervention, and sometimes they're not even there. But I believe they *should* be there. They should, sort of, you know, guide the discussion, be there as a speaker and organize the discussion, because sometimes people get too carried away. I mean, it's normal, because law is a fairly social topic and you can really expand on it and talk about some other things in relation to law ... I, personally, ended up not going to the student-led seminars last year because it was a waste of time. Some people talked about stupid things, 'Oh, I've done this last night'. I mean, is it the place to talk about your social life, during the student-led seminars? It's not. But people do, because they can't help it. (Hakan, law student)

Some students – though, amongst the English and American studies, law and education students this was a small minority – preferred to be spoon-fed information in lectures rather than to participate in small-group discussions. For these students, the most satisfactory seminars were those which operated as lectures:

I find lectures more valuable than seminars ... partly because the lectures are the main source of information ... like, the skeleton of the course. Er ... and, sort of, ... the seminars, I don't find *that* helpful ... in the way they're done. (Clive, law student)

ONE-TO-ONE INTERACTION

We categorize as one-to-one interaction all of the occasions on which students engaged in course-related one-to-one exchanges with tutors. This was the least frequently employed mode of teaching and typically included individual tutorials whose purpose was to provide oral pre-assessment and/or post-assessment guidance and feedback, impromptu discussions through which students sought clarification of specific course-related content, and written feedback on coursework which had been submitted. Most one-to-one teaching of this kind, with the exception of written feedback on coursework, was discretionary and generally instigated by the student. As a result, our students' experience of it, in quantitative terms, varied and, since many reported having had very few such one-to-one exchanges with tutors, it is the mode of teaching on which we have the fewest data.

The consensual view amongst our student interviewees was that the existing discretionary one-to-one teaching provision was perfectly satisfactory. In response to our questions, all responded that they would not prefer an 'Oxbridge-type' system of more regular one-to-one teaching. The reasons underlying this unanimous view varied; a minority of students spoke of feeling intimidated by, and lacking the confidence to enjoy, one-to-one exchanges; many said that they enjoyed and benefited from interaction with other students in teaching groups and would not want to see this form of teaching replaced; some indicated a preference for being spoon-fed through didactic teaching approaches; and some queried the cost-effectiveness of individual tuition.

There emerged two clear preferences in relation to one-to-one, course-related interaction between students and tutors. The first, which also has implications for small-group teaching, was for teaching groups to be sufficiently small to allow students adequate opportunities for engaging in one-to-one exchanges with tutors within group discussions. Since this is an issue which overlaps considerably with that of students' willingness to participate in group discussions, it is examined in depth in the next chapter. The second preference, which all of our students shared, was that tutors should be available and willing to engage in one-to-one exchanges. Invariably, our interviewees identified availability, accessibility and approachability as key characteristics of good tutors. The following representative comments were responses to our asking students to identify what makes a good tutor:

> Somebody who'd be easily approachable, that you can go and see any time ... somebody who you can go to at any time and just ask them questions about anything you need to know, and ... er ... go out of their way to help. (Daniel, physics student)

> Well ... er ... they've always got time for you. They know ... er ... a lot about everything, really ... Er, you can talk to them about anything ... they're just prepared to talk to you whenever you want to talk. (Claire, physics student)

> They need to know what they're talking about ... approachability – very important ... you can learn a lot from chatting to them ... er ... availability ... er ... I think they should care about the students ... be more broad-minded to students' needs, I think. (Alan, law student)

> Approachable, being friendly, always having time for the students ... well structured ... and organized. (Hakan, law student)

> Someone who's approachable and friendly ... I think they've just got to be more open, really – free for you to come and talk to them. (Dorothy, law student)

> Someone who doesn't seem as though they've got, sort of, more pressing ... more important things to do, and doesn't, sort of, dismiss undergraduates as, sort of, time-wasters. Someone who will make time ... and come up with answers to problems, and that sort of thing. (Fiona, physics student)

Someone who knows their stuff, so, obviously, they *do* have to be putting time in on research. Er ... someone who, in a seminar, will give enough prompting and direction without spelling it out ... er ... and someone who's always willing and available for the students to talk to. (Karen, English and American studies student)

It became clear that, whilst they were satisfied with the relatively small amount of one-to-one teaching which occurred within the models of course delivery which existed in their departments, students nevertheless wanted the assurance that, should they need individual teaching, it would be readily available and willingly given to them.

LEARNING NEEDS AND PREFERENCES

Referring to what, at the time of writing, is the current trend towards the promotion of innovation in teaching and learning in higher education, Utley (1997b) suggests that 'the focus of university teaching is shifting away from the corpus of knowledge in favour of the process of learning. And that means the lecture can no longer be the central plank of university study.' Similarly, the Dearing Report (NCIHE, 1997, pp. 114–18) promotes a 'new look' teaching and learning in higher education, which exceeds the mere transmission of knowledge through didactic methods, embracing a more student-centred ideology and incorporating mechanisms for developing intellectual skills and analytical competence:

students must have access to more than just the articulation of knowledge in the form of books and lectures. They also need practical experience that rehearses them in the professional or scholarly skills of their field, and the opportunity to develop and express their own understanding and point of view in an environment that gives constructive feedback. (NCIHE, 1997, p. 114, para. 8.3)

A successful student will be able to engage in an effective discussion or debate with others in that field, relying on a common understanding of terms, assumptions, questions, modes of argument, and the body of evidence. Learning also involves acquiring skills, such as analysis and communication, but these in isolation do not constitute learning. (NCIHE, 1997, p. 115, para. 8.6)

Putting aside for the moment consideration of tutors' job-related needs, the 'new look' teaching and learning culture which universities are being encouraged to adopt, which veers more towards individualized, participatory, active learning, is, based on the evidence of our findings, superfluous to requirements, from a student perspective. We emphasize that we do not, by any means, accept this as an adequate rationale for resisting change. We fully appreciate the merit of the argument that, since they are involved in a learning process, students are not necessarily best qualified to recognize what is in their best interests, particularly in the long term, and that they may not be the best judges of what they need. We also acknowledge that our students' general disinclination towards change is more likely to reflect ignorance which stems from lack of experience of that which change might bring rather than a conviction that it would be detrimental to their needs and interests. Essentially, our students were probably, for the most part, happy with the status quo because they had managed to adapt comfortably to its requirements and because they knew nothing else. It worked for them. Yet it does not follow that a different approach would not work equally well, or even better.

However, when consideration of the increased pressures on academic staff to perform well in both teaching and research is added to consideration of students' perceived needs and preferences, it is difficult to justify sweeping changes to course delivery which cannot be clearly justified on the basis of empirical evidence and which may potentially be detrimental to the quality of tutors' working lives. Utley's (1997b) suggestion that the prominence of lectures should be reduced is one such sweeping change. Our evidence reveals the potential of lectures in university teaching to be such that, as a mode of course delivery, they should by no means be dismissed out of hand as ineffective. We were given many accounts of lectures which, as we have illustrated in this chapter, seemed effective at promoting learning, and in the next chapter we provide evidence of how good lecturing is capable of engaging students' interest in their subject and of motivating them. Certainly, the wider range of methods of course delivery recommended by Dearing (NCIHE, 1997, pp. 114, 115) is to be welcomed, but these new methods could supplement, rather than replace, existing methods and, in doing so, enhance teaching and learning in higher education.

Chapter 4

Getting Involved

INTRODUCTION

In the previous chapter we examined students' assessments of the usefulness as vehicles for conveying course-related information of the various modes of course delivery. This chapter develops that examination by shifting the focus to students' levels of involvement with their courses, and the factors which influence these. Our interpretation of 'involvement' in this context is wide, encompassing attitudes towards, enthusiasm for, commitment to and participation in courses in their entirety, as well as specific course aspects and components. We examine the extent to which, and the reasons why, in relation to their courses, students feel involved and actually do get involved. We therefore focus both on attitudes and on behaviour.

This chapter contributes towards identifying students' study-related needs. It begins with an overview of the general extent of our students' reported levels of involvement, then goes on to identify more specifically the factors which emerged as determinants of the different levels of involvement, and, finally, examines the implications of these findings for meeting students' needs.

LEVELS OF INVOLVEMENT: AN OVERVIEW

As we pointed out in Chapter 2, one of the limitations of our study, which arose out of sampling bias, was that we were unfortunately unable to procure a student sample which was representative of the full range of motivation levels and study-related attitudes in the wider student population. Our student interviewees were, as a result, fairly well to very well motivated to study, displayed fairly to very positive study-related attitudes and reported fair to good levels of participation. None reported attitudes which might categorize them as disaffected. However, in some cases, in comparing and contrasting their own attitudes with those of their peers, our students provided reports of examples of more negative study-related attitudes which we have incorporated, where appropriate, into our evidence in an attempt to convey with a little more accuracy something of the nature and range of student involvement.

In this section we present a general picture of student involvement, distinguishing between reported attitudes and reported behaviour through two sub-sections, *Motivation* and *Participation*.

Motivation

To varying degrees, and with no distinction between the four subject sub-samples, all of our students reported positive study-oriented attitudes. Just over half of the sample described their attitudes as being predominantly work-focused, but encompassing a concern to balance their study commitments with a good social life. The following comments are illustrative of this level of commitment:

> I lie somewhere in the middle ... er ... I'm certainly not first-class honours material, but ... er ... I do a fair amount of work, but I like to combine it with a fairly busy social life. (Fiona, physics student)

> I don't want to, sort of, come to university just to, sort of, work. I mean, you may work very hard and not end up with anything spectacular in the end, so, I mean, it has to be a give-and-take sort of thing. Do your work and get a balance. (Graham, physics student)

> I mean, I want to do well – to get a 2i, I hope – but, I'm not going to get a first – I don't *want* to, because I think you don't get the mix – you wouldn't get the social life as well. (Angie, law student)

> I didn't really come to university to party ... but I think that *did* happen in my first year, and I found it very hard to find a balance. And, since then ... since I settled into this course, I've been quite fixed, I think, on doing well in my degree, you know, coming out with either a 2i or a first. (Poppy, education student)

The remainder, just less than half, of the sample were more exclusively work-focused and emphasized that studying, rather than socializing, was their main purpose. The extent to which this seemed to be the case varied. Some students reported that they endeavoured to ensure that their lives were not entirely devoted to studying, but did include socializing and leisure activities:

> My main reason for coming to university was to do my degree and, as far as I'm concerned, that's the most important thing. But I also recognize the importance of, like, the social life, and getting involved with other things, but, as far as I'm concerned, it's not my main priority. (Felicity, education student)

> I'd probably say that I was here to get a first ... and if I don't get one I will be ... very disappointed. But, secondly, I'm here to have a good time, and to meet people, and to have new experiences. Er ... but, mainly, I think it's the first, really. That's what's driving me, and that's what keeps me here ... I'm a bit of a workaholic ... I don't go out *too* much ... Whatever else is going on, the work always comes first. (Yvonne, education student)

Others, a minority, seemed to be almost entirely work-focused:

Well, I'm twenty-eight, so I'm not your average, sort of, eighteen ... nineteen-year-old entrant. And I've worked for eight years before, so I came here, not to socialize; I came here to get a degree ... er, and I want a *good* degree; I don't want a 2ii or a third. I want a 2i, preferably, and I do spend a lot of my spare time working ... A lot of what I *do* do is ... self-taught, if you see what I mean. Although we're given the ideas here, a lot of the time, obviously, is reading and finding out for yourself. (Grace, education student)

I'm a bit of a perfectionist. I get very, very stressed about every single essay ... sleepless nights ... and I'm writing through the night and sleeping all day ... that kind of thing. (Jane, English and American studies student)

I never thought I'd get to university, so to be here is an absolute achievement as far as I'm concerned, and I'm just *thrilled* to be here ... I keep on top of my work. Every single essay I had to hand in the first year was handed in ... I never asked for an extension ... I keep up with the reading. I read voraciously over the summer. I just read *everything* – in fact, I virtually read the whole of the literature part of the course! (Nancy, English and American studies student)

I've found, since I've joined the course, that I do love it ... What I want to do is achieve my potential, which, I hope, will be very high ... Most of my non-contact time, when I'm not looking after my family and home affairs, is taken up with studying ... Certainly, 95 per cent of my free time is taken up with it. (Tina, English and American studies student)

It became clear throughout their research interviews that this minority of students whose work focus seemed, in some cases, almost to verge on obsession share a concern to prove themselves capable of high achievement. In all cases, this concern seemed to represent a response to self-doubt and fears of inadequacy. Many of this minority of interviewees were mature students for whom this experience of higher education offered a second chance of academic success; a means of compensating for previous lost opportunities. Those who were not mature students typically manifested low self-esteem and low self-confidence, which some attributed to their failure to excel academically before coming to university. The common characteristic shared by this minority group was that they had something to prove to themselves, and their degree course was the vehicle for doing so.

Participation

The general picture to emerge of student participation was broadly positive. Most of our students reported being conscientious in respect of attendance and fulfilment of course requirements. The exception was the physics students' attendance at examples classes, which was poor to the extent that none of our interviewees had attended any of these classes during their second year. Within this generally positive picture, however, there emerged a diversity of participation levels in relation to the various specific elements of the four courses, and with respect not only to attendance but also to levels of engagement with particular types of activities. The nature of this diversity, and the reasons underlying it, are examined more specifically in the next section.

LEVELS OF INVOLVEMENT: INFLUENTIAL FACTORS

There are no simple, straightforward reasons why some students find a lecture on electro-magnetism absorbing, whilst others struggle to keep awake during it, or why some will have no qualms about voicing their views to a large seminar group, whilst others prefer to sit silently in a corner. The reasons are complex and reflect the intricacies of human motivation, which in turn are determined by differences in contextual circumstances and the individual differences which constitute the heterogeneity of human groups.

Our research findings revealed a diversity of student involvement in different aspects of their courses which was underpinned by the inter-relationship of two factors: the individual student her/himself and contextual circumstances, or, respectively, presage and context variables. Cutting across this inter-relationship of underlying factors was the added dimension of three different considerations which influenced the levels and nature of involvement: interpersonal, strategic and affective considerations. Amongst our sample there was no evidence of what we acknowledge as a fourth potential consideration: responsibility. Our findings reveal that the nature and the extent of student involvement were influenced by the combined effects of students' individual characteristics *and* prevailing contextual circumstances, in conjunction with *at least one* of the three considerations which we have identified. Something of the complexity of this combined interplay is conveyed through the specific findings which we present below, in three sub-sections: *Interpersonal considerations*, *Strategic considerations* and *Affective considerations*.

Interpersonal considerations

To varying degrees, students' participation in, and sometimes their attendance at, different course-related activities was determined by consideration of the rest of the group. Several students' references to this interpersonal consideration revealed it to be a quantitative issue, rather than one which is related to individual personalities.

Group size

Group size emerged as the key determinant of levels of active participation. Several students, for example, identified lectures, which accommodated between 20 and 220 students, depending on the course, as being inconducive to student interaction, since most students were insufficiently self-confident to speak out in front of so large a peer group:

> occasionally there's a lecturer that likes to ask questions, and does actually expect an answer off someone ... but most people don't really ... feel able to respond, even if they *do* know the answer. (Fiona, physics student)

> When you've got 150 people I wouldn't *dream* of asking a question. (Cathy, law student)

> The small classes I find, you know, a lot better. There's one lecture that we had last term in design and technology which was – there was only about six of us in the group. Er,

that was really good, 'cos ... er ... the lecturer was asking questions and the individuals were answering back. But in the lectures where there's, like, 100 people you can't really do that. (Daniel, physics student)

It was not just in lectures that students were unwilling to respond to questions: in large seminar groups, too, many students spoke of either their own or others' reluctance to interact:

I think the size of *all* seminar groups is too large. They're fifteen to twenty, and it does take an awful long time for people to feel confident to speak in that sort of forum. (Julie, education student)

If there's fifteen people in a seminar group and you have a discussion, there's no way that everybody's going to talk, so it's better to be in smaller groups. Then, even if you haven't got the confidence to speak in front of fourteen others, you can ... er ... speak in front of your little group and it, kind of, gives you a boost to have said something. (Jane, English and American studies student)

There was, amongst our sample, variation in students' reported enthusiasm for participating in seminar discussions. This seems principally, but not exclusively, as we point out in a later sub-section, to stem from a combination of two factors: group size and individuals' self-confidence, and did not relate to subject discipline. Some students manifested a definite preference for active, rather than passive, participation:

When I come to a seminar group I've always prepared my work. I always like to prepare so I can answer questions. I'm one of these – you may have gathered – quite a loud mouth in seminar groups. I tend to take over sometimes. I just, you know, run rampant with my mouth. (Alan, law student)

I think I *would* prefer more interaction ... I think you get *much* more benefit from seminars if you've got the students leading it, because they've got some commitment to the seminar. (Julie, education student)

I *love* seminars. They're the single most important part of the course ... If I hadn't actually been told by a student who I met last year – who's a third-year at Liverpool – and she was going, 'I've never spoken in seminars, ever', and I couldn't believe it at first. I thought everybody was like me ... I do get far more out of talking than I do out of reading criticism ... out of reading articles in *New Literature*, or whatever. I get a lot out of ... just personal contact, so any way I could increase that would be better for me. (Nigel, English and American studies student)

I think there's nothing worse than coming away, actually, from a seminar and thinking, 'I didn't say a *word*' ... I'm never afraid to make a fool of myself, unfortunately. (Jenny, English and American studies student)

I feel quite comfortable contributing. I don't mind at all; I'm quite happy to ... I normally have quite strong opinions on some things, so I say them ... I like contributing, and I like listening to what other people have to say. (Ruth, education student)

There were, however, across all subject sub-samples, students who spoke of how their lack of self-confidence deterred them from speaking out in front of what they considered to be too large a group:

When I first came ... I think a lot of the people at this University are southern ... and a lot of the tutors are southern, and you get this accent 'thing', and you're about to open your mouth, and then the person next to you speaks, and it's this ... I don't know ... just a different accent. It's so cultured, and you sit there and think, 'That's it. I'm not opening my mouth – ever!' And in the first year I don't think I talked much at all. And it was just because I thought, 'There's no chance. They'll either ... not understand what I've said, or they're just going to laugh and think I'm a country bumpkin.' ... If you're not prepared, it's good that you've got a large group because you can hide. But ... er ... I think, sometimes, if they were smaller groups you'd get more out of it because it would be more of a one-to-one basis, and if you didn't understand things you're more inclined to say, 'Excuse me, I don't understand', and have *five* people turn round and look at you as if you're stupid, rather than thirteen people. (Denise, law student)

I know, myself, I feel uncomfortable speaking up in seminars, because of the size of the group. It doesn't inspire confidence in people – especially if you're not used to talking up ... I can go away and work confidently on anything, really, but, when it comes to speaking up in the seminar about the same subject that I've just read about ... I don't seem to have that confidence to do it. (Yvonne, education student)

My idea of a seminar was six or eight people, but there's been a lot of problems with staff–student ratios, and there's about twelve, to fifteen, in each seminar group ... which isn't that good, I don't think ... I'm quite quiet in the seminars ... I don't really say that much ... Sometimes people say things. Sometimes, in a seminar where I haven't spoken and the tutor asks a question, and, in my head, I know the answer, and then my heart starts thumping and I start panicking and wait for someone else to come up with it. And then when they say it, I think, 'Well, there's nothing to it. I could've done that.' But, at the time, it's just ... panic ... Every time I see my personal tutor I say, 'I *wish* I could speak. I wish I could get the guts to do it.' ... Last week only four people turned up for a seminar and I spoke for the first time. But then, this week, the other fifteen turned up and I was the quiet one again. (Jane, English and American studies student)

Group dynamics

It was not simply group size which inhibited active participation. The group dynamics which influenced the extent to which students were prepared to get involved in course-related activities evidently involved an intricate interplay of interpersonal factors, including group composition, familiarity with other group members, body language, the atmosphere within the group and the presence of specific individuals, or 'types':

It's very dependent on the group and the size of the group. I mean, if I'm comfortable with the people I'm with, then I can contribute quite a considerable amount. But, if I feel ... I don't know ... we're in with a lot of the drama students and they take the lead in a lot of discussions, and that puts a lot of people off ... a lot of people I know, who're in the same position as me, take a back seat because there's people dominating the seminars.
Interviewer: So, do you feel intimidated?
Yeah, definitely! ... and I know, from talking to a lot of people who I mix with, that it's quite a widespread thing ... It does put people on edge and makes people sit back and be quiet ... And I can often think of ... you know ... relevant points I'd like to make ... and I won't say them ... I'll just keep them to myself, even though they'd probably, you know, be a good contribution to the discussion. (Oliver, education student)

The seminars ... I think it's variable, depending on who's in the group and how you interact with each other ... If you've got one shy person in a group of people who're very confident, then you, personally, aren't going to get much out of it. You can scribble down everything that everybody else says, but you don't necessarily understand it. And that's where I put myself. But, in other seminars, where I feel more comfortable with people, you're prepared to talk and so you get more out of it. (Karen, English and American studies student)

I didn't like the student-led seminars at first. I thought they were really intimidating – especially when you don't know people ... but you get used to them ... The entry requirements are quite high, and everybody's very clever, and most people I've spoken to say they end up feeling really intimidated, and everybody else seems so much cleverer than them. (Angie, law student)

The seminar system fails, most weeks, because if people haven't done the reading you can't get a discussion going. Er ... they don't know what they're talking about and you end up with one or two people talking. And if only one or two of you talk, then you feel a bit, sort of, like you stick out like a sore thumb, and everyone's thinking, 'Oh, that person's done the reading. That person's a swot.' So you don't tend to talk, and you don't *want* to talk, and the session, in the end, fails, and nobody gets anything out of it ... I *started* contributing. I used to contribute, at the beginning, and I contributed occasionally. I did yesterday, because I felt I had something reasonable to say. But, after a while, you give up. You think, 'Well, everybody else doesn't want to, so why should *I*?' ... And you feel a bit ... intimidated, in some ways, I suppose. (Ursula, education student)

I think, sometimes, it's the composition of the group. There's a lot of people on our course that're quite intimidating. Er ... I don't know whether anybody else finds that, but, certainly, *I* do. You get the feeling that there's a lot of – I don't know; it's almost bitchiness ... you just feel like people are talking behind your back. (Yvonne, education student)

This sample of comments conveys not only the diversity of the factors which inhibit students' willingness to become actively involved in group discussions, but, also, something of the complex interplay between presage and context variables: that is, the student her/himself and contextual circumstances. Our findings revealed an intricacy in the group dynamics which influenced students' participation, and which precluded the application of formulaic explanations of why students were willing or unwilling to speak out in groups. It was not simply a straightforward equation of self-confidence levels and group size. Some students made little, or no, contribution to group discussions, not because they lacked self-confidence but because they were unwilling to exert themselves to compete for opportunities to speak. Others, conversely, were motivated by the need to compete for a part in the discussion. Some, evidently, were intimidated into a low-participatory, or even non-participatory, role by threatened peer perceptions of their deviance.

Involvement in group discussions depends on a myriad of factors, such as: the student's overall level of self-confidence; interest in the subject; mood and feelings on the day; level of preparedness; group size; familiarity with others in the group; perceptions of the tutor; the tutor's attitude and approachability; and perceptions of the relevance of the discussion. Clearly, with so many, and other, dynamic variables to consider, there are limits to the extent to which departmental, or even course-team, policy on course delivery may be successful in encouraging greater participation. It seems that the means of potentially most effectively motivating students to become more involved in group activities lies with the group tutor who, through his or her own interaction with the rest of the group, becomes an integral component of and a controlling influence on its dynamics.

The tutor's role

GROUP MANAGEMENT

While there was diversity amongst our student interviewees in their responses to factors such as group size and group composition, there was unanimity in their recognition of course tutors' influence on student involvement. Several students spoke of tutors' influence on group dynamics, revealing a general acceptance that tutors have an important part to play in controlling the direction and level of discussion, the extent and distribution of student participation, and the overall success of the session. However, whilst there was consensus in relation to recognition of tutors' influence, students differed in their preferences for the style and the nature of tutors' involvement in and control over groups. The range of views amongst our students is illustrated by two law students' very different perspectives on tutors' intervention in seminars:

> I actually prefer ... lecturer-led seminars to student-led ones ... Most of the students aren't that willing to take part, so you really need a focus, which has to be the lecturer ... I always like to prepare, so I can answer questions ... and all the other students, like, haven't prepared because they know that the lecturer's going to go away for forty-five minutes and they can just sit there! ... Now, if he stayed for most of the time, I mean, yes, go away for ten or twenty minutes, or whatever, to let people just formulate their answers, but come back. And if we can have a half-hour or forty-minute discussion, it'd be really, really good. And he did that two weeks ago ... and we had a very, very informative discussion, and it was *very* good. But most weeks he doesn't do that. (Alan, law student)

> I think student-led seminars encourage people who're quiet to actually say something. I mean, lecturers are pretty good ... they do try to encourage everybody to join in, but there are some people who really are shy and reserved, especially overseas students ... and so I think it's less intimidating when fellow students are coaxing you, rather than when a lecturer turns to you and says, 'Well, what do *you* think?' (Cathy, law student)

Several comments highlighted tutors' potential for encouraging students' contributions to discussion. It was clear that this potential was perceived by students to be an individual characteristic: a quality which they found easy to recognize, but difficult to describe. Essentially, tutors varied considerably in relation to how students responded to them. Some had gained reputations which ensured that their courses were always oversubscribed. They secured good attendance rates and encouraged widespread participation in their courses' activities. Others were avoided because of their intimidating or annoying attitudes. Some were considered to be too laid-back and laissez-faire in their attitudes to student involvement, and some conveyed a lack of interest in, or concern for, students' work, which discouraged involvement.

The range of tutors' propensity for motivating students is reflected in the following illustrative comments:

> In seminars, particularly, some tutors are much easier than others to say things in front of. You have to have a lot of nerve, in *some* seminars, to actually say anything. And, like, last year I just didn't *dare*, half the time ... But, yeah ... there's some tutors that're easier to talk to in the seminar. (Doris, law student)

> Education, this year, has been absolutely superb for me. The tutor, who's a bought-in ex-head ... well, she is so down-to-earth, you can say anything to her. She gets on absolutely brilliantly with everybody. I mean, she's got a really bubbly personality, and everybody feels they can say anything to her, and the group discussions have been brilliant! Everybody's contributed, and she has a certain way of making sure that everybody *does* ... but not in a horrible way, she, like, invites people in a friendly sort of way, which is the right sort of attitude ... whereas, *last* year's ... er ... I didn't learn anything at all. Because I had such a bad one *last* year, I feel that *this* tutor is so much better ... last year, I think it was his first time with older students and ... we got the impression that he was ... still thinking he was in school with 13- to 14-year-olds, and he was very nervous with us all. (Grace, education student)

> Stephanie, last year's tutor, was very, sort of, emotional. One minute she'd be okay with you, and the next minute she'd be having screaming ab-dabs at the whole group, and I found that very unsettling; I didn't feel comfortable to talk to her about how I feel, and give my best to it, really ... Because of this irrationality every now and then, I felt that ... if I *did* say something, I didn't know what sort of comment I was going to be met with, so I'd really rather not, and just turn up, be there, and do all the things I *should* do and ... you know ... that was it. (Hazel, education student)

> It's a brilliant course! Ben [the tutor] is ... *everybody* shouts and screams and jumps up and down in *his* class, you know ... He comes in with a mug of coffee, and tells jokes, and it's ... you know, you're completely at ease. (Cathy, law student)

> I think, actually, maybe, you know, students are a little bit in awe of the tutors, and perhaps fear them a little bit. One of our tutors is so ... er ... well, she's really superb ... but sometimes she terrifies you with the things she *doesn't* actually say, in seminars. And you think, you know, 'If I *do* say anything, it's bound to be utter rubbish', because this person is so knowledgeable ... their very presence tells you they know *everything*. You know, she'll, sort of, sit back and ... and not say too much ... and, I think, sometimes that just can be a bit ... not *intimidating*, because I think that's an unfriendly word to use, but ... daunting. (Jenny, English and American studies student)

It became clear as we collected and analysed our data that the role of tutors is crucial in influencing participation levels and getting the best out of all students, in order to engineer a successful session. Success often depended on striking a right balance between encouraging and intimidating; on knowing when to invite comments and when to let the discussion flow undirected; on deciding whether to give an opinion or whether to wait for a pertinent point to emerge. It also required tact in handling the individuals within the group, in preventing more vociferous students from dominating, without discouraging their involvement and risking stifling the discussion. Several of our student interviewees manifested an awareness of the difficulties of this role, which were identified particularly clearly by an English and American studies student:

I think it's a very difficult balance for tutors. And I think the balance is ... multifaceted. It's about not, in any way, intimidating people, but being able to be encouraging, or to stimulate the conversation. It's about not ... you know ... turning it into a mini-lecture, but, you know ... getting feedback from people, and I think it's a really delicate balance. But some people seem to achieve it better than others, I think ... I've just been to a seminar, now, with someone who *I* respond to in a particular way ... and I think he is, obviously, very knowledgeable about his subject ... obviously he's been teaching for a very long time ... er ... and, listening to the other students talking about him, the responses are completely different, so that's another element in the balance of things ... you know ... the number of different personalities and ... er ... styles to be catered for ... *I* respond better to a very, sort of, positive ... a very, sort of, *direct* style ... I mean ... one particular seminar tutor who I had last year who I found absolutely tremendous and, at the end of the year, sort of, really felt that I'd gained a lot, because of this tutor, over the whole course. Er ... but I know other people who found her style, sort of, over-bearing, really ... (Tina, English and American studies student)

Considering the multifaceted nature of the task of orchestrating an effective group discussion, and the numerous variables which need to be taken on board, it is quite remarkable that the process is as generally successful as students and tutors believed it to be. The complexity of the task and the challenge which many of our tutors considered it to pose explain why this form of teaching has job-fulfilment potential. Yet our findings revealed our tutors to be, for the most part, unaware of the level of anxiety which some students, albeit a minority, experienced in seminars. Since they were unaware of this, tutors were, therefore, also unaware of the extent of their potential for boosting or lowering students' self-confidence and of their capacity for enhancing or damaging students' self-esteem.

We are able to provide a graphic illustration of the indirect effects on students' self-esteem of tutors' management of seminar group discussions. Earlier in this chapter (p. 53) we included a quote from Jane, an English and American studies student, which conveys something of the extreme anxiety that she frequently undergoes in seminar groups, when her personal need to contribute orally is unfulfilled because her lack of self-confidence prevents her from opening her mouth. Jane described how her heart starts thumping and how she formulates the answer to a question in her head, but is too nervous to articulate it. Yet she identified one particular option component of her course as an exception to her usual experiences:

I was interested right from the beginning, and was speaking, and felt at ease speaking.

She made a comparison with other components of her course, and described her typical behaviour in, and attitude to, these:

But, in seminars where I find it harder to settle in, to find out what kind of things we have to know and talk about ... er ... I find that I get myself into the role of the quiet one. And it makes it such a big deal if I would speak, that everyone would think, 'Wow! She's said something after two terms', that, even if I *did* have something to say, by that point, I don't. I keep it to myself.

Then, in response to being asked what had distinguished the seminars where she felt able to contribute, she identified, first, before making reference to other interpersonal factors, one particular organizational feature introduced by the tutor:

> The very first seminar we had, the tutor went round each person – she just asked them what their preconceptions were about the American South ... which forced everyone to speak first of all, and it, kind of, broke the ice. Also, there were third years in the group as well, and I didn't know anyone and I didn't feel that ... er ... I wasn't really bothered what people thought about me saying something, because I didn't know them and I wouldn't really see them outside the seminar ... so I just said whatever came into my head.

Finally, she described the effect which her participation had on her self-esteem:

> But then, once I'd done it ... For people who are really confident and talk all the time, it sounds silly, but for people who find it so difficult to talk, ... to have said something, and everyone's listened ... and, maybe, even writing it down – is just an amazing feeling! ... At the beginning I tended to talk a lot of rubbish – and everyone did – but then, when I started really getting interested and researching on my own, then, to have an intelligent conversation about literature, in front of everybody, with the tutor, was just ... amazing!
> *Interviewer: Did you feel it raised your self-esteem?*
> Yeah, definitely! ... But, then, by the same token, when I don't speak in the other seminars, I come out feeling like a nobody ... feeling, kind of, useless.

ENGAGING STUDENTS' INTEREST

Whilst many interviewees recognized tutors' capacity to influence students' active participation in course-related activities, all of our student sample acknowledged that tutors' potential for fostering enthusiasm for, interest in and generally positive attitudes towards their courses was considerable. Our findings reveal that, quite apart from whether or not they chose to participate actively, and, in some cases, irrespective of the amount of knowledge or number of skills which they acquired, students' feelings towards their courses were largely attributable to how well their tutors engaged their interest: how they put the subject across. This corroborates the findings of Gibbs and Harland (1987), whose questionnaire survey revealed the importance on students' attitudes to their courses of tutors' 'enthusiasm, openness and commitment' (p. 165). Tutors' qualities as teachers, it appears, not only determined what students learned but also how they felt about what they learned. Several students suggested that tutors' evident interest in and enthusiasm for the particular course component that they taught was contagious:

> I think it's the person themselves ... their character. I mean, we've had two lecturers so far for constitutional law. The first one, it was *very* hard to be interested because he was very slow ... er ... I don't know, he just didn't seem to have an interest in his subject, I think. So it was, like, coming across as, 'This is this', and he was very opinionated as well, which was difficult to work from because he was supposed to have, like, quite a neutral background. But the lecturer we've got *this* term's very good. I don't know what it is. He's very open ... he's very approachable ... you know. (Dorothy, law student)

> He's very good ... very good indeed. I mean, I'd really rate him as a tutor. You just find yourself electrified by listening to him ... It's his obvious enthusiasm ... the way

he changes his voice patterns … but, it's what he knows about his subject – history. He's obviously enthusiastic, and that counts for a lot. If somebody's enthusiastic and enjoys their subject … and they've got a charisma – there's a charisma there … And then, there's the education course. Last year I absolutely hated education … this year I absolutely love it, and it's purely down to how it's been put across, I really do feel strongly about that … This year I can't wait to get to the lectures. I really enjoy them, and it's given me a whole new dimension. Last year I was seriously thinking, 'Well, what am I doing?', you know, 'If this is what education is all about, is this really what I want, to go into teaching?' And, now, I'm, sort of, thinking, 'Yes, and I can take it with both hands!' … I mean, the content has got to have *something* to do with it … but if you've got a tutor that's … reasonably on track, they'll make the first year delightful, if they've got it there. (Hazel, education student)

Tutors' delivery style – the way in which they communicated course content to students, through lectures or seminars – was also considered to be an extremely potent influence on students' attitudes towards their courses:

In my constitutional law seminar, the seminar tutor's got a very … monotone voice, and it puts me to sleep sometimes. But, I don't think it causes that many problems for other people. I think it's just, kind of, an expectation thing, really. I go into the seminar thinking I'm not going to enjoy it, and so I don't enjoy it. (Deborah, law student)

The equal opportunities issue very much interests me, anyway, so I suppose I'm quite fired up about that, anyway, but … even … it possibly couldn't have interested me as much if it hadn't been for the lecturer. She's had a way of talking about it and making me think about it more than, I feel, the person I had last year would've done. (Grace, education student)

I recently went through a lecture course run by a particular chap, Ivan, … and he was one of the best lecturers I've ever had … He was inspiring … he was interesting … he was … I really wanted to salute him and say, 'Thank you' … I wanted to say, 'Thank you very much' … He really, sort of, grabbed you and said, 'Hey look!' (Harold, physics student)

The maths tutor went round the group, asking people to pull teddy bears out of the sack, and, again, even with *our* age group, people were going, 'Can *I* do one? Can *I* do one?', which is exactly what would happen in a classroom. And then he stopped for a bit and then he said, '*Now*, how many d'you think there are in here?' Er … he hadn't asked enough people to pull teddy bears out of the bag for us to see a pattern … and, so, he carried on asking people to pull these teddy bears out … but, you know, it took quite a while to establish the pattern, and, I mean, by the end of this, sort of, activity a couple of people had walked out because they were bored … er … it was … I don't know, I mean, there were only about five of us concentrating, in the end, that could see the point of this activity. (Felicity, education student)

Similarly, tutors' attitudes to students could either win them over or antagonize them to the point of losing their interest:

Well, I had a lecture yesterday, actually, and … basically, the tutor stood in front of the class and he said, 'I'm waiting …' And he was waiting for us all to shut up. And then … er … he started to go on about … 'You're not exactly gaining my respect in this class, because you're talking when I'm talking', and, 'I expect respect from you', and all this … I felt like we were five-year-olds, really, in a class … I just felt really patronized and I just couldn't be bothered to listen after that, really. (Yvonne, education student)

The gentleman who runs the second-year laboratory at the moment, his attitude is very much . . . 'Oh, fucking hell, what d'you want now?' And . . . a lot of people *aren't* – a lot of people are very passionate about it . . . I think my personal tutor's very good, and he's always got time for me . . . but, I think, what happens is that particular people are put in charge of, like, say, a particular subject, and they have to mark, maybe, eighty or ninety different students, and so, because of that repetition, they get very complacent and they get very . . . blasé about it. And what happens when you're the ninety-seventh person to go up to him and say, 'Where's my mark?' or, 'Has it been done?' or, 'What did you think of it?', not surprisingly, the attitude comes over as being very . . . blasé . . . and it's very painful. (Harold, physics student)

Strategic considerations

Our findings revealed many examples of students' levels of involvement being determined by the strategies which they adopted in order to excel in, or simply to cope with the demands of, their courses. Essentially, strategic considerations informed a prioritization which was reflected in differential involvement in various course components and course-related activities. Students ranked these course components and activities on the basis of their perceived relative value, and they prioritized accordingly the time and effort to be expended on involvement in them.

Strategic considerations involved cost-benefit equations which assessed the cost-effectiveness, in relation to time and effort, of participation. Cutting across strategic considerations, presage and context variables shaped the nature and the extent of their influence and determined the bases of the different criteria for value which were applied.

We interpret a strategy as simply a plan of action, and so, accordingly, all approaches to study are, in this sense, strategic. In this chapter, however, we confine our examination of students' strategic considerations to those study-related strategies prompting courses of action which were directed towards purposes reflecting a variation on those intended by the institution. Two such strategies, which are inter-related, were particularly prominent: assessment-oriented prioritization, and time and effort prioritization. We examine each of these below.

Assessment-oriented prioritization

A small minority of our students, from amongst those who reported being conscientiously study-oriented to an extreme which in some cases verged on obsession, or workaholism, appears to have been intrinsically, rather than extrinsically, motivated to study. These students seemed to want to learn for the sake of learning: to extend their understanding, to develop their intellectual capacity and to absorb information in a voracious quest of knowledge. The majority of our sample was, however, to varying degrees, essentially assessment-focused. Their attitudes to studying seemed to be similar to those summed up in a law student's description of himself:

> I don't believe anyone just sits down and studies for the fun of it. I mean, I love law, that's why I'm doing it – I really love it ... but, still, I don't sit down and say, 'Oh, I've nothing to do, let's read a couple of pages of a law book!' (Hakan, law student)

These students' involvement in their courses was influenced by consideration of how, and in what ways, they might best meet course assessment requirements. To them, the value of course components and course-related activities was determined by how useful they were for assessment purposes. We emphasize that it was by no means the case that students tended only to attend those sessions, or to undertake those activities, which were clearly advantageous with respect to course assessment preparation. None of our sample, since it was representative of those who are reasonably to very motivated, admitted to adopting the minimalist approach to course-related involvement which one student identified:

> students are going to do ... the majority of them are going to do as little as they can to get the right mark to get through their degree. (Colin, education student)

However, some provided second-hand evidence of low levels of involvement amongst their peer group:

> One girl who was in my seminar group last year, I think I saw her *twice* in all the seminars for the whole year! She hardly went to *anything* – she didn't go to any lectures ... She passed! I think she had to re-sit her exams, but, as far as I know, she's on the course again this year. (Cathy, law student)

> Last week I was in a lecture, and this particular lecture is a late one – it's four o'clock till five on a Monday, which is difficult for me, with children; I'd had to make childcare arrangements ... and I saw this chappie in there that I know, and I said to my friend, 'Gosh, so-and-so's in here', I said, 'He must've swapped from another option'. So I spoke to him last week, and that was the *first* lecture he'd attended on that option! (Nancy, English and American studies student)

There were amongst our students many reports of levels of participation which exceeded assessment-focused requirements, but it was, nevertheless, the case that, when faced with the need to prioritize, course assessment-related needs were a prime consideration. The extent of the influence of assessment-oriented prioritization varied amongst the majority for whom this was a strategic consideration, and was manifested in diverse ways. One student spoke of how her course option choices were influenced by assessment-related considerations:

> Definitely, next year, I'll be looking at who's teaching the courses, rather than what their content is ... and looking to see that I can get a solid basis from the course to do the exam well and do the course work well, rather than be that interested in it. (Fiona, physics student)

Others clearly placed greater emphasis on activities which were assessed than on those which were not and which were, accordingly, relegated to being considered peripheral:

> I go for the information which will help me in the exam. I don't, sort of, go for the, sort of, the 'extras' which aren't relevant for the exam. (Clive, law student)

> I have great intentions about doing things, but rarely get round to doing them. Er ... I tend to put most of my work into essays and the seminar feedbacks that we have to give ... and the revision. (Colin, education student)

Variations between students in the extent and the nature of their assessment-oriented prioritization reflected individuals' different study-related needs and the different attitudes to study which underpinned these and, as such, they constitute the presage variables to which we have referred. Representing the context variables which also cut across strategic considerations was a specific manifestation of assessment-oriented prioritization which was peculiar to the physics students, and which applied to this entire sub-sample. All of our physics student interviewees admitted to having failed to attend any of the weekly examples classes during their second year. Two main reasons, which many of the students combined into a single, dual-factor, excuse, were offered for this non-participation. One reason was that attendance at examples classes offered students no advantages in relation to course assessment since, even though they might include content which would feature in exam questions, the answers to the questions discussed in examples classes would be pinned up on noticeboards. The other reason was the inconvenient time at which examples classes were held. This second reason reflected prioritization of time and effort, rather than assessment-oriented prioritization and we therefore examine it in more detail in the next sub-section.

Time and effort prioritization

The tendency of many of our physics students to combine them into a single excuse for non-attendance at examples classes demonstrates how inter-related are the two forms of prioritization which we identify. The particular circumstances making attendance at these classes an issue which involved time and effort prioritization were: second-year students, in accordance with university policy, lived off-campus; examples classes were timetabled late in the day; and the other second-year physics classes that day finished around midday. The inconvenience for students which this represented is explained through one student's comments:

> Personally, I haven't been going this term. Er ... the examples classes have been up and running but ... er ... being in the second year, and living about ten miles away, they're actually at very awkward times, and you, sort of, end up spending about ... five or six hours on campus in between your early morning lecture, and then they've decided to plonk these examples classes at the end of the day. Whereas, I'd rather, like, head on home and do my own reading up ... which is probably a bit silly, but it seems to be what a lot of people *are* doing ... They were well attended last year, the maths examples classes, because we were on campus and it's a lot more convenient to have a five-minute walk, rather than hanging around all day. (Fiona, physics student)

These sentiments were shared by all of the physics students and, in response to our asking students if they could think of ways in which their course could be improved, some identified more conveniently timed examples classes as the best, and in some cases the only, potential source of improvement.

Yet, in the case of physics examples classes, inconvenient timing was not the only issue to influence the prioritization process. The low assessment-related value afforded to these classes was equally important an issue when considered in conjunction with that of timing. It was undoubtedly the combination of these two factors which resulted in what our evidence suggests was complete non-attendance, not only on the part of our sub-sample but also, by our interviewees' accounts, of the entire second-year cohort of physics students. It is likely that, despite the classes' low assessment-related value, convenient timing of the classes would have had the effect of securing some students' attendance. It is likely, too, that inconvenient timing would deter only a minority of students from attending the classes if their assessment-related value were high.

It is impossible to separate time and effort prioritization entirely from that which is assessment-oriented, since the assessment process is integral to and prominent in the process of studying for a degree. It is for this reason that it is upon assessment that students' goals are focused. Assessment is the vehicle used for gaining a degree and, as such, it shapes their study-related needs. Prioritization of time and effort involves students' making choices when faced with competing demands on their time and energy. It involves cost-benefit calculations, but the currency being calculated is gains and losses in the assessment process which leads to a degree. Time and effort prioritization certainly includes, typically, consideration of what will take the least time and involve the least effort – although even this is subject to variation amongst individuals, reflecting a myriad of presage variables – but this consideration is in conjunction with consideration of what will yield the most gains, and result in the least losses, in the assessment process.

Affective considerations

It is very difficult to isolate evidence of the influence of students' affective feelings for their subject, or, more specifically, for their courses, from the influence of the other two considerations that we have identified. Clearly, as we have demonstrated with the findings examined in an earlier sub-section, interpersonal factors, such as tutors' attitudes and delivery styles, are capable of influencing the ways in which students perceive their courses, and, sometimes, even the subject itself. Strategic considerations, too, are not entirely detached from affective considerations, but incorporate them into their integral prioritization process.

Nevertheless, whilst acknowledging the underlying interrelationship between all three considerations, we did find some evidence of the influence of affective considerations on students' involvement in their courses which seemed to be relatively independent of interpersonal and strategic considerations. Data constituting this evidence were provided by a minority of students, but we consider it important to mention that approximately a quarter of the student sample referred to the extent to which they felt inclined to participate in course-related activities being influenced by how well they liked their subject, how interested in it they were and how passionate they felt about it, either in its entirety or in relation to specific components:

Er ... I think it's different with different subjects. In some subjects I'm really active, and I really speak a lot. But ... er ... in my constitutional law seminar I don't enjoy the subject at all – it's not that I don't *understand* it – it's just that I don't enjoy it, and so I find it really difficult to bring myself to actually speak in the seminars. (Deborah, law student)

I'm definitely not a swot! I mean ... er ... I tend to, sort of, like ... leave it to the last minute a bit. I mean, I did quite well last year, but, like ... I do tend to leave it to the last minute. I mean, I can't *stand* physics – I hate it! I can't stand it. ... I just, sort of, did it at the time because it was something I could actually do. ... I think A level killed *me* off – I couldn't stand A level physics. And it was merely a case of, sort of ... finding a degree to do which I *could*, ... but I can't stand it ... It's like ... I think it's a very hard course, and then ... so, like ... if you're not that interested in it, it makes it even more difficult when you have to really work to understand it. So ... I just leave it to the last minute. (Greg, physics student)

I *can* be a perfectionist. It depends ... if something interests me, then, probably, I *am* a perfectionist. Er ... I can spend hours and hours doing things just because I want them to be right – *if* I'm interested. (Valerie, English and American studies student)

It's normally things that I'm interested in that I prioritize more time to, and the subjects that I'm not so interested in, I tend to rush those a bit more ... not to give my 'all' as much. (Ruth, education student)

As these comments indicate, affective considerations influence students' attitudes towards their courses, which, since they underlie the motivation to work, influence participation in turn. Yet, whilst students clearly feel more inclined towards study when they are interested in, enjoy or have a passion for their subject, affective considerations alone are relatively insignificant as an influence on involvement in course-related activities. Our findings revealed them to be very much a supplementary influence, overshadowed by interpersonal considerations and eclipsed by the most potent influence of all those which we have identified, strategic considerations.

IMPLICATIONS FOR MEETING STUDENTS' NEEDS

The findings presented in this chapter reveal both diversity and commonality amongst the student sample, in relation to their involvement in their courses. On the one hand, diverse preferences for levels of participation in small-group discussions, for example, or for more tutor-independent learning, as well as different preferences in relation to tutors' delivery style, make it difficult to suggest ways of encouraging participation which will meet all study-related needs. Some students, as we have illustrated, are happy to sit in obscurity at the back of a lecture hall or seminar room, keeping their heads down, listening to what others are saying and recording what they consider to be useful. Others wish they could find the courage to participate actively, but seldom find themselves able to do so, and experience low self-esteem as a result of their perceived inadequacy. Others relish the opportunities which small-group teaching sessions offer for voicing their opinions and debating issues with tutors and fellow students. Any study-related needs which this varied picture reflects are clearly not common to all and therefore cannot be considered core needs. Rather, they reflect a range of study-related preferences which could be accommodated through methods of course delivery incorporating something for everyone: opportunities for discussion in very small sub-groups, larger group exchanges, and more passive involvement, as well as both tutor-independent and tutor-directed learning.

Emerging very clearly as a common concern, however, was the need to fulfil assessment requirements. This took precedence over all other considerations in students' decisions over the extent and nature of their involvement, and we identify it as a core study-related need. The implications of this for teaching and learning and for departmental and institutional policy development are that measures to introduce changes, whether they be innovative methods of course delivery or teaching approaches aimed at saving tutors' time or at coping with larger groups of students, are unlikely to win the approval of students if they do not also prepare them for course assessment. It seems to be the case that, for tutors who wish to encourage greater student participation in their courses, the key to success lies not so much in stimulating or interesting them – though this certainly helps – but in ensuring that what is provided is recognized by students as being of assessment-related relevance.

Chapter 5

Meeting Students' Needs: A Framework for Course Design and Delivery

INTRODUCTION

Chapters 3 and 4 have focused respectively on the prominence of pertinent information as a study-related need and on students' preferences for the various ways in which they are able to access such information. The picture presented by the illustrative examples in these two chapters is one of students as a heterogeneous group, with diverse views and tastes, reflected in a wide range of preferred ways of learning. This diversity will be familiar to anyone who has tried to implement modifications to course content, delivery or assessment in the light of student feedback and has become exasperated at the impossibility of reconciling conflicting evaluations into planned changes which will satisfy everyone. As we illustrated in the two chapters which precede this one, students differ, not in relation to subject-specific factors but on a much more individual basis.

Some preferred to be lectured at, others to participate in discussions. Some preferred conventional lectures which presented large amounts of information in a clear, coherent way; others preferred lectures in which students' participation was encouraged. Some wanted to understand what was being presented, some were content with being informed.

Considering the large number of presage variables which are applicable to analysis of our findings in relation to students' preferences, the diversity is not unexpected. Yet it was only in relation to study-related preferences that differences between students were evident. In relation to what students perceived to be their study-related needs, our findings revealed a basic commonality.

There is a clear distinction between study-related needs and study-related preferences. Addressing the issue of what distinguishes students' 'wants' and 'needs', Bailey (1993) implies that wants are usually determined by students themselves, and needs by academics. In the context of our study, the study-related needs to which we refer are, as we explained in Chapter 2, their own needs, as perceived by the students. Study-related preferences are related to needs, but are distinct from them in that they reflect what students would ideally like, but which, unlike needs, are not perceived as absolute necessities.

This is a period of great change for higher education in the UK. The effects of recent reforms have been to set in motion the process of altering the nature and the notion of higher education. The need for redefinition, greater clarity and cohesiveness in relation to the aims, the purpose and the form of higher education is widely recognized (see, for example, Barnett, 1997a; Barnett, 1997b; Harvey, 1996; Hague, 1996). The university of the twenty-first century will be a 'new-look' university. As Harvey (1996, p. 183) points out:

> higher education itself must be transformed ... What is needed is that academics embrace the new paradigm of higher education and embrace transformation as a positive rather than regrettable step away from the traditional values of the cloister.

A key component of the transformed higher education will be a changed conception of the student constituent, in relation to its role, its status, its position and its needs. However this conception emerges, whether it adds definition to the developing image of students as clients (or customers) or whether it is more aligned to Harvey's (1996, p. 183) notion of students as the recipients of an institutionally designed empowerment package, it will require an understanding of student needs and preferences so that it may either, in the first case, endeavour to meet them or, in the second case, endeavour to transform them. Empirical evidence of diversity, and analyses of how the nature of this diversity is determined by complex causal relationships, contributes much to understanding students' perceptions of their study-related needs, and the origins and determinants of their preferences, but it is, on its own, of limited use for policy-making and practical application, on account of its unwieldiness. The rationale for undertaking any piece of research is not only to contribute to the development of theory but also to apply that developed theory to policy and practice. In order to be meaningful, then, the practical implications of research findings need to be informed by a mechanism which combines both elucidation and generalizability and reflects a level of analysis which incorporates understanding of what accounts for the diversity manifested by the findings into the identification of the 'lowest common denominator' explanation of them. As a mechanism for the practical application of our research, we have developed out of analysis of our findings a framework for understanding course components' acceptability with students. We present and illustrate this below.

A FRAMEWORK FOR 'STUDENT-ACCEPTABLE' COURSE DESIGN AND DELIVERY

Our framework has three components, reflecting the three areas of consideration which it incorporates: students' perceived study-related needs;

students' study-related preferences; and course-related influences on the satisfaction of study-related needs and preferences. We examine these through a three-stage incremental process. First, we present a model of an incremental sequence of what our students identified as those essential aspects and features of following a first-degree course and which we refer to as study-related needs. Second, we match each specific study-related need to illustrative examples of the range of aspects and features of following a first-degree course for which our students expressed a preference. Third, we match each specific study-related need, and the examples of study-related preferences associated with it, to examples illustrating the various features of degree courses and the ways in which they are delivered, which have the potential to satisfy that need and its associated study-related preferences' example.

A model of study-related needs

Our research findings have revealed core study-related needs, as perceived by students, which are common to all students amongst our sample and, therefore, represent the 'lowest common denominator' to which we referred above. These core needs are incremental in the sense that they form a progression, which we illustrate in Figure 5.1. We do not imply that the progression reflects an increase in educational value associated with the different needs, merely that it represents increasing proximity to the gaining of a degree. We have identified five needs, each on a different level, demonstrating the cumulative, or incremental, nature of the composite picture of study-related needs. Since we consider these to be core needs, we have chosen to end our model, in the context of this book's focus, with the need to gain a degree. Clearly, though, the picture does not end there, and our students varied in the extent to which, and in the clarity with which, they identified more far-reaching needs. Some failed to identify needs which went beyond gaining a degree.

The most basic need identified was the need to receive appropriate information. Some students identified this need more explicitly than did others, but reference to it was included, sometimes repeatedly, in some form or other in all students' interviews. Information which was considered necessary included the course syllabus and what students needed to know about the organization and structure of the course, and course-related university and departmental procedures.

The second-level need in our model is the need to acquire specific knowledge, skills and experience. This constitutes a natural progression from the need for appropriate information since it involves students' processing the information which they receive, through cognitive assimilation, in order to transform it into knowledge or, through applying it to practical use, to develop specific skills or to gain specific experience(s).

At the third level, which represents a self-evident progression from level two, is the need to utilize the acquired knowledge, skills and experience in participation in course components. Participation in course components

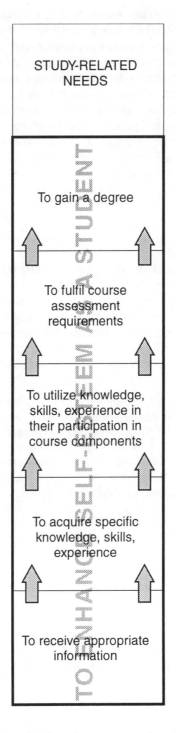

Figure 5.1   Perceived core study-related needs

includes all occasions when students fulfil course requirements or avail themselves of course-related participatory opportunities.

The need to fulfil course assessment requirements, at level four, reflects the assessment-oriented prioritization which most of our students practised. It also represents a progression from level three to a narrower focus on one specific course component.

Level five is represented by the need to gain a degree, which all of our students identified as the primary purpose of their being at university. Obtaining a degree was, without a doubt, the goal upon which they all focused: all of their study-related core needs, as our model illustrates, were subsidiaries of this over-arching need, and were formulated out of its constituent parts. Finally, pervading all of these five core needs was the need to enhance self-esteem as a student.

The model of students' core study-related needs, which reflects students' own perceptions of their needs, not only highlights the features of studying for a first degree upon which students focus, but it also serves to illustrate how narrow that focus is, in comparison with what is typical of tutors, in terms of their perceptions of students' needs.

Needs are determined, in part, by goals, and it is fundamentally in relation to educational or study-related goals that the disparity between students' and tutors' perceptions arises. Packwood and Sinclair-Taylor (1995, p. 218) outline a higher-education learning process which, in terms of the cognitive demands that it places on students, exceeds the process suggested by our model:

> There are certain distinctive features which characterise the learning process at HE level. Students are required not only to acquire an extensive technical knowledge of their subject area but also the associated skills involved in applying that knowledge within a profession or an academic discipline. This knowledge goes well beyond the acquisition of detailed factual knowledge; it involves the development of conceptual understanding and critical thinking about the subject matter.

Similarly, Chalmers and Fuller (1996, p. 4) refer to goals which have been identified by university tutors:

> It is important to note that while specific goals were discipline-related, they were not directed at accumulation of knowledge of specific content of a discipline, but at the more general principles of critical thinking and understanding.

Yet, if the educational goals of higher-education tutors include the development of conceptual understanding and critical thinking, our research evidence suggests that they are not necessarily shared by students. This incongruence between students' and tutors' goals is well recognized. Elton (1996a, p. 65), for example, points out that 'some students' motivation for learning may differ from what their teachers would like it to be, at least in the order of importance given to them'. Wankowski (1991, p. 74) suggests that:

> Students' attitudes to teaching and learning at university are most likely to derive from their *wants* and, consequently from their expectations of how their *wishes* are to be met or fulfilled on entering an institution of higher education.

Considering, then, that students' overriding *want*, on embarking on a degree course, is, for the most part, to be awarded a degree, this becomes the goal upon which they focus and which determines their needs; the wider goals of their tutors are excluded on the grounds of their perceived superfluity.

Chalmers and Fuller (1996, p. 5) describe how the incongruence between students' and tutors' goals manifests itself:

> It would seem that many students complete university without achieving the intended goals of university education. These students achieve only a basic understanding of the discipline they are studying. They are able to recite facts, manipulate jargon, and survive the assessments, but lack awareness of their own limited understanding of the principles of the discipline.

They attribute students' failure to achieve the goals set by their tutors to their seeing learning in relation to a hierarchy of six specific conceptions, derived from several sources (Chalmers and Fuller, 1996, pp. 5–8).

Progressing through each level of the hierarchy, beginning at the lowest, these conceptions of learning are: a quantitative increase in knowledge; memorizing and reproduction; applying knowledge; making sense or abstracting meaning; interpreting and understanding reality in a different way; and changing as a person (Chalmers and Fuller, 1996, pp. 5–6). Supporting Wankowski's (1991, p. 74) suggestions that students' attitudes to teaching and learning are shaped from the *wants* and *wishes* which they have when they enter university, Chalmers and Fuller (1996, p. 5) identify students' conceptions of learning as the beliefs which they hold about what learning involves and what they intend to achieve through study, and which are influenced by their current goals and motives. Since their goals and motives are focused narrowly upon successfully completing their course and being awarded a degree, students' conceptions of learning generally fall within the parameters of the lowest levels of the hierarchy.

Certainly, our research evidence supports the idea that students' study-related goals and motives tend to be, for the most part, so narrowly focused on the assessment-oriented path which leads to a degree that they equate to the lowest conceptions of learning. Indeed, our model of study-related needs reflects only the first three 'quantitative' conceptions. Yet it is important to draw a distinction between students' conceptions of learning and their perceived study-related needs which emanate from their goals. Although our study was not intended to uncover views about the nature of learning and the wider purpose and aims of higher education, our findings nevertheless revealed evidence that some students' conceptions of learning were at a higher level than their reported study-related needs would suggest. However, it is impossible to know how widespread this was, since the evidence emerged, to some extent, incidentally and was not gathered systematically.

Whilst it is very difficult to try to match specific comments made by students during research interviews as examples of specific conceptions of learning, it is possible to identify evidence of conceptions of learning which seem to be higher than those reflected in the study-related core needs identified in our model. Several students, for example, spoke of the importance of formulating their own opinions, rather than simply accepting those presented by tutors, or presented in texts:

> There's one lecturer who tends to put forward, very strongly, his own view ... and sometimes it's nice just to get an objective view so you can form your own opinion around that. (Angie, law student)

> We're not given enough opportunity to do our own learning and think for ourselves, sometimes. Things are just rammed down our throats and we have to accept that that is that. (Yvonne, education student)

Some highlighted the importance of learning, rather than simply acquiring information:

> Some lecturers just don't seem to communicate ... they don't seem to keep the essence of what's going on ... and so it just becomes a load of information; it doesn't become a concept, or an idea, which, of course, is incredibly important in physics. (Harold, physics student)

> I probably enjoy the lectures most because I like learning new things, whereas, the labs, they're not really about learning new things. They're, maybe, expanding on something that you do know, but it's basically, er ... practical work, which is not so ... oh, I can't think of the word – educational ... It doesn't teach you as much ... Some lecturers actually ask questions in lectures, which, I think, is a better way to do it because it gets us all thinking, instead of just copying down and not thinking what we're writing. (Claire, physics student)

Yet it became clear, as we analysed our data, that, although some students clearly seemed to hold conceptions of learning which were more sophisticated, and of a higher order, than those suggested by the needs identified in our model, these more sophisticated conceptions reflected students' study-related *preferences*, rather than their *needs*.

A model of study-related needs and preferences

The key distinction between what students implicitly ranked as needs and what they implicitly ranked as preferences is the perceived indispensability of the needs, in relation to students' goals. This resulted in prioritization which put needs before preferences. Several students spoke of how, for pragmatic reasons, their study patterns had to be designed in order, first and foremost, to meet the core study-related needs, and, only if time were available, to satisfy their preferences. One example of this prioritization is provided by the comments of Graham, a physics student. On the one hand, he spoke of his preference for developing an interest in his subject and, in doing so, enhancing his understanding and appreciation of it:

> I find it interesting hearing about tutors' research. It keeps you interested in your subject as well, to, sort of, be able to talk to people who're actually researching something new, and have got something to tell you ... In the first year I just, sort of, got down and did my work, and when it came to the exams, and when you start reading through your notes, you have a deeper understanding ... and then, as you *really* understand, you get really interested in the subject. So, I think, yeah, it's really good to get that interest. It

helps you in the work. You enjoy the course much more. It stops it becoming ... just going off to lectures, writing notes and doing questions.

Clearly, this presents a picture of a student who is evidently much nearer to achieving some of the kinds of learning goals which his tutors are likely to hold than are students who typically go to lectures simply to build up a set of revision notes which will facilitate their passing examinations. Yet, on the other hand, Graham referred to his prioritization of time which involved his missing out parts of the course which were not essential for assessment purposes:

> I haven't actually attended any examples classes ... I did in the first year, and they were quite helpful because you could go along and get information. But, also, I find, when it comes to exams, I've got, like, enough work in my notes – they're complete enough and comprehensive enough to get all the information I need from those.

Similarly, Jane, an English and American studies student, provided another example of this type of prioritization. She spoke first of how she had developed intellectually whilst following the course, to the extent that she considered herself capable of critical analysis and reflection:

> At school we were spoon-fed opinions on literature. We were told what to think. And when I came here in the first year I was, kind of, waiting for an opinion to write down, and we were given, maybe, two or three, maybe one. And, for the first six months, I was just completely baffled ... and then I started to learn to develop my own opinions ... which I *didn't* at school ... Lecturers tend to take it in turns to give lectures ... and have different ideas, and contradict each other. But, I mean, as long as you've got your head screwed on, you can – you learn, by the second year, you learn to just follow your own ideas, and other people's are either interesting, or they're not. But you don't really base your ideas on theirs by the second year ... I mean, some lecturers love poets, and others hate them ... It's quite interesting, seeing both sides of the input. Also, we're encouraged to look at criticism, which is also conflicting opinions, and you learn to just pick out the best bits of each one, and make it your own.

Again, this suggests an approach to study which is far wider and encompasses much more than simply acquiring knowledge and using it to pass examinations. Jane also spoke of a passionate love of her subject, and how she had expected this to be fostered during her undergraduate years:

> I took English because it was a hobby. Reading was a hobby. I love reading. I, kind of, lived from book to book in a fantasy world. I mean, my idea of being a university student was to have a passion about the subject that you're doing.

But this conception of learning, which, as with our earlier examples, is more sophisticated than the conceptions suggested by our model of core study-related needs, remained to a large extent unrealized in Jane's case. She spoke of demands on her time which forced her to prioritize in favour of meeting the assessment-oriented needs:

> Coming here has killed that passion, to some extent, because we're always under pressure to read. One week I had *Middlemarch* and *Roots* to read, in the same week! And we're skimming all the time, and if you get to a difficult bit you tend to skim over it because you haven't got time. And then, when you're reading, you're thinking, 'Well, what will I be able to say about this in the seminar?', instead of just reading for pleasure ... which is one of my regrets.

Figure 5.2 illustrates the relationship between specific study-related needs in our model and specific study-related preferences, of which we provide a range of examples. Study-related preferences varied from student to student, giving our sample the heterogeneity to which we have referred earlier and which has been illustrated through the students' comments in Chapters 3 and 4. Whilst it is possible that, in the case of some students, what we have identified as preferences may actually constitute real, self-esteem-related, needs, our model presents study-related preferences as, for the most part, optional extras to the fulfilment of the core study-related need with which they are aligned on our model, bearing in mind that they are not confined to alignment with one need.

Some students, for example, prefer to have their need for appropriate information met in a way which allows them to be interested in the information which they are receiving, and/or in a way which involves their participating actively, rather than passively, or in a way which allows them to seek clarification about some aspects of the information. Clearly, these preferences, along with the needs with which they are aligned, have implications for and relate to features of course design, delivery and content.

A model of study-related needs and preferences, and course-related influences on their satisfaction

Students' study-related needs, as identified in our model, are met through specific course-related features, which have to become even more specific and clearly defined in order to satisfy associated preferences. Figure 5.3 illustrates, with a range of examples, the relationship between needs, their associated preferences, and specific course-related features.

It is important to note that, whilst each course-related feature listed in our model influences the extent to which the core study-related need with which it is aligned is satisfied, it does not necessarily have the potential to satisfy any of the associated preferences, though our selection of examples generally includes those features which have the potential to satisfy at least one preference, and usually most of the preferences, with which they are aligned.

Applying the model to course design and delivery

If they are to be acceptable to students, course design and delivery must, at the very least, accommodate the core study-related needs identified in our model. At the lowest level, in order to provide students with information which is appropriate for their assimilating it into knowledge, skills or/and experience, which they might then utilize in their participation of course components, in order to satisfy the requirements of course assessment and be awarded a degree, it is essential: that the knowledge and expertise of tutors designing and delivering the course render them competent to provide the information, in one form or another; that tutors are sufficiently available and/or approachable to provide adequate opportunities for information to be conveyed to students; that lectures are structured and delivered in such a way

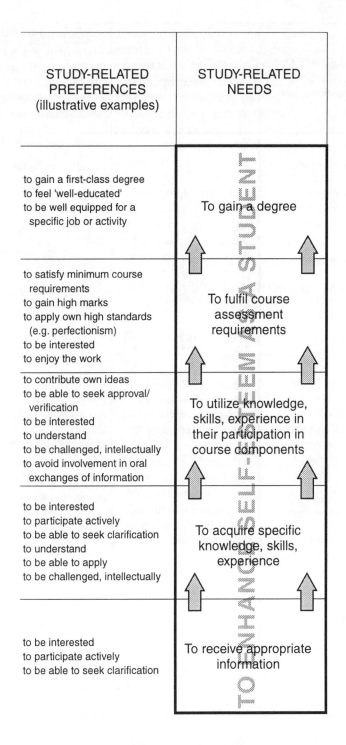

STUDY-RELATED PREFERENCES (illustrative examples)	STUDY-RELATED NEEDS
to gain a first-class degree to feel 'well-educated' to be well equipped for a specific job or activity	To gain a degree
to satisfy minimum course requirements to gain high marks to apply own high standards (e.g. perfectionism) to be interested to enjoy the work	To fulfil course assessment requirements
to contribute own ideas to be able to seek approval/ verification to be interested to understand to be challenged, intellectually to avoid involvement in oral exchanges of information	To utilize knowledge, skills, experience in their participation in course components
to be interested to participate actively to be able to seek clarification to understand to be able to apply to be challenged, intellectually	To acquire specific knowledge, skills, experience
to be interested to participate actively to be able to seek clarification	To receive appropriate information

TO ENHANCE SELF-ESTEEM AS A STUDENT

Figure 5.2   Study-related needs and associated study-related preferences

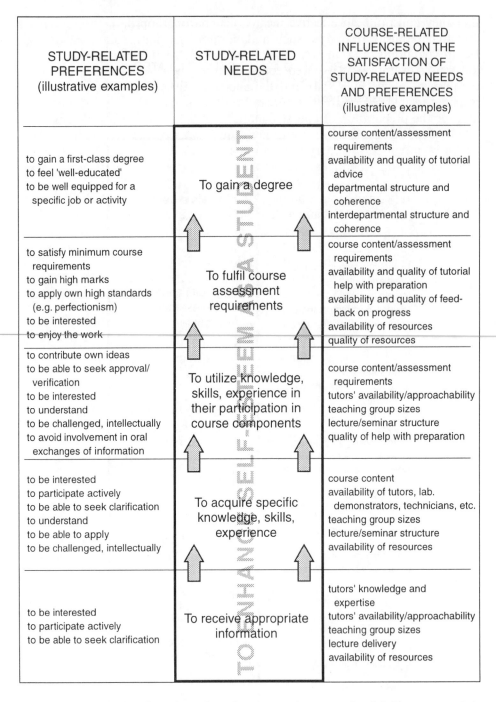

STUDY-RELATED PREFERENCES (illustrative examples)	STUDY-RELATED NEEDS	COURSE-RELATED INFLUENCES ON THE SATISFACTION OF STUDY-RELATED NEEDS AND PREFERENCES (illustrative examples)
to gain a first-class degree to feel 'well-educated' to be well equipped for a specific job or activity	To gain a degree	course content/assessment requirements availability and quality of tutorial advice departmental structure and coherence interdepartmental structure and coherence
to satisfy minimum course requirements to gain high marks to apply own high standards (e.g. perfectionism) to be interested to enjoy the work	To fulfil course assessment requirements	course content/assessment requirements availability and quality of tutorial help with preparation availability and quality of feed-back on progress availability of resources quality of resources
to contribute own ideas to be able to seek approval/ verification to be interested to understand to be challenged, intellectually to avoid involvement in oral exchanges of information	To utilize knowledge, skills, experience in their participation in course components	course content/assessment requirements tutors' availability/approachability teaching group sizes lecture/seminar structure quality of help with preparation
to be interested to participate actively to be able to seek clarification to understand to be able to apply to be challenged, intellectually	To acquire specific knowledge, skills, experience	course content availability of tutors, lab. demonstrators, technicians, etc. teaching group sizes lecture/seminar structure availability of resources
to be interested to participate actively to be able to seek clarification	To receive appropriate information	tutors' knowledge and expertise tutors' availability/approachability teaching group sizes lecture delivery availability of resources

(Vertical text in centre column, bottom to top: TO ENHANCE SELF-ESTEEM AS A STUDENT)

Figure 5.3   Study-related needs and preferences, and course-related influences on their satisfaction

that they constitute an effective means of imparting appropriate information; and that requisite resources, such as laboratory facilities, course handbooks, lecture handouts and library books, are available. Clearly, in this list of illustrative examples of required course features there are implications for the recruitment of teaching staff and the allocation of staff to course teams and teaching-related responsibilities, for staff professional development and training, and for the preparation of course material and the organization of resources.

These implications take on another dimension, however, if course features are to be intended to satisfy not only the core study-related needs which are common to all students but the range of study-related preferences as well. This added dimension is the need to incorporate the flexibility required if any attempt is to be made to accommodate the diversity of different preferences. This involves trying to build into course design and delivery mechanisms which provide something for everyone: something for those who do not wish to participate actively in seminars or lectures, and something for those who do; something which allows those who wish to develop their own original ideas but which is sufficiently structured for those who prefer to have more guidance; something for those who wish to work independently, and something for those who prefer to work in a group, or team.

Those who provide the courses will vary in their responses to these implications, and responses may be institutional, departmental or even at the level of course teams. Responses will be influenced by course providers' conceptions of: teaching and learning in higher education, the aims of higher education, the purpose of universities, the role of tutors and the responsibilities of students, and pressure from external accountability mechanisms. They will also be influenced by consideration of the needs of tutors. The most effective response is likely to be course-provision policy which represents a compromise by aiming to satisfy the needs of students and tutors. In the final chapter of this book we examine some of the issues involved in developing such policy.

Part III

The Tutor Perspective

Chapter 6

Tutors' Work

INTRODUCTION

Although there is an abundance of research-based literature on higher education and, within this, many studies of different aspects of academics' work, there are few which provide comprehensive accounts of the nature of academics' working lives and of their work-related attitudes. The major studies in this area are those of Halsey, whose three surveys (Halsey and Trow, 1971; Halsey, 1979; Halsey, 1995) portray the changing role and status of British academic staff from the period of expansion of higher education initiated by the 1963 Robbins Report to 1989, when higher education had been affected by the changes reflecting the Conservative government's policy shift. Halsey's work is distinctive in its representativeness and as an accurate portrayal of what being a British academic involves. However, his surveys were large-scale and involved the collection of data which are predominantly quantitative. As such, they reveal interesting trends and are generalizable and informative, but present what is, for the most part, a surface picture of academic life which does not delve deeply into examination of individual perspectives and attitudes. More illuminative in this respect is Becher's (1989) study of academic culture, but his narrower focus on what are essentially epistemological considerations and his narrower sample create a more detailed, but less complete, picture.

This chapter makes a further contribution towards describing the nature of academics' working lives. It outlines some of the main aspects of their work which our sample of tutors reported and, as a prelude to addressing how they feel about their jobs, examines the concepts of job satisfaction and morale and outlines the findings of published research into influences on attitudes to work.

TUTORS' WORK: WHAT THE JOB INVOLVES

With the shortage of empirically based descriptive literature on academics' working lives, some of the most illustrative sources of information about what the job involves are to be found in works of fiction or autobiographical accounts. Many of these portray the privileged lifestyles of Oxbridge dons whose decline is analysed in Halsey's studies. Rothblatt (1996) refers to a nineteenth-century example:

> Open Joseph Romilly's diary and notice how a don amused himself in 1842: a miserable rainy day in February, he scribbles, but an excellent dinner with venison. Archdeacon Hoare is fond of rhyme and jingle, the queen is looking pale and ill, and, by the way, the college has met to revise statutes but not seriously. He saw an old washerwoman hunting for her spectacles and can find no one at home in Trinity College. A *Don's Diary* perhaps, but Romilly had little else to do even though he was the Cambridge registrar.

Whilst changes effected by government policy on higher education have eroded away the culture of academic life which this nineteenth-century illustration represents, remnants of the privileges enjoyed by Oxbridge academics reflect the advantaged extreme of a diverse range of workplace cultures which are to be found in different higher-education institutions. This diversity reflects, and is determined by, levels of funding and institutional traditions and foci. What this means is that what academics do at work varies depending on where they work. Crace (1993) refers to 'a two tier system of academic staff' and distinguishes between the two extremes, Oxbridge and the new universities:

> Mr Weale's working life is very much that of the traditional Oxbridge don's. 'From time to time I am away at a conference and I do attend official meetings at the Treasury and at the Central Statistical Office now and again, but an average week consists of three hours lecturing and from six to seven hours of tutorials. The rest of my time, apart from the odd afternoon dealing with college business, is devoted to research, which I consider the main part of my job.' ... In the new universities the situation appears significantly different ... Lynette Hughes is in her first year as full-time lecturer in computer science at the University of Hertfordshire, formerly Hatfield Polytechnic. Like Martin Weale, she has three hours lecturing and seven hours of tutorials a week. The difference is that she has 30 students in each tutorial ... 'I reckon that I spend about 50 hours a week either teaching or preparing to do so', she says. 'As for research, I don't have time for it.'

This distinction is similarly evident between more established universities and Oxbridge, according to a young academic who has worked at both (Janes, 1997):

> I obtained a research post at Oxbridge. Having been faced with a freeze on book purchase at my first institution, it was with relief that I was able to work with not perfect but better facilities. Once again, however, I was faced with the same yawning gap in modern British culture between public images and the reality of university life. Oxbridge dons are supposed to live in rarefied worlds of scholarship far from everyday concerns. I was rapidly to discover that the main difference from where I had been before was that both places were desperate for money but only the latter was having any success in

getting any. How can a sixties university attract donors to 'enhance excellence' when the place is so obviously falling apart?

However, transcending the diversity in workloads and working conditions which arises out of inequalities in funding is a shared recognition of the nature of academics' work. Whilst, on the one hand, what academics do at work depends on where they work, this disparity is quantitatively rather than constitutionally related. There is evident consensus, if not unanimity, in identifying the components of university tutors' work – at least, from the perspective of rhetoric. It is when the rhetoric is translated into reality that the inevitable disparity becomes apparent in relation to prioritization and proportionability.

It is generally accepted that university tutors' work has three main components: teaching, research and administration. In some cases, depending on the discipline, a fourth component, consultancy, is added, but this is widely considered to be an optional extra. Halsey (1995, pp. 184–6) describes how, between 1964 and 1989, recognition amongst academics that both teaching and research are essential components of their work has gradually incorporated acceptance that administration is the third component. He applies this recognition to new universities (polytechnics, at the time of Halsey's study) as well as old, distinguishing between the respective priority afforded to teaching and research by old university and new university staff, and accounting for the inevitability of this distinction with reference to funding differentials. Nevertheless, Halsey (1995, pp. 185–6) reports an enduring consensual acceptance that university tutors' work involves both teaching and research:

> In short, the subjective experience has been that scholarly and scientific ideals about teaching and research have persisted as a relatively stable expression of the traditional conception of the academic life through a period of expansion and vicissitude; but performance has in reality been at a lower intensity for both. A leaning towards the research is more strongly defined as appropriate to the university than the polytechnic, though this expected bias is stressed more by university than by polytechnic lecturers, who tend to see research responsibilities as having more even claims in the two types of institutions.

The tripartite nature of university tutors' work was borne out by our research findings. With the exception of the two bought-in education tutors, all of the academics in our sample described their work in relation to the three components: teaching, research and administration. Precisely what the work involved, within these three categories, varied more in relation to tutors' seniority and/or particular management role than in relation to subject, although there were some subject-related variations. Certainly, the 'myriad of duties' which Dominic Janes (1997) identifies as part and parcel of a lecturer's job and which include 'writing, marking, tutoring, examining, form-filling, photocopying and justifying my own position' were similarly incorporated into all of our tutors' day-to-day work.

Most striking was the generally broad similarity of the nature of the tutors' work, across all four subjects, and particularly amongst tutors of similar status and seniority levels. We attribute this to the strength of institutional culture, through which a very strong research focus permeated. Whilst there were a few slight exceptions, patterns and quantities of teaching contact for tutors below readership rank were fairly uniform. Most taught three or four different courses and averaged twelve hours' contact time per week. This usually included undergraduate and postgraduate teaching and supervision, and typically involved lecture delivery, smaller-group teaching and individual tutorials. There were departmental variations as to which of these three teaching approaches was the most prevalent. The physics department's main mode of formal teaching was lecturing, and this accompanied the practical work which students carried out in the laboratories. Education, English and American studies and law courses were generally taught through weekly lectures and smaller-group seminars, although many option courses involved seminar teaching only. The nearest equivalent to seminar teaching for physics tutors was small-group examples classes, but, as we pointed out in Chapter 4, in reality these seldom took place since students failed to take advantage of them. For education tutors, a unique additional feature of what was categorized as teaching was the supervision of students on school practice placements. This involved pre- and post-practice tutorials and observation visits to schools.

Apart from the two who were bought in, all of our tutors identified research as a key component of their work. Whilst the nature and topic of research inevitably varied between the four subjects, the implicit 'regulations', conditions and expectations associated with research activity did not vary. Academics were expected to be engaged in research and/or scholarship, to write and have published, as appropriate, research reports and articles in refereed journals or books and, again where appropriate, to chase external funding for research projects. Research could be carried out independently or collaboratively, and tutors had autonomy in deciding what to research; no constraints – departmental or institutional – in relation to choice of area of study were reported.

Reflecting individuals' areas of interest and expertise, fields of study amongst our sample were wide-ranging within, as well as between, departments. The education tutors were all engaged in educational research which, typically, investigated issues and areas which either had a direct bearing on educational practice or policy or contributed to the development of educational theory, or both. This would often involve their gathering data about human behaviour or attitudes, which they might obtain through research interviews, questionnaires or observation. Their research samples might include, for example, schoolchildren, teachers, parents, school governors, policy-makers, students or fellow academics, and they disseminated their findings by publications and conference papers.

English and American studies tutors did not engage in empirical research, but undertook literary research in their own, specialized fields. One had an international reputation in her field. Another, a junior lecturer, spoke of her developing research interests:

I'm interested, really, in nineteenth – early twentieth – century fiction; British and American. I'm interested in women writers ... I'm interested in constructions and journalism as well. I'm interested in the market-place at that period, and the construction of authorship.

She then illustrated the nature of her research activity:

> I've put together an anthology of stories by women writers at the turn of the century and I have to write little pieces of biographical data at the end of it ... And there's one writer, and I can't find *anything* out about her whatsoever, and I've been to every source I can. (Louise, English and American studies tutor)

Amongst the law tutors, one spoke of having carried out a large research project for a government department, one referred to her research as 'applied' and another considered herself atypical because she undertakes empirical research:

> I do empirical research – not many people in law do empirical research. A lot of law research is ... going into the library and finding out about things ... I look at practice ... things like social services practice. (Avril, law tutor)

Although some physics tutors referred to two or three large research groups within their department, all of those whom we interviewed were involved in research which they carried out, for the most part, independently or, as two tutors described it, 'in loose collaboration'. Christine, a theoretical physicist, outlined what her research typically involved:

> I work on theoretical models ... also, I make large use of computers ... but I wouldn't be involved in testing it by an experiment. The sort of experiments that would be involved are, typically, er ... well ... quite a few are carried out outside of the University because they need a sort of national centre, you know ... to take the measurements, for example ... It's, sort of, loose collaboration. The other theorists are at other universities – there's a couple in this country, and a couple in America, who I work with ... and now we've got electronic communication that's a very effective way of communicating ... And the experimentalists ... again, it's people who're, sort of, scattered around. (Christine, physics tutor)

As a category denoting a component of tutors' work, however, the term 'research' applies not only to the research activities themselves but to associated tasks, such as, where applicable, the preparation of research bids, participation in research team meetings, liaison with sponsors and funding bodies and the dissemination of findings through publications.

Administration appears to be the most diverse of the three components of tutors' work. There is a range of routine administrative tasks which seemed to be incorporated into all tutors' jobs. Most of these are teaching-related, such as the preparation of course documentation and teaching materials, marking, attending course team meetings, and writing letters to students. Other, more 'heavy-duty,' administrative tasks constituted important departmental, or even faculty, jobs and demanded considerable time and, in some cases, knowledge, expertise or political awareness. These positions typically included deputy chair of department, director of studies, examinations secretary, admissions tutor and chairs of committees. Amongst our sample, these 'heavy-duty' administrative responsibilities were taken on by tutors whose status or whose experience and length of service afforded them seniority. They were generally considered too onerous or time-consuming to be undertaken by tutors serving the three-year probationary period.

In order to develop an understanding of tutors' job-related needs, which is one of the purposes of this book, it is necessary to examine their attitudes to their work, and, more specifically, to uncover what influences job satisfaction and morale. Our tutors' job-related attitudes, and the factors which influence them, are examined in the next two chapters. In the following section we review the evidence available in the literature in this field of what factors affect how people feel about their work.

ATTITUDES TO THE JOB

Since it was pioneered in the 1930s, the study of employees' attitudes to their work and, more specifically, of job satisfaction has contributed a substantial body of knowledge about what makes people happy or unhappy with their jobs. Locke (1969), for example, estimated that by 1955 over two thousand articles on the subject of job satisfaction had been published and that by 1969 the total might have exceeded four thousand. Much more has been written since then.

There are, however, conceptual problems related to researching job satisfaction and morale. These emanate from a lack of both clarity and consensus about what is meant by the terms. It is therefore important to examine and address the main problems and to explain precisely how we define 'job satisfaction' and 'morale' before presenting our findings in the chapters which follow.

Job satisfaction and morale: definitions and distinctions

The essential underlying conceptual problem associated with researching job satisfaction and morale, and which is familiar to those who work in this field, is that there are no agreed definitions of the terms. Any assumption that there is universal agreement about what is meant by these terms is ill-founded. Amongst those who have made serious attempts to resolve the conceptual complexities of morale, for example, there is no consensus over issues such as the dimensionality of morale (see Evans, 1992a) and whether it is a group or an individual phenomenon (Guion, 1958; Stagner, 1958). Indeed, the conceptual difficulties are notorious. Guion (1958) refers to the 'definitional limb' on which writers about morale find themselves and, as Smith (1976) points out, use of the term has often been avoided in order to eliminate the problems of defining it. Williams and Lane (1975), employing a chameleon analogy, emphasize the elusiveness of the concept. Redefer (1959a, p. 59) describes it as a 'complex and complicated area for investigation' and one which lacks a succinct definition, whilst Williams (1986, p. 2) writes that 'attempts at defining and measuring morale in the literature seem like a quagmire'.

Conceptual analyses of satisfaction are similarly problematic and diverse. A range of definitions of job satisfaction is evident, and the disparity amongst these relates both to the depths of analyses of the concept and to interpretation of it. Moreover, not all of what are passed off as definitions *are* actual definitions. Some are merely descriptions of possible consequences of job satisfaction or lists of its characteristics.

Schaffer's (1953, p. 3) interpretation is one of fulfilment of individuals' needs:

> Overall job satisfaction will vary directly with the extent to which those needs of an individual which can be satisfied in a job are actually satisfied; the stronger the need, the more closely will job satisfaction depend on its fulfilment.

Sergiovanni (1968) also supports the personal-needs-fulfilment interpretation and draws attention to the evident link between Herzberg's (1968) Motivation–Hygiene Theory and Maslow's (1954) Theory of Human Motivation, based upon a hierarchy of human needs.

Lawler (1973) focuses on expectations, rather than needs:

> Overall job satisfaction is determined by the difference between all those things a person feels he *should* receive from his job and all those things he actually *does* receive.

Locke (1969), however, dismisses both needs and expectations in favour of values. He defines job satisfaction as 'the pleasurable emotional state resulting from the appraisal of one's job as achieving or facilitating the achievement of one's job values' (p. 316), whilst, in relation specifically to the job satisfaction of teachers, Nias (1989) accepts Lortie's (1975) interpretation of job satisfaction as a summary of the total rewards experienced.

Kalleberg (1977, p. 126) identifies both job rewards and job values as determinants of job satisfaction, which he defines as 'an overall effective orientation on the part of individuals toward work roles which they are presently occupying'. Katzell (1964, p. 348) adopts the all-encompassing term 'frame of reference' to include 'values', 'goals', 'desires' or 'interests'. He refers to 'job features which a person perceives as attractive or repellent, desirable or undesirable', and interprets job satisfaction as 'a response to the activities, events and conditions which compose the job'. Similarly, Rosen and Rosen (1955, p. 305) use the rather generic term 'desires'. The source of much of this disagreement lies with the hierarchical positions, as determinants of job satisfaction, of what Katzell (1964) identifies as the different 'frames of reference'. It arises over whether, for example, needs determine values or values determine needs.

A second, more specific, conceptual problem associated with the lack of agreed definition of 'job satisfaction' is the ambiguity of what is meant by 'satisfaction'. This ambiguity, and the methodological problems which arise from its having failed to be recognized, are examined elsewhere in detail by one of us (Evans, 1997a). Essentially, the conceptual problem stems from the application of the word 'satisfaction' to something which results from circumstances which are satisfactory or/and from circumstances which are satisfying. Evans's (1997a) analysis of this problem culminates in her suggesting a bifurcation of both terminology and definition, and we adopt and apply to our examination of tutors' satisfaction her terms *job comfort* and *job fulfilment*. Job comfort 'relates to the extent to which the individual feels comfortable in his/her job. More specifically, it is about the extent to which the individual is satisfied with, but not by, the conditions and circumstances, of his/her job' (Evans, 1997a, p. 327). Job comfort is obtained passively. Job fulfilment, on the other hand, relates to that which is satisfying, rather than satisfactory. It is an attitude which reflects, and is derived from, a sense of having made a valuable contribution: a feeling of having achieved something, a mental pat on the back. Job fulfilment is not obtained passively. It involves and is a reciprocation of some kind of personal effort, activity or contribution. It is a 'return' on self-evaluated job performance. We adopt Evans's (*ibid.*) definition of job fulfilment as 'a state of mind determined by the extent of the sense of personal achievement which the individual attributes to his/her performance of those components of his/her job which s/he values' and her definition of job satisfaction, which incorporates both job comfort and job fulfilment, as 'a state of mind determined by the extent to which the individual perceives her/his job-related needs to be being met'.

Finally, another conceptual problem associated with research in this area is that job satisfaction and morale are sometimes used synonymously. Smith (1976) criticizes American studies for confusing morale with satisfaction, or at least for failing to distinguish between them. His distinction is that job satisfaction is a static, shallow concept, whereas morale is dynamic and forward-looking. He illustrates this by pointing out that 'high morale may exist in a situation where many job dissatisfactions exist and are being overcome' (p. 144). Guba (1958), on the other hand, sees high morale as dependent upon achievement of a high level of satisfaction. Satisfying acts require less expenditure of energy than do unsatisfying acts, he argues, and so satisfaction is necessary to avoid expending the requisite energy for morale.

The interpretation of morale which we adopt is that of Evans (1992a), who defines it as 'a state of mind determined by the individual's anticipation of the extent of satisfaction of those needs which s/he perceives as significantly affecting his/her total [work] situation' (p. 169). This incorporates the notion of morale as an individual, rather than a group, phenomenon, and quite distinct from group cohesiveness, which, Evans suggests, is often misinterpreted as morale. Evans's distinction between morale and job satisfaction is one of temporal orientation: satisfaction is perceived as present-oriented and as a response to a situation, whereas morale is perceived as future-oriented and as anticipatory. Thus, for example, the state of mind which represents individuals' responses to change in their working lives is job satisfaction, but the anticipation of how change will affect their job satisfaction in the future constitutes morale. This interpretation accommodates Smith's (1966) explanation that high morale may exist alongside job dissatisfaction.

Factors influencing job satisfaction and morale

The literature in this field incorporates a wide range of specificity, reflecting levels of analysis of research-generated data and of key concepts, as well as research sample constitution and, in some cases, data-collection techniques.

Evans (1997b) has identified within this range four levels of understanding, or stages of elucidation, in relation to what affects morale and job satisfaction levels.

The first level has as its basis, for the most part, conventional wisdom and common-sense, but over-simplistic, reasoning. Sometimes it may be based on research findings, though these will tend to emanate from quantitative surveys, often using large samples. It is exemplified by assumptions that pay and centrally imposed conditions of service and policy are key influences on employees' attitudes to their work. It is the underlying rationale for the notion of performance-related pay, and it attributes job-specific recruitment or retention problems to low pay and/or unpopular conditions of service and professional demands. This level of understanding evidently assumes much homogeneity among professional groups and among employees in general. Applied to university tutors, level one would be represented by assumptions that the morale of the profession will have been lowered as a result of the deterioration of working conditions arising out of recent higher-education reforms.

Halsey's (1995) attribution of low morale and dissatisfaction among academics to the proletarianization of the profession and the erosion of professional standing, status and privilege represents this level of under-standing:

> senior common room morale is low. In 1989 as many as 37 per cent of university teachers and 39 per cent of their polytechnic colleagues had seriously considered leaving academic life permanently: the comparable percentage among university staff in 1964 had been 23. The underlying explanation was, I believe, anticipated by the Weber and Veblen forebodings of 1918: the key word is a long and alien one – proletarianization. (p. 124)

> But discontent for the academic profession as a whole is linked to loss of status and deterioration of working conditions ... The vast majority of university and polytechnic staff are convinced that public respect as well as appreciation from politicians and civil servants has sharply declined over the past decade. (p. 134)

Similarly, a survey carried out in 1996 by the Association of University Teachers (Thomson, 1997) reveals evidence of an assumption that pay is a factor enhancing recruitment and retention: 'The survey reveals 89 per cent of the respondents agreed that academic pay ... was too low to attract and hold staff of necessary calibre.'

The second stage of elucidation of what affects employees' morale and job satisfaction is generally based upon empirical research, but its underlying analysis is under-developed. It moves away from a homogeneity basis towards typologies and trends, exemplified by studies which reveal factors such as employees' age, seniority and status, institutional culture and subject discipline to be key variables influencing job satisfaction and morale levels. The paucity of research specifically on university tutors' morale or job satisfaction makes it difficult to find examples of studies, in relation to academics, which fall exclusively within this category. Some of Halsey's and Trow's (1971) findings partially represent level two, insofar as they present typologies of academics in relation to, for example, teaching and research orientations, attitudes to professional status and professional power, and attitudes towards expansion. Referring to their typology of academic orientations, for example, they explain:

> our analysis suggests that basic differences in academic orientations are represented not in a continuum but more accurately by a typology. One dimension of this typology refers to the conception of the university as either an élite, or as a relatively open and popular institution. The other dimension points to conceptions of the university teacher's primary role as either a creator of knowledge or as a teacher and transmitter of values and culture. (Halsey and Trow, 1971, p. 455)

Yet they also clearly recognize the limitations on elucidation of analysis which identifies typologies:

> These stark polarities of course do not do justice to the complex views and attitudes held by individual university teachers nor do they capture the nuances of thought and feeling by which men manage to maintain conceptions of the universities and of their academic roles which reflect *both* expansionist and élitist values, and which accept *both* teaching and research as legitimate and complementary functions of the university. Nevertheless, ... men do differ in the emphasis they place on these values, the priorities they put on their embodiment in university organisation, and in the allocation of both national and personal resources. (Halsey and Trow, 1971, p. 455)

Similarly, in education, though not higher education, settings, Lowther *et al.* (1985) and Dixit (1985) identify, respectively, age and teaching experience as determinants of teachers' job satisfaction levels, and Halpin (1966) identifies six typologies of schools' organizational climates, categorized according to the behaviour typically manifested by headteachers and staff, each of which fosters different levels of institutional morale.

The third level of understanding is a subtly enhanced variant of the second, incorporating greater depth and sophistication of analysis, and focusing on narrower, more specific, typologies which have emerged from empirical data. This level moves towards recognition of the significance both of heterogeneity within groups and of match or mismatch between individuals and the contexts in which they work. It is exemplified by studies such as that of Vancouver and Schmitt (1991), which supports the 'contention that organizational goals are an important point of comparison between individuals and the organizations in which they find themselves' (p. 348), and which 'confirms the idea that person–organisation fit relates to positive employee attitudes and intentions' (p. 350). Another example of this level of analysis and understanding, relating specifically to teaching in higher education, is Redefer's (1959b) study of teacher morale at New York University:

> Teachers and administrators make the mistake of thinking in monolithic terms with respect to morale. They assume that morale is a matter of salary level as though most teachers and professors were motivated *solely* by the pay envelope ...
>
> The morale status of a faculty may be expressed by the equation, $M = f(P_I, P_C, P_A, P_H)$. In other words the morale status of the individuals who compose a staff is a function of P_I (the person's feeling about his position and the acceptance and possibility

of achieving his objectives), P_C (the person in relation to his professional community-school neighborhood, parents, fellow teachers, and students), P_A (the person in his relation to administrators, supervisors, and administrative relationships), and P_H (the person in relation to himself and his profession). These are variables of the morale status of the teacher. The morale status of teachers had no causative relation to sex, marital status, or salary level. Human relations factors stand out as the basis upon which staff morale is built. (Redefer, 1959b, p. 136)

At the fourth level are studies such as those of Herzberg (1968), Kalleberg (1977), Schaffer (1953), Sergiovanni (1968), Lawler (1973) and Locke (1969), which are not necessarily education-specific nor directly research-based. This is a level of in-depth analysis and recognition of the need for conceptual clarity and precision, and many of the studies representing it, as pioneering analyses of employees' attitudes to their work, are considered seminal.

This level of understanding, recognizing the inaccuracies associated with crude generalization which ignores individualism, focuses upon the lowest common factor in relation to determinants of job satisfaction amongst individuals. Analysis at this level seeks commonalities and generalization, but it seeks commonalities and generalization which are accurate, because they are free from contextual specificity. Studies representing this level therefore claim wide, if not universal, applicability and any job-specificity or profession-specificity, which tends to be confined to being in relation to research samples, is dissolved through the incrementally diluent process of analysis which uncovers the lowest common factor. Level four has contributed much to elucidation not only of what morale and job satisfaction are but also of what, fundamentally, are their determinants. At this level, suggested determinants of job satisfaction are, typically, fulfilment of individuals' needs, fulfilment of expectations, or congruence of values, as indicated in some of the definitions and interpretations of job satisfaction and morale presented in an earlier section of this chapter.

The wide range of elucidation represented by literature in the field means that it is not a simple and straightforward task to draw upon published evidence of what influences job satisfaction and morale. The main source of difficulty lies in the lack of rigour in relation to conceptual clarity which is applied to many studies. Work representing the first three levels of understanding identified above generally neglects consideration of how key concepts may be defined, and seldom incorporates discussion of what is meant by 'job satisfaction' or 'morale'. Oshagbemi (1996), for example, reporting the findings of his survey of the job satisfaction of UK academics, writes:

teaching contributes more to the university teachers' satisfaction than research, which, in turn, contributes more to overall satisfaction than administration and management. (pp. 365–6)

In contrast with teaching and research, where they generally expressed a high level of satisfaction, the university teachers were dissatisfied with their administrative activities. (p. 396)

We found from our survey that, on the whole, university teachers were generally fairly satisfied with their job. They were particularly satisfied with teaching and, to a lesser extent, research. Another area where they also derived great satisfaction was the interaction with colleagues. (p. 398)

Yet his failure to provide any definition or interpretation of job satisfaction greatly reduces the usefulness of his work and thereby impoverishes it. Not only is it impossible to ascertain from the information provided whether Oshagbemi's references to 'satisfaction' or 'satisfied with' equate to what we, adopting Evans's (1997a) terminology, identify as job comfort or job fulfilment, but it is also unclear what conceptions of job satisfaction are held by the survey respondents. It is, however, important to know whether the sample was, for example, indicating greater satisfaction with the organization-related facets of teaching than with those of research, or whether its responses indicate more positive self-assessments of individuals' own progress and success in teaching than in research, or whether teaching was a greater source of fulfilment than was research. There is a clear distinction between being more satisfied *with* teaching than research, and being more satisfied *by* teaching than research, which, though it is fundamental to understanding what influences job satisfaction, is too often neglected.

Not all work on academics' job satisfaction is so unclear. Without necessarily including conceptual analyses, or distinctions between what equates to job comfort and what equates to job fulfilment, some writers make much more explicit the nature of the job-related attitudes which they report. Ashcroft and Foreman-Peck (1994, p. 47), for example, refer to 'social satisfaction' and satisfaction which is derived from the completion of tasks:

if your task satisfaction comes from doing the work better than others would, you may find it hard to delegate. If your satisfaction comes from working as near to perfectly as possible, deadlines may be hard to meet. You may find social satisfaction from being the sort of person who always says 'yes'.

Similarly, Rowley (1996a, p. 14) uses the terms 'gratification', 'frustration' and 'dissatisfiers' to good effect:

Most staff gain gratification from working with students and witnessing the achievement and development of those students. This is associated with having a professional pride in their work. It is important for them to be accepted by the students when they work as a leader and facilitator. Frustration may develop from dissatisfiers which prevent staff from doing a good job, including poor timetable organization, inadequate maintenance of educational equipment, or too many assorted demands on their time.

Drawing upon his research findings, Becher (1989, p. 123) distinguishes between academics' reported sources of pleasure and 'boring' or 'unsatisfactory' facets of their work:

The sense of personal pleasure to be derived from research activities was widely acknowledged, and there was not a single interviewee who confessed to being 'turned off' by, or uninvolved in, even its routine aspects . . . This is not to say that there are no boring or unsatisfactory facets of an academic life. The most common candidates under this heading were administration, committee work and marking undergraduate essays and exam scripts (the actual process of teaching was generally held to be enjoyable and worthwhile, and could sometimes be found to have a broadening effect on one's research).

The paucity of research on university tutors' attitudes to their work makes it difficult to gather empirical evidence of factors influencing job satisfaction and morale which relate specifically to academics. This problem is, moreover, compounded by the conceptual superficiality of much of the available work, with the result that it is impossible to identify, with any reliability, generalizable patterns of academic-specific sources of job comfort and job fulfilment.

Studies which focus more widely on employees in general, rather than on specific jobs or professions, particularly those studies representing the fourth of what we refer to as levels of understanding, have identified factors which influence job satisfaction and/or morale levels. Probably the best-known study, and one which is distinct from many others representing level four by the specificity incorporated into the identification of influential factors, is that of Herzberg (1968). Based upon research of engineers and accountants in Pittsburgh, Herzberg's Two-Factor Theory, or Motivation–Hygiene Theory, of job satisfaction distinguishes between two sets of factors: motivation factors, which are intrinsic to the work, and hygiene factors, which are extrinsic to it. The distinction lies in the capability of each set of factors. Motivation factors, of which Herzberg identifies five – achievement, recognition (for achievement), advancement, responsibility and the work itself – are capable of motivating or satisfying employees. Hygiene factors – salary, supervision, interpersonal relations, policy and administration, and working conditions – are not capable of satisfying or motivating, but they are potential sources of dissatisfaction. It is upon this distinction that Herzberg's theory hinges.

The Motivation–Hygiene Theory has been applied to, and tested in, education contexts (see, for example, Farrugia, 1986; Nias, 1981; Young and Davis, 1983), though we are not aware of its having been tested specifically with higher-education tutors. However, one of us (Evans, 1997a) has incorporated into her reconceptualization of job satisfaction a basic critique of Herzberg's work. The underlying problem identified by Evans (1997a) is Herzberg's failure to offer any definition or interpretation of job satisfaction. This threatens construct validity within his own study and provides insufficient conceptual clarity to enable other researchers to draw adequate meaning from his work; most importantly, the lack of conceptual rigour results in his misguidedly developing what he believes to be a theory on work motivation and satisfaction out of what is, essentially, nothing more than ambiguity within the terminology. Herzberg's hygiene factors, Evans (1997a) suggests, are those which would generally influence how satisfactory a job is considered to be, and motivation factors relate more to the extent to which the work is satisfying. Evans (1997a) points out that there is no evidence in his work that Herzberg acknowledges this ambiguity of the term 'job satisfaction'. She writes:

Indeed, his theory emphasises what has often been regarded as a revelation; that the opposite of satisfaction is not dissatisfaction, but 'no satisfaction', and that the opposite of dissatisfaction is not satisfaction, but 'no dissatisfaction'. The issue is, I believe, much more simple and straightforward. Since one category relates to factors which are capable of satisfying, then, clearly, they *are* distinct and separate. But realisation of this should not form the basis of a theory; it merely follows on from awareness that there are separate, but related, components of what has tended to be regarded as a single concept. (p. 322)

It is this lack of recognition of the ambiguity of the term 'job satisfaction', arising out of neglect of conceptual analyses and definition of key terms, which, Evans (1997a) suggests, imposes serious limitations on the process of testing Herzberg's theory. She refers to the example of Nias's (1981; 1989) application of the Motivation–Hygiene Theory to her sample of school-teachers, and offers conceptual misunderstanding as a more likely explanation for the slight disparity between Nias's and Herzberg's (1968) findings than attitudinal distinctions between their respective samples:

What is more likely than Nias's findings failing to corroborate Herzberg's, though, is that her and Herzberg's interpretations of the concept of job satisfaction differ, and that those of Nias's teachers who reported deriving satisfaction from extrinsic factors were actually satisfied *with* them, rather than *by* them.

Since Herzberg fails to make explicit his interpretation of job satisfaction it is only possible to make assumptions. I have already suggested that he interprets it narrowly, confining job satisfaction to involving satisfying elements of work. His exclusion of extrinsic factors, such as salary and working conditions, as satisfiers is consistent with this assumption. Those specific extrinsic factors which Nias (1989, p. 89) identifies as satisfiers would have been excluded by Herzberg because they fall outside of the parameters of what, to him, job satisfaction is all about. They may be satisfactory (or unsatisfactory) to teachers but they are unlikely to be capable of satisfying. Nias's interpretation of job satisfaction is evidently wider, though, and incorporates both satisfactory and satisfying elements. The extrinsic factors which she identifies as satisfiers lie within the parameters of her interpretation of the concept. Thus, what are interpreted as, and presented by, one researcher as research findings which fail to corroborate those of another researcher may, in fact, be nothing of the sort. Herzberg's theory is challenged and its applicability to education settings questioned when, all the time, the lack of agreement is more likely to be conceptual. If this is, indeed, the case, then the misconception has its origins firstly in the failure (on Herzberg's part) to define the key concept under study and, secondly, in failure to recognise the ambiguity associated with the concept. (Evans, 1997a, pp. 323–4)

The conceptual difficulties associated with researching morale and job satisfaction prompted Evans to develop her own definitions of the terms, and to suggest a bifurcation of terminology, in relation to job satisfaction, to which we have referred earlier in this chapter and which we adopt for our research.

Ascertaining precisely what aspects of their work tutors found satisfying and satisfactory, or unsatisfactory, was essential to our identifying their job-related needs. We therefore applied much thought and precision to the formulation of our interview schedule and, in particular, to the wording of specific questions, in order to minimize threats to construct validity (see Evans, 1997a).

Since there is evidently very little work specifically on academics' job satisfaction upon which to draw, and since much of the available work on the wider topic of employees' job satisfaction is impoverished by a lack of conceptual rigour and clarity, we had a limited amount of material to guide our inquiry. The most valuable work in the field is that which represents what we have referred to as the fourth level of understanding, but this level lacks the contextual specificity needed to be informative in a way which may influence policy and practice. Pointing out, for example, that job satisfaction is influenced by the extent to which employees gain from their work what they feel they ought to gain may reflect conceptual sophistication and in-depth analysis but it contributes little towards identifying precisely what are the sources of job satisfaction, and hence the job-related needs, of UK academics. What we wanted to do was to present findings which represent a fifth stage of elucidation of what influences job satisfaction levels: a stage which combines the conceptual sophistication of level four with the requisite contextual specificity for informing policy decisions. These findings are presented in the next chapter.

Chapter 7

Chasing the Ideal

INTRODUCTION

Tutors' perceptions of their job-related needs are developed out of their comparisons between what they consider to be the realities of their actual jobs and the conceptions which they have formulated of their ideal jobs. Often this will be an unconscious process, but it is clear that those aspects of their work which tutors identify as unsatisfactory are considered impediments to their achieving the sort of working conditions that they would, ideally, like. The removal, or at least reduction, of these impediments therefore constitutes a job-related need, although the essential, underlying need is to achieve the ideal.

In the context of this book, tutors' job-related needs are important because our examination of teaching and learning in higher education incorporates consideration of the needs of both parties: students and tutors. If our findings reveal, for example, that tutors find teaching a constraint which impedes their achieving their ideal of predominantly research-focused work, then our suggestions for policy which aims to be effective in meeting tutors' and students' needs must incorporate facilities for accommodating the need for less teaching and for more research on the part of tutors. The key to discovering job-related needs lies in uncovering the individual's conception of what is, at any one time, her or his ideal job. Underpinning this conception of the ideal job are sources of job fulfilment and job comfort, to which we referred in Chapter 6. Clearly, the ideal job will include what are perceived as sources of job fulfilment and positive job comfort factors, and it will exclude those aspects of the job which are unsatisfactory.

This chapter contributes to the process of identifying tutors' job-related needs by uncovering conceptions of job-related ideals, as revealed by sources of job satisfaction and dissatisfaction. It highlights what academics want from their work, the extent to which they achieve what they want, and the consequences of this. It reveals the complexities, conflicts, crises and personal triumphs of individuals who make up a professional group and identifies what can be done to meet more of their job-related needs.

TUTORS' JOB SATISFACTION

There was considerable consensus amongst our tutors in identifying sources of job satisfaction. We were struck by the overall similarity of responses to our questions about the constituents of tutors' 'ideal', and what gives them a 'kick' or a 'buzz'. We emphasize that this was similarity, rather than uniformity. There were some atypical comments, but despite the slight disparity which these created there emerged a distinct impression of a group of similarly minded individuals who shared broadly the same professional values and vision. We attribute this to acceptance of, and immersion in, a strong institutional culture. It is not unreasonable to expect – and, indeed, our interview-generated evidence supports this expectation – that some degree of homogeneity occurs amongst people who are exposed to a common workplace environment and culture and whose general acceptance of the values and expectations present is implied by their choice to remain there. This is certainly an oversimplification which neglects consideration of many variables and detailed analysis of cause and effect, but it was our strong impression that, notwithstanding some evident dissension, most tutors broadly accepted and supported the values and vision which shaped their institution's prevailing ethos.

The sources of job satisfaction and dissatisfaction identified by our interviewees included both job fulfilment and job comfort factors, and we examine these separately.

Job fulfilment

Fulfilment from teaching

We had anticipated that tutors who, by implication, accepted, or indeed endorsed, their university's strongly research-oriented culture would be likely to manifest a preference for the research-focused elements of their work over those which fell into the teaching and administration categories. This was not entirely the case. Certainly, research was identified by all eighteen permanent tutors as enjoyable and, in nearly all cases, as satisfying, but its superiority over teaching as a source of job satisfaction was not as great, nor as widespread, as we had expected. Out of the full sample of twenty, sixteen made it perfectly clear that they valued and enjoyed their teaching role and included it as a constituent of their ideal job.

Qualifications to this assessment related to the quantity and the nature of teaching which tutors said they would, ideally, like. Six tutors admitted that they already, or very nearly, had what they considered to be their ideal jobs, but the remaining ten who were happy to retain a teaching role said that reduced teaching loads and/or teaching which was confined to specific groups of students (usually postgraduates), to specific courses, or which allowed them to interact in ways which they preferred, would enhance their job satisfaction. The following comments illustrate the range of desired refinements to their teaching roles which tutors identified:

> Ideally, I would have a job in which I could ... have a number of graduate students who I'm supervising – (that's the problem now, because I'm on probation, so I can't properly do that yet, anyway) – er ... whose work I was interested in ... where there seemed to be some sort of reciprocity going on ... Er ... I would perhaps run a MA course, or contribute to a jointly taught MA course, I'd be interested in doing that, too. (Louise, English and American studies tutor)

> I would, ideally, want to teach small groups of students – up to twelve – I think twelve is a very good number. I would want to ... I have no problems with undergraduate teaching, except that education students have a particular need ... which is not quite ... university teaching as I ... er ... define university teaching, in as much as they actually want you to give them the answers, as opposed to want you to help them to ... develop themselves as learners. Ideally, I would want to work with students who want to develop themselves as learners. I would want to operate a feminist pedagogy, as opposed to this very top-down model, which, to some extent, we're constrained to do by the nature of education ... I would have small groups of committed students who would be happy to operate in a semi-autonomous way. (Stephanie, education tutor)

> I'd like to be responsible for my own course ... I would like to design it ... be totally responsible, to design it, to teach it and to be responsible for the seminars, responsible for the examination questions, be responsible for setting essay questions, etc. I mean, that sounds rather ... autocratic, perhaps, but that's ideal, I think. (Otto, law tutor)

> Certainly, in my ideal job, I wouldn't wish to try and be teaching more than two different courses at any one time, because I think it's very difficult to do justice to ... er ... you know, ... that ... in terms of preparation and so forth. (Maurice, English and American studies tutor)

These various idealized modifications reflect what tutors reported valuing about teaching. Many tutors spoke of the sense of fulfilment which they derived from passing on knowledge, skills or understanding, from being instrumental in enabling students to grasp something which had previously eluded them, from feeling that they had made an impression, exerted an influence, challenged, empowered, enabled; that they had made a difference in someone else's life:

> Well, the thing which gives *me* the most pleasure is if a student walks through the door and says, 'I've got a problem. It's the following ... Can you help me?' And then you stand and talk for half an hour, or an hour, and at the end he says, 'Ah! I see the light.' Because that's about the only point at which we actually feel – or *know* – that you've taught them something. (Bernard, physics tutor)

> when a lecture's gone well, when a seminar's gone well, and I see them thinking, 'Yes!', or when one of them says to me, 'I think I'd like to do what *you're* doing' ... that's a good feeling. But I think the other thing is ... when I get *real* satisfaction, and when I really do get a lot of satisfaction, is when I talk to a student who's got problems ... and we both ... and we can discuss this ... and we both have a sense that the problem becomes overcome

in the conversation, and they go away feeling better ... and, I don't mean in a sentimental way – or even an emotional way – that they go away feeling better, that I've cured their problems – I can't possibly do *that* – but, they have more self-confidence ... or they have more ... fight. (Louise, English and American studies tutor)

Er ... there's a certain reward in seeing someone actually 'get it' ... Er ... you're trying to impart, and it's difficult for them to accept what you're thinking when you're trying to engage them in ... again ... in the approach ... you know ... 'This is what I want to do', er ... and to get them to acknowledge that – to see, from their faces, 'Yeah, this would be good as well', er ... you do get quite a big kick out of that. (Brian, law tutor)

I like to challenge people. I like them to ... yes ... to actually *look* at their practice – I said, today, 'If you can only learn to be reflective, and retain that ability throughout your career, then I shall be pleased. So that you can actually respond to today's issues, current research, and actually enhance your teaching through that.' (Janice, bought-in education tutor)

The potential for acquiring ideas and the contribution which teaching could make to their intellectual development, and, more specifically, to their research activities, was also valued. This did not always arise out of interaction with students. Sometimes ideas and plans for research projects originated from the necessity of reading up on a subject which had to be taught or from course design and preparation:

The course I was given as my first lecture course when I can here ... I knew nothing about it. However, on reading about it, I think it's a fascinating subject, and I like it. And so I'm using the concepts of it in my research.
... The interaction with young people ... for me, it's quite interesting. I mean, sometimes they will actually come up with ... silly questions which are ... not so silly ... And I think there's a certain synergy involved in this all the time. I feel very strongly that teaching and research should be kept together – *very* much so. I think it's really important ... I find researching, on its own ... not so entertaining as when I'm teaching at the same time. (Ivan, physics tutor)

Some of the best revisions to writing that *I* feel I've made ... you know ... when I've had stuff in draft form, have been as a result of teaching ... It's not necessarily direct feedback on what you're writing, but ... it's a very good means to clarify your own thinking ... actually to teach something. (Ken, education tutor)

The teaching prompts new ideas and leads me down new paths, and gives me insights into the research that I'm doing ... An example ... would be my current research ..., and some of those ideas that I'm working on are the result of teaching a statistics course to undergraduates here ... So ... when a student on a course says something that surprises you, you immediately go away and reflect on it and that, occasionally, leads you down some ... some sort of aspect ... and re-channels the research that you're working on. (Stan, education tutor)

The importance of the link between teaching and research, which is referred to in some of the quotes above, was highlighted by all eighteen permanent tutors. Tutors who had experience of teaching topics which were unrelated to their research interests or expertise ranked this as much less fulfilling than teaching which was informed by their own research. Not only was the synergy of research and teaching considered important but the advantages of teaching as an expert, as a specialist in the field, were also valued. Teaching those subject areas which one is researching was identified as a vital part of the cycle forming the process which reflects universities' essential purpose: to be continually acquiring up-to-date knowledge, through research and scholarship, and to pass on this knowledge to those who may make use of it:

> I firmly believe in the, sort of, symbiosis between research and teaching ... And that *does* happen – and it *must* happen ... er ... for one to stimulate the other. (Ted, physics tutor)

> I would like to teach ... er ... in areas where I do my research, that's the only, sort of, ... er ... requirement I have in respect of teaching. I like to teach, I like teaching, I wouldn't want to have a research job – an exclusively research job – but I want to teach in the areas where I have been doing my research ... I'm lucky that research and teaching don't really clash. Most of the things I research I can feed back to my students and it makes for an easy lecture. I have just written an article, I can walk into the lecture theatre and give an interesting lecture. I think that's ideal – that's the ideal situation – that's how it *should* be. (Otto, law tutor)

Fulfilment from research activity

Whilst the dissemination of research findings through teaching was widely considered to be valuable, research on its own was a source of fulfilment to all of our eighteen permanent tutors. There was only one case of a tutor's ranking another job component – in this case, managerial administration – higher than research as a source of job fulfilment. Several tutors gave teaching and research equal ranking, but, for the majority of our interviewees, research was the most enjoyable and fulfilling part of their work. Precisely what elements of their research activities satisfied tutors varied, depending on, amongst other factors, the nature of the research, career stage and experience, personality traits and, leading on from this, preferred ways of working.

Networking, cultivating research links outside the university, building up one's profile and reputation and making a name for oneself were sources of satisfaction to some tutors:

> Last year, when I was on leave, I got very ... excited, really. It was wonderful, because I went all over the place. I went to Finland, I went to Iceland and to New Orleans twice, and I went to ... you know ... I gave talks all over the country, and I do like that, yes ... I like that aspect of it. (Meryl, English and American studies tutor)

> My book ... has been very widely reviewed and has had good reviews, er ... not just in this country but in Australia and New Zealand, and the States ... and it's very nice to get a review from an American journal, or an American research journal, which talks about this work being very innovative, and the person has gone away and read the book and developed it, as well ... so *that's* exciting. (Jenny, education tutor)

Indeed, recognition in various forms seemed to be an important job fulfilment factor, which was referred to specifically by eight tutors. Some highlighted the importance of recognition within the university of the achievements of its staff, and some spoke of peer recognition amongst the wider research community:

> I think university recognition is what's important. (Ben, law tutor)

At the moment, what inspires me most is the freedom I have to develop myself in a certain direction. And then, of course, at the end of that you want recognition ... Recognition from people I admire ... I would be wanting to be recognized, for example, in Holland by some people who have influenced me a lot, or in Germany and France. That would give me a kick ... to develop an international name in a very small area. (Otto, law tutor)

My promotion ... was a recognition of the research that I'd been doing ... Getting the readership was an acknowledgement both of the importance of the area, and the fact that my research was good. (Ken, education tutor)

There was, however, disparity in the ranking which tutors afforded to recognition as a source of job fulfilment and, in particular, in the ways in which recognition was perceived. One tutor was dismissive of it:

It's very much my *own* satisfaction. I've given up with peer recognition ... There's a lot of people that know what they're doing, that appreciate what *I* do ... so, I don't mind that. But, I'm very happy with – that's what gives *me* the best kick. (Ivan, physics tutor)

Others emphasized the greater importance of what underlay recognition. For them, recognition was not valued as an end in itself:

Well, clearly, I think most people enjoy ... positive feedback from whatever source ... whether it's somebody saying that your article is good enough to be published, or whether it was a student saying, 'That went well', so, yeah, I recognize that. But I think there are more important, but less tangible, and less easily described things. Er ... I actually enjoy discussing, and feeling that I'm making more sense of, a difficult idea ... But, you know, I'm constantly – in the back of my mind – struggling with various ideas, and ... when I have a discussion with someone ... and something *seems* to come out of that ... that gives me a definite buzz. (Stan, education tutor)

I think the recognition is unimportant. Er ... it's only a means to an end. The recognition is only important if people ... er ... *read* my book ... and say, 'Ah, here is a new way of assessing the views of _____. This is something *I* can do, I can go out and apply those ideas.' That's what's important to me – it's not the recognition *per se* ... it's not important. (Jenny, education tutor)

I was, sort of, terribly gratified because people really knew me, and knew the book, and felt it had made an important contribution to scholarship – which I didn't know. (Meryl, English and American studies tutor)

What is highlighted in all of these quotes is the fulfilment derived from making an intellectual contribution to a body of knowledge, feeling that one has played a part in developing understanding or in advancing theory. This aspect of research – the intellectual creativity which it fosters – was the overriding source of job fulfilment. Whether pursued independently or collaboratively, it is a means of enhancing self-esteem as an academic and as an intellectual:

The best days, when I've just, sort of, walked six inches off the ground ... er ... it's just realizing something ... or discovering something that really does happen. (Ivan, physics tutor)

I *love* doing my research ... I love everything about my research ... Also, because a lot of what I do is dealing with nineteenth-century work that other people haven't written about, so I'm very often coming across things which seem to me to be quite new ... One writer, I couldn't find anything out about her, but I had half an hour between two seminars yesterday, and I rushed to the library, and I *found* her! And it was just thrilling! And I came back, terribly excited! (Louise, English and American studies tutor)

I think ... that feeling of being 'on the edge' of something new, of finding something new ... is what satisfies me about the research ... I think it's exciting when ... if you're with a team of two or three people ... you've almost got some kind of reinforcement that what you're doing is new, novel ... and is going to inform the debate. (Maggie, education tutor)

My research has been in two main areas ... and I do get a *huge* amount of satisfaction and excitement from working in those areas, partly because ... a lot of the work has been collaborative, and I enjoy working with other people ... I think it's very stimulating ... you get new perspectives on things – not just within the department, but outside the department ... So, there's something *socially* which is exciting about working with other people. Intellectually, it's exciting to feel you're doing things which are new. Er ... and, related to my large scale survey ... there's the feeling that you've fed in, at some level, into policy development ... er ... and the DfEE were on the phone to me about the survey and, you know, what it might mean in terms of revising practice. Now, I don't feel that that survey is particularly associated with me as an individual, and I'm not bothered by that at all. Again, all that matters is that the policy-makers have been made aware of it, and it seems to have affected their responses. (Jenny, education tutor)

Fulfilment from administrative tasks

For a minority of tutors administration seemed to be, to some extent, a source of job fulfilment, though in all cases except one its fulfilment potential was ranked lower than that of teaching and of research, and it generally seemed to be less emphatically regarded as fulfilling. Five tutors referred to the administration components of their jobs as being at least enjoyable, and some comments were suggestive of fulfilment. One tutor, Sandra, clearly found managerial administration a definite source of job fulfilment. All of this minority of tutors held what we have identified as 'heavy-duty' administrative roles, and it was to these, rather than the day-to-day routine administrative tasks which fell to all of our tutors, that they referred.

It seems that what distinguished administration from teaching and research as a potential source of job fulfilment is that it is essentially an unwanted component of tutors' jobs. Sandra is the only one of our sample who welcomed administrative work; all of the others gave the impression of being very willing to dispense with it, even though they were, in some respects, fulfilled by it. The minority to whom we refer above, seemed to derive some fulfilment out of their resignation to make the very best of, and to make an effort with, what was the least favourite part of their work. The attitudes which they conveyed are best illustrated by selected comments:

Well, I rarely get positive pleasure out of administration ... I mean, it's a job which has to be done, and which, you know, if you do it reasonably efficiently, and get to keep things moving, is reasonably *satisfying*, but it's not *pleasurable* in the same way that doing a scientific experiment is pleasurable. (Bernard, physics tutor)

I think, in terms of pleasure, at the moment, I would place research at the top. Er ... I wouldn't *always* have said that ... I would probably put it in: research, teaching, administration order, only that's a *slightly* false order, in so far as I think there *is* a problem that if you're in any department and there are administrative areas to be covered ... er ... the pain of not ... er, if they're not being done well would actually be so demeritorious of your situation in the *other* two areas that ... you know ... one tries to do the administration in order to ease the pain, rather than because it's such fun in itself ... I enjoy my role as _____ up to a point. Er, ... I mean, it partly is, I suppose, subject to the kinds of pleasures – if that's what they are – that a lot of those people who do those kinds of administrative jobs will talk about. This ... er ... you know ... obviously, in some cases, working with colleagues you find amenable to work with. (Maurice, English and American studies tutor)

I've always been a reluctant administrator, but I've always had to do it, and I've always had a lot of it. But I have a new role now ... which is an organizational and, sort of, management role ... Er ... I find myself enjoying it very much more than I thought I would, because, what I'm finding is that there's scope for lots of ideas, er ... so I like to do the research, and I like to do the administration. (Ken, education tutor)

Sandra, an education tutor who had held a succession of 'heavy-duty' roles related to administration or management, was atypical amongst our sample with respect to the satisfaction derived from administration. In her interview she reflected on the different roles that she had held:

I felt that, between us, the Chair of Department and I did create some kind of sense of department in those three years ... er ... that we did make people feel a bit more secure. Er ... and I also felt ... and this is going to sound arrogant ... that quite a lot of that was down to me ... Er ... and I think that gave me a lot of satisfaction. I actually enjoyed that ... very much ... Being Chair of _____ was more of a buzz ... because of the wider range of interests. And it was more of a challenge to my personal confidence, because I didn't know the people, and I didn't know the set-up, and I had to learn all that ... But, I think, in the feeling of having an impact on something – even though it was a much smaller thing – there was equal satisfaction in doing that management job. And I really enjoyed those three years, and I really felt that I had put ... *my* own stamp on things. (Sandra, education tutor)

Not all of what were identified as potential sources of job satisfaction incorporated sufficient opportunity for challenge and for tutors to make a contribution or an input, which could give rise to a sense of personal achievement. Elements of tutors' work which lacked the potential for personal achievement, but which were, nevertheless, influential on levels of job satisfaction, are categorized as job-comfort factors and are examined below.

Job comfort

Job-comfort factors are probably best described as those things which one likes or dislikes about one's work: factors which affect the extent to which one is comfortable at work. They are, in a broad sense, working conditions. They may be positive or negative. The positive job-comfort factors tend often to go unnoticed and are less likely to be highlighted. They are the little, seemingly unimportant and taken-for-granted things which combine to provide satisfactory working conditions. Negative job-comfort factors, on the other hand, are generally very much noticed. They are the irritants and inconveniences which act as constraints on work performance and efficiency, the hurdles which have to be jumped over in order to carry out work responsibilities, the annoying, upsetting or depressing elements which become the subjects of moans and complaints. They are the discouraging aspects of work, the 'flies in the ointment' which one would remove, if possible. Whilst comfort factors may constrain or facilitate the emergence of job-fulfilment factors, they are distinct from job fulfilment factors because they are independent of the activity or intervention of the person whose job comfort they influence.

Positive job-comfort factors

Because they are so often taken for granted, very few positive job-comfort factors were identified by our tutor interviewees. Responses to the questions, 'What do you like about your job?' and 'What makes a good day?' invariably prompted discussion of what emerged clearly as sources of job fulfilment, rather than job comfort. Nevertheless, several job-comfort factors either emerged in the course of the interview conversations or were specifically identified. Many of these reflected broad consensus amongst the whole sample, such as the freedom of choice and of ways of working which academics enjoy in relation to the research and scholarship components of their work:

> Probably, for me, the great privilege of being an academic is being able to read what you want and think what you like, and someone gives you money for it ... I mean, that's what I really see as, I suppose, the strength of it. (Brian, law tutor)

> The freedom inspires me and that is something you would not find in a university of the continent. I am a junior person ... er ... and I can do what I want, basically. On the continent I would be told by my professor, 'This is what you're going to do. This is your desk. This is the research we're going to do, and good luck!' (Otto, law tutor)

The variety of the disparate tasks and activities was also a source of job comfort:

> What do I find interesting about *this* job? Well, at least you do different things, that's the good part of it – lots of different things. And even the more closely you look at one particular subject, the more diverse it appears to be. (Ivan, physics tutor)

> What I like is the balance of things. (Ken, education tutor)

> I love the variety in the work I do. (Janice, bought-in education tutor)

And the pleasure and benefits of collegiality, of good staff relationships and of working in supportive departmental environments were highlighted:

> We, pretty regularly, ... about once every three weeks, or so ... we have what we call 'research informals', where we go round to each other's houses, and it's a sort of social event with a research bent to it ... We feel a little bit privileged because ... there are other groups around in the department, but I don't think they have the same ... team ... feeling ... and, also, actually, we quite like each other, just as people. I think a large element is just the, sort of, social aspect of it. (Stan, education tutor)

I like my colleagues. My commitment is actually to my colleagues. I like my colleagues very much. (Louise, English and American studies tutor)

I think it's just quite a nice department ... I mean, certainly, I've found the chairman of department very supportive ... if you've got any problems ... and he'll make a point of ... well, we'll have lunch, maybe, twice a term ... which is important ... to feel that the chairman is interested in me. Yeah ... it's a very supportive environment. (Brian, law tutor)

Negative job-comfort factors

Negative job-comfort factors, the unsatisfactory aspects of the work, were more readily identified. There were variations in the precise forms of the unsatisfactory circumstances and conditions which tutors identified, but what they all had in common was that they were perceived as constraints. By constraining, or in some cases even preventing, tutors from pursuing what they consider to be the more valuable and fulfilling components of their work, negative job-comfort factors created barriers between tutors and their 'ideal' jobs. Tutors wished for their reduction or removal, even though, in many cases, this was unrealizable. The more realizable their removal was perceived to be, though, the more their presence was resented, and the more this provoked frustration and dissatisfaction.

Three broad categories of negative job-comfort factors emerged, related to time, resources, and interpersonal constraints.

TIME-RELATED CONSTRAINTS

Time-related constraints were, quite simply, tasks which were unenjoyable and/or unfulfilling and whose performance demanded time which was unwillingly given and was considered misdirected. Reflecting its predominant status amongst our sample as a source of job fulfilment, not only was research excluded from the list of time-related constraints, but other activities were considered constraining because their performance reduced the amount of time available for research. Teaching in general was not identified as a constraint, but specific teaching-related conditions – typically, group sizes and the nature and size of teaching loads – were the source of several complaints which, for the most part, were made half-heartedly. School practice student supervision, which was undertaken by the education tutors, was, however, highlighted as a significant unsatisfactory element of their teaching-related responsibilities, and those education tutors who considered themselves to have already fashioned or to be approaching their 'ideal' jobs had very little, or no, school practice supervisory responsibilities:

At the moment it's extremely inefficient, because, as a subject mentor, I spend most of my time travelling between schools, and between the University and schools, and relatively little time *in* school. So, that's both unfulfilling and ineffective in its current role. (Stan, education tutor)

I think one of the reasons why ... er ... next year is closer to my 'ideal' job than this year is that I've got sufficient money to buy myself out of teaching practice supervision. And that will make a tremendous difference ... It's an absolute *nightmare*, the teaching practice supervision. (Stephanie, education tutor)

> I haven't found teaching a constraint ... but ... I would've done if I'd not – I think I would've found school practice supervision a constraint, and it can be a very big chunk of time ... Er ... because I've had research funding I've been able to buy myself out of school practice supervision over the last couple of years, and I think that's made a big difference. And I think my attitude would be very different if I were still having to do that ... because of the disproportionate amount of time that takes up. And I don't feel it really feeds into anything else ... I mean, the teaching, as I've said, I think, feeds into research, and I don't really feel the school practice supervision does. (Jenny, education tutor)

The most widespread source of dissatisfaction was tutors' administrative responsibilities. These were identified most emphatically by over half of the sample as a major time constraint. Some complaints were made by junior members of staff who resented having to carry out routine administrative tasks which they considered to be a misuse of their skills and qualifications:

> I'd be very happy to dump the admin ... I do timetabling in this department and I really think it's a very onerous job. I really can't see why it's a job which an academic should do ... er ... and that's not a judgemental position, it's just about what I would be best at doing, and where my skills lie ... And I think there's a lot of form-filling which I have to do, which, again, seems crazy ... Tasks which, previously, we might've passed on to the clerical staff, we tend to do ourselves now. So if you're writing an exam paper you'll often do it all yourself on your computer and simply hand in a disk ... and that seems, to me, again, not really to be a very good use of our time ... So, I think there are all sorts of administrative *little* things like that, which you might not necessarily notice, that you pick up very quickly. (Louise, English and American studies tutor)

> I find that I'm standing at the photocopier being, you know ... a very well paid ... photocopyist – if there's such a word! (Stephanie, education tutor)

The most vehement complaints about the constraints of a heavy administrative load came from more senior tutors, who had what we have identified as 'heavy-duty' administrative jobs. Four tutors fell into this category of reluctant, overloaded administrators:

> I regard myself as *inundated* with administrative jobs ... My life feels, administratively, extraordinarily over-burdened. I feel that that's what I spend most of my time doing. I take paper work home at night and weekends ... er ... and that's all departmental and faculty paperwork. And my research and teaching really are *very* much ... marginalized – certainly, in term time, ... and only recently has the department agreed to give us teaching relief for administrative burdens. So, the first few years I was on things like the University's academic policy committee, and I was chairing a University committee looking into the work of staff–student liaison, and ... I was on Faculty Board and departmental committees, and things like that – and doing a full teaching load. So, actually, my research ... my research got stuck around a project that I wanted to do ... but I felt I could never *get* to the project – I could never really think it through. (Meryl, English and American studies tutor)

> Ever since I've been a member of the academic staff I've never been able to find fifty per cent of my time for research purposes. Er ... and, at the moment, it's virtually nil because of the administrative work which I have, in connection with my role as _____. So, it's *far* from ideal at the moment ... Pretty well every member of staff has a fairly significant administrative job to do. And I think most of them might well say that they actually spend more time on the administrative job than on the actual active teaching.

That's the thing that I use most of *my* time on – and always have, really. For every hour of teaching, I probably do two hours of preparation and two hours of administration connected with the course. (Bernard, physics tutor)

You shouldn't have to do the amount of – you know ... timetables! All the stuff *I* do for the second-year course, really, it's a waste of academic expertise. I'm not trained as a secretary, or a book-keeper ... it's just a waste of my own brain power ... a waste of expertise! ... there's an awful waste of academic expertise and energy ... by them being expected to do ... administrative and secretarial matters which could be done by other people less highly qualified. I'm not being snobbish, but, you know, not everybody *wants* a Ph.D. in theoretical physics, you know. There are jobs for the people with different skills ... er ... and it just seems a waste – you know – why employ somebody at our level if ... our level isn't being exploited to the full? (Ted, physics tutor)

My administrative role is *huge*! ... I seem to be administering all these flaming links throughout the world! So, you know, I mean, it's down to the mundane ... like, you know, two people from Chile are arriving next month – where are we going to house them? ... you know, I've spent the whole morning, I suppose, when I thought I'd be working on my paper that I've got to give, trying to figure out a number of these administrative matters ... You know, you do spend a lot of time ... running committees, or ... you know, the things you have to do ... er ... appointments committees ... As I get older, and, therefore, a more senior – but still a junior – member of staff, I do an awful lot of things – like, I'm an appraiser ... er ... you know, you become, sort of, a repository of knowledge – which brings more committee work, more administration at *that* level. (Beverly, law tutor)

RESOURCES-RELATED CONSTRAINTS
The resources-related constraints that were identified were very specific and varied, and included faulty equipment:

I can't get a blackboard to work! I think that's disgusting! ... *I* shouldn't have to waste *my* time and energy, ringing up people after every lecture, and having to apologize to students that they can't read my writing, because the bloody board doesn't work! (Ted, physics tutor)

insufficient equipment and inadequate funds for specific equipment:

There are certain forms of under-resourcing ... Er ... under-resourcing in terms of, you know, money to do other, sort of ... some of the peripheral things that research involves ... and ... er ... arguably, resources for machinery – even, sort of, the technical machinery – to, sort of, facilitate *my* research. (Maurice, English and American studies tutor)

and poor facilities, resulting from inconvenient site locations:

I actually enjoy being able to say to colleagues, 'Let's go for coffee,' or 'Let's go for lunch, and let's talk about issues that're important'. That's very difficult to do here, where this department is situated, and I *bitterly* regret that because, the sort of learner I am, and the way I operate is an active learner, so I like to be in a busy, buzzing environment, and I'm quite happy to sit over a cup of coffee and thrash out the contents of a unit of work, or whatever it might be. That's very difficult to do on this part of the campus, so I find that that's awkward ... Moving the entire department to another site, where it's much more in the heart of the university, ... I wouldn't *hesitate* in saying that that would be the best move possible. (Stephanie, education tutor)

INTERPERSONAL-RELATED CONSTRAINTS

Interpersonal-related constraints are unsatisfactory conditions or situations arising directly from the behaviour and/or attitudes of others in relation to the individual who is constrained. These constraints were identified by only a small minority of tutors, and there were no references to constraining collegial relationships. Two education tutors spoke of their dissatisfaction with what they identified as the unhelpful attitudes of some of their department's secretarial support staff, outlined by one tutor:

> I find the attitude of some of the secretaries very difficult ... er ... and I find myself placating them in order to get things done. (Stephanie, education tutor)

The other source of constraint in this category was students. In this respect there were subject-related distinctions amongst the sample. Law and English and American studies tutors, whose courses recruited high-achieving students with extremely good A-level grades, made no references to their students' intellectual capacity or general quality being constraining. Indeed, several of these tutors included amongst their sources of job fulfilment references to the high calibre of their students and spoke of how this facilitated course delivery. Physics and education tutors, however, interacted with what was perceived as a generally lower-calibre student body, and several of these tutors spoke of the constraints which this imposed on their teaching and, as a result, on their job fulfilment:

> You don't get the feedback from students. You don't seem to get any reflection on their classroom experiences. They don't seem able to relate their classroom experiences to the issues that I address in lectures ... There is a relevance and a relationship there, which the students can't identify ... or aren't willing to discuss ... I'm very surprised, actually. It's very confusing, because, on the one hand you get this information that they've got particular grades at A level, and yet, when you mark their coursework ... their expression is poor ... the way they express their ideas is poor ... Rarely can they use apostrophes correctly ... their spelling is atrocious ... er ... and it does bother me. (Maggie, education tutor)

> There's a range in the academic ability of the students. Some of the spelling and grammar leaves a lot to be desired, and I hadn't really expected that. (Janice, bought-in education tutor)

> Of course, if we selected the best – and only those who're really up to it – er ... we would have to spend less time on teaching ... the job would be more rewarding, because talking to good-quality students is more pleasurable than, talking to ... nerds. (Bernard, physics tutor)

> *Interviewer: What would improve your job?*
> Well, in the first instance, improving the ... the quality of intake ... you know ... these people can hardly read, you know. They certainly can't write! They can't spell, they can't punctuate, they can't write reports, they can't write decent essays ... They can't even fill in, correctly, an exam registration form! ... If you look at the first-year course now, and the first-year course I taught when I came ... the first year course in 1968 was more like the *final* year now! (*laughs*) – that's exaggerating, but you know what I mean. (Ted, physics tutor)

UNDERSTANDING TUTORS' MORALE AND JOB SATISFACTION: A FIFTH STAGE OF ELUCIDATION

In the last chapter we referred to four levels of understanding, or stages of elucidation, in relation to what influences morale and job satisfaction. The fourth level, which incorporates the greatest conceptual sophistication, has revealed factors such as the degree of congruence between individuals' values and those reflected in the nature and responsibilities of the job, or the extent to which individuals' expectations are met at work, to be influential on levels of job satisfaction. As we point out in Chapter 6, however, for practical purposes this level of understanding has limitations arising out of the difficulty in applying the generalizability of its findings to specific job-related contexts. For the purposes of policy-making or recommendations for practice, greater elucidation is necessary on how the influence on morale and/or job satisfaction of the lowest common factors identified at the fourth level of understanding manifests itself in specific job contexts. In this section we provide that elucidation and, in doing so, develop a fifth stage, or level, of understanding.

Reflecting the fourth stage of elucidation, we have shown how university tutors' job satisfaction, which incorporates both job fulfilment and job comfort, is determined by perceptions of proximity to one's ideal job. This constitutes the lowest common job satisfaction-influencing factor. Our findings have also revealed a common factor influencing job fulfilment to be the tutor's perception of having made a contribution, in relation to some aspect of her or his work, which allows him or her to feel a sense of significant achievement. It is this sense of significant personal achievement which underpins job fulfilment, and we develop this relationship and explain the actual job fulfilment process more fully in Chapter 9. Analysis of our findings alongside those of Herzberg (1968), to whom we refer in Chapter 6, yields a difference in the significance afforded to specific factors as influences on job satisfaction. Herzberg (1968) identifies five factors which are capable of satisfying: achievement, recognition (for achievement), responsibility, advancement and the work itself. We place the last four of these as subsidiary to achievement as job fulfilment-influencing factors, since they may all, in effect, be cancelled down to this lowest common factor, in so far as they either contribute towards, or reinforce, a sense of achievement. Recognition, for example, reinforces individuals' sense of achievement, and the work itself is the vehicle for arriving at, and therefore contributes towards developing, the feeling of having made an achievement. Yet our tutors, whilst reflecting a great deal of homogeneity, differed in some respects as to what allowed them to experience the sense of significant achievement which was a constituent of their ideal job. Precisely how, and why, they differed is important to understand if the research findings are to be applied to any practical purpose. It is this information which represents a fifth stage of elucidation.

Amongst our sample of tutors job fulfilment was achieved through research, through teaching and, in some cases, through administration, although the relative ranking afforded to each of these as sources of fulfilment varied from tutor to tutor. In her examination of schoolteachers' morale and job satisfaction, Evans (1997b) identifies three interrelated variables – professionality, relative perspective and realistic expectations – which account for the diversity amongst her research sample in relation to sources of job satisfaction and dissatisfaction. These variables are equally applicable to our tutor sample.

Professionality

Professionality is not the same as professionalism (see Hoyle, 1975). It is a professional-oriented perspective which incorporates values and vision. Applied to university tutors, professionality would incorporate epistemological perspectives, reflected in the value afforded research, and views, for example, on the function of universities, the purpose of higher education and the role of university tutors. Professionality underpins attitudes to students and, to a lesser extent, views on responsibilities towards them. It reflects ideologies. It is, in a sense, a professional-oriented stance. Evans (1997b) found that, in the case of schoolteachers, job fulfilment was strongly influenced by the degree of congruence between individuals' professionality orientations and the professionality reflected in the climate of the institution in which they work. Professionality 'clashes' lead to dissatisfaction, whilst a good match, indicating shared values, is more likely to lead to greater job satisfaction. Similarly, in our study, the generally high level of job satisfaction reported by tutors is attributable, in part, to what we found to be a general consensual acceptance of, and in many cases support for, the university's prevailing institutional ethos. This ethos seems to have incorporated a strong focus on research with a concern for teaching quality, reflecting recognition of the importance of externally imposed quality assessment mechanisms and acknowledgement of the need to keep up with the changing face of higher education and to meet the demands which it imposed. This was not a university which allowed itself to be left behind; it was one which kept abreast of the times and which fashioned itself accordingly. As long as their professionality orientation did not place them significantly at odds, ideologically, with this institutional culture our tutors were able to sustain acceptably high levels of job satisfaction. Most of our interviewees did, to varying degrees, fall into this category, exemplified by the willingness of Louise, an English and American studies tutor, to conform to expected work patterns:

> I still feel very tired because last year I did so much. But, again, it's part of the academic performance. I knew that ... I'm a young academic, I had to do a lot of performing last year, in order to get a body of stuff that would be published in the next two years ... So I did it ... There was a hoop ... I jumped through it.

A minority, however, found it difficult to accept some of the features of institutional culture which conflicted with the views and/or ideologies determining their professionality, and these features became sources of dissatisfaction. One such example was Ted, a physics tutor, who was scathing in his criticism of the university's administration:

I don't ask them to give my lectures in physics, so the people in the 'Kremlin' over there shouldn't expect me to do their bookwork ... It's as simple as that ... Now, those people are paid to do nothing other than administration ... Now, in the first instance – you can imagine – academics might have gathered together to set up a university, and they might have said, 'Well, we need somebody to help us to keep track of things ... and administer a bit for us ... let's take on some people' ... It's now the other way round! ... They now, sort of, act as managers, and dictate, and say, you know, 'You should be doing this, and ... blah, blah, blah, blah'. And, every year, there's more and more ... er ... load being passed and – God knows what they *do* most of the time! I honestly do not know.

Not all professionality clashes reflected dissonance between individuals and institutional culture. Sometimes it was with externally imposed ideology that tutors' professionality was at odds. Bernard, for example, clearly disapproved of the changes to the higher-education system which have brought universitities increasingly under outside control:

What I get *most* angry about ... well, not really 'angry', but, you know ... the thing that makes me ... sort of angry ... contemptuous too ... is the increasing ... interference, from outside, in what we're doing – outside the University ... I mean, the fact that we've had imposed on us ... research assessment exercises ... that we've had imposed on us ... er ... quality assessments. I really resent this, because I don't believe that these things are necessary ... I don't believe that they're working efficiently ... er ... I believe in autonomy for universities. That's what the Royal Charter is all about – it's saying, 'You are able to ... educate these young people, and we trust you to do it'. And I very much resent the fact that we're no longer trusted to do it. And I don't see that most of the decisions which are being made ... about what we should be thinking about ... most of them make very much sense, as far as I'm concerned.

Relative perspective

Relative perspective relates to how tutors view their work in relation to other factors. Such perspectives incorporate prioritization and comparison, and are seldom static, but will tend to fluctuate in response to reprioritization and re-evaluation that may result from changing circumstances and experiences.

Factors which determine how tutors consider their work include comparative experiences, comparative insights and the circumstances and events which make up the rest of their lives: their non-work selves. Tutors view and place their work as it relates to factors such as these. Comparative experiences, for example, could be previous jobs; comparative insights may include knowledge of how another department or institution is run, or how a comparable system, such as that of another country's higher education, operates; and consideration of their non-work lives would involve the prioritization which is a prerequisite of putting the job into perspective.

The outcome of having a relative perspective on their jobs is that tutors, having compared their current job-related circumstances with the factors which constitute their evaluative yardstick, are able to rate these circumstances as either relatively satisfactory or unsatisfactory. Those tutors, for example, for whom the work context represented an improvement upon their previous work-related situations viewed it relatively favourably and were, predictably, more satisfied than were those who perceived a deterioration of work-related conditions. Moreover, if it were anticipated that the favourable conditions would persist, high morale was also experienced. Stephanie, an education tutor, spoke of how much closer to her ideal job she considered herself to be moving, compared with her experiences during previous years:

> Next year I will be teaching an area in which I have expertise which will take me one step closer towards that ideal job.

Similarly, Ken, who was also an education tutor, illustrated the nature of his relative perspective, which involved his favourably comparing his department's current management with the preceding one:

> The management at that time didn't seem to be capable of understanding ... what the priorities *ought* to have been with the work that I was doing. And I was asked to do totally inappropriate jobs, in my opinion ... Some negotiation went on ... but the simplest course of action seemed to be to do the job quickly ... er ... and without any pleasure or enjoyment. Er ... but, I was asked to do *inappropriate* things, that were unrelated to my strengths and my main interests. Er ... I might say that that situation is radically different now.

On the other hand, the relative perspectives of Ted and Bernard, both from the physics department, result in their comparing their current job-related situations unfavourably with those which prevailed during their early careers. Regretting the end of the golden age of academic freedom from accountability and external regulation which, unlike many of our tutor interviewees, they had experienced, and lamenting over what they considered to be the undesirable results of the series of reforms to higher education of recent years, they manifested comparatively low job satisfaction and morale.

Realistic expectations

Realistic expectations of their work contexts do not necessarily reflect tutors' 'ideals', but, rather, those expectations which they feel are realistically able to be fulfilled. Such expectations reflect values and ideologies, and will be partly influenced by professionality and comparative experiences and insights. In this way, the three factors which we identify as underlying what diversity there was amongst the attitudinal responses to their work context of our tutor sample – professionality, relative perspective and realistic expectations – are clearly interrelated. It was the non-fulfilment of their specific realistic expectations of students' ability which gave rise to this being a negative job-comfort factor for some tutors, such as Maggie, Ted and Janice, whose complaints about low-calibre students are presented above. In contrast, Meryl's realistic expectations of her students' ability were clearly being met, resulting in what was a negative job-comfort factor for her colleagues in other departments being a positive job-comfort factor in her case:

> *I* feel these students could teach themselves. They've all got three As at A level – they're very bright ... they ... you know, with a bit of library training they could go off and read the books, they write good essays ...

What diversity there was within our sample was most apparent with respect to attitudes to the teaching component of their jobs. The next chapter focuses on the different ways in which our tutors operated as teachers.

Chapter 8

Tutors as Teachers

INTRODUCTION

In Chapters 6 and 7 we described the main and varied features of tutors' work and identified successful teaching as a widespread source of fulfilment for 80 per cent of our sample. This chapter focuses more narrowly on the teaching component of tutors' work, which we interpret broadly as those aspects of their jobs which involve interaction with students. Teaching, in this context, could, therefore, range from lectures to brief, informal, course-related conversations with individual students.

As we pointed out in Chapter 1, internal and external pressures are being placed on tutors to improve their performance in all aspects of their work. As part of this process the teaching-quality assessments undertaken by the funding bodies have focused attention on the quality of teaching. Our book is not intended to be a teaching manual containing guidance on how to achieve high grades in this assessment process. However, through an exploration of the range of teaching roles undertaken by tutors, this chapter includes descriptions of what tutors consider to be innovative and effective teaching. These examples of good teaching are important inclusions since they contribute towards clarifying concepts of innovation and excellence in teaching, and inform the debate about whether or not the nature and style of university teaching ought to change. Of greater significance, however, within the remit of our book is consideration of the contribution teaching can make to meeting tutors' job-related needs. The main underlying issues, in this chapter, therefore, are the importance which tutors place upon teaching as an integral part of their work: the priority level and ranking which they afford it, and how their attitudes towards this aspect of their jobs are translated into teaching preparation and performance.

AVAILABILITY TO STUDENTS

Whilst, generally, our sample of students expressed a high level of satisfaction with the teaching they received and with the availability of tutors, they also recognized differences in the attitudes of individual tutors to teaching, manifested through differing levels of commitment and differing degrees of involvement in, and time for, teaching.

Tutors' own educational backgrounds will clearly have an impact on their attitudes to teaching and their conception of the nature of the responsibilities associated with this component of their work. Whilst we did not collect detailed data on the educational backgrounds and experiences of tutors, we feel it is worth including the somewhat atypical example of Otto, a law tutor, who, having been educated on the Continent, held expectations of the role of university tutors which were somewhat less student-centred than those of most of his colleagues:

> But I feel that ... er ... in the law school we spoon-feed students too much and, of course, I come from a different educational background. In Holland ... er ... the system is *entirely* different. I'm not saying that is the ideal model, but I *know*, ... er ..., that Dutch students, German students, the system is much more impersonal. You don't get the kind of guidance you get here. The German students and Dutch students are more independent. They do not have this kind of expectation that lecturers hold them by the hand and say, 'Oh, this is a book. Open it.' ... I couldn't care less if students don't turn up. It's *their* responsibility. (Otto, law tutor)

Although Otto's educational background rendered him atypical amongst our sample, his interpretation of what teaching, in the widest sense, involved in terms of tutor commitment was by no means distinct. The range of views in relation to what responsibilities tutors ought to undertake, in their roles as teachers, and how available to students they should be, included some which were congruent with those of Otto, as well as some representing the other end of the spectrum.

Otto's views reflect a culturally determined concept of higher education which embraces the notion that the onus of responsibility for their learning lies with students. For the most part, though, it was not so much concepts of higher education, but competing pressures, which underpinned our tutors' willingness to be available to students and which shaped their interpretations of the teaching roles and responsibilities of academics.

The influence of competing pressures presented by the other components of their work, such as research and administration, upon tutors' prioritiza-tion of teaching is vividly illustrated by the contrast between the time devoted to teaching by Nicholas, one of the bought-in tutors in our sample, and by permanent tutors, such as Meryl and Ken, who had considerable adminis-trative loads within their departments:

> It still takes me hours, and hours, and hours to mark assignments and fiddle about with them. I'm very conscious when I'm second marking, or someone's second marking mine, that I want to do justice to what the students have done. And I spend two/two and a half hours on each assignment reading and re-reading, trying to be as fair as I possibly

can ... I mean, this week, I was able to give groups three-quarters of an hour to each question, and then offer a 20- to 25-minute individual tutorial. And, to the final year students – those who wanted it – *another* 20-minute tutorial at the beginning of next term ... because my time can be fairly flexible, so, yeah ... they have that sort of opportunity. (Nicholas, bought-in education tutor)

I think that what I would say is that, actually, *teaching* is almost a kind of afterthought in my daily life ... you know ... it's a, sort of, interruption of paperwork. Which is ... not the way life should be, and I don't enjoy that ... er ... I think, what I ... well, my *feeling* is that I would like to have less teaching, but I think that's only because I don't have time to do it properly. And so, I always feel that, when students come into my room, that I'm ... I really haven't given enough time and space to this work. (Meryl, English and American studies tutor)

I think we've *got* to be ... available ... to students, to give them advice, to give them help, and so on, but at appropriate times and in appropriate ways ... There are situations that crop up where you just drop everything, because someone's in dire straits ... er ... but, somebody knocks on the door and says, you know, 'I want such-and-such a form', but they shouldn't be coming to *me* for it, and, you know ... I'm not going to waste my time doing that ...

I mean, somebody quite inappropriately knocked on the door the other day – and I was trying to complete something for the ESRC which had to go off, I was also due up in Oxford that afternoon – and this person was quite cross because I wouldn't see him just at that moment. Well ... I mean ... he got short shrift really ... (Ken, education tutor)

Nicholas was able to dedicate a significant amount of time to his work with students because, as a bought-in tutor, he was not expected to carry out research or administration duties. Ken and Meryl were subject to many work-related demands on their time and had to make decisions about the amount of time they could afford to devote to working with students. All permanent tutors, because of the competing pressures arising out of the tripartite nature of their jobs, were faced with similar questions, but some nevertheless identified work with students as their major priority:

I feel a, sort of duty, to the student. Teaching is what you have to put at the top of the list of priorities. (Christine, physics tutor)

The priority would be the student – at least to find out what the student wanted. That's also because I'm a senior tutor, so I have to be responsible for a number of both academic and personal crises. Er .. so, yes, I would be responsive to the student, first ... It's also that ... you know, my research is ... perhaps a bit of a 'movable feast'. One of the things of being an academic, I think, is that you can have control, to some extent, over your own time. That tends to be the research element. And, therefore, I do think that ... well ... I can move that bit, but the students are less flexible and less able to do that. (Ben, law tutor)

The institutional ethos of the university, which we briefly describe in Chapter 7, greatly emphasized the importance of research activity for full-time tutors. This imposed particular pressures on all tutors, who were expected to contribute significantly to research activity in addition to maintaining high standards in their teaching and administrative responsibilities. Time spent with students, therefore, potentially prevented tutors from focusing on other aspects of their work. However, despite all tutors being placed under these pressures, they responded differently and developed their own strategies for dealing with student access. These strategies reflected their own prioritization, and there was considerable disparity amongst the sample. Many adopted an open-door policy, believing that their responsibilities as teachers should take priority over other aspects of their job:

I feel I *ought* to be available to students. My view is that one ought to be available, more or less, within reason ... (Maurice, English and American studies tutor)

You make yourself accessible. I suppose, as well ... you do things which make the students ... come and discuss things with you outside the lecture room, as well as in it ... Part of it is also appearing as a human person who they can talk to, and want to talk to. So one tries to present that sort of image ... (Stan, education tutor)

However, some tutors admitted, implicitly or explicitly, that they did not welcome interruptions to their work from students arriving unexpectedly at their doors:

I have office hours, and I fob off students. I'm really quite ruthless. (Meryl, English and American studies tutor)

So, ideally, I would not see students too often. I would be available for one hour a week which is more than enough ... (Otto, law tutor)

Interviewer: Do you get them knocking on the door?
No, because I discourage them from doing that, and, er, what I would normally do would be to get them to come straight up at the end of the session and make an appointment then ... If it happens to be a session where I've got a bit of time afterwards, actually to see me immediately. And then I'd also look to save time by seeing a group of people together who happen to be working on the same essay title. (Ken, education tutor)

It's inevitably an intrusion because if you're in your office you're planning to do something. It's very difficult to refuse to see people. I find it impossible to refuse to see people since you're very visible ... you're there. There's a suggestion that if you're there you're also available.
Interviewer: Do you resent *having to see them?*
... I would prefer – and I've suggested to them – that there are particular parts of the week when they do come to see me ... er ... and I would prefer they did that so that I'm thinking about the issues that they're likely to raise, rather than interrupting something else. (Maggie, education tutor)

The impression which we gained, in the course of our interviews with academics, was that the university management, whilst valuing, and recognizing the need to promote, effective teaching, nevertheless afforded teaching lower priority than research. This was reflected in the perceptions which our tutors held of their institution's promotion policy and to which several referred:

Everybody, to a man, realizes that the way to get promoted is to do good research and sacrifice teaching ... Er ... but some people, nevertheless, do a *very* conscientious job in the teaching and put a lot of time into it. And I think, to be honest, that they are carrying – on the teaching side – the staff who are pursuing research very vigorously ... I'm not too worried about that because you could put the argument the other way round and say that the staff who're pursuing research vigorously are also carrying the people who're spending more time on teaching ... So, it's just that the research side produces the promotions, whereas the teaching side does not, and this balance of people doing slightly different things is fine, except from the point of view of promotion. (Bernard, physics tutor)

I think that one of the tragic things about the whole promotion process at this university is that ... what is *not* rewarded, is things like ... er ... the sort of people – and I'm not talking just about myself here, actually, 'cos I'm talking very much about other colleagues who've not been promoted – the sort of colleagues who are anxious to introduce new courses, who are anxious to make changes, who *do* rewrite their lectures, who do, sort of, take their teaching very seriously, and regard, you know, a course that's been run in the same way for five years as a real failure, and feel that, you know, it should be ... it should be transformed, it should be changed. (Meryl, English and American studies tutor)

Despite these research-focused pressures, the relatively high level of autonomy given to tutors in this university allowed them much flexibility to impose, and work towards, their own standards of effectiveness in teaching. As an institution-specific influence, the autonomy given to tutors outweighed the pressure to conduct research and allowed individual views about the relative importance of teaching to determine work-related priorities. Diverse attitudes towards responsibility to students and the importance of teaching were, therefore, able to be found, even within the same department:

There is a big variation, I think, in the way in which different staff in the department respond to ... er ... casual visits ... I take the attitude that, if I'm here in my room, and if I'm not with somebody else, and ... well, by and large, I can always spend time with the student ...

And so, I say to the students, 'Look, talk to us. *We're* here, *you're* here. The reason you're here and not at home is because you're in contact with us. You've got to talk to us, and don't be frightened of coming ... You *might* sometimes get a sharp grunt, because someone's in a bad mood ... don't worry about that; at heart we're pleased to see you, and we're happy to spend time with you.' But it doesn't happen enough. (Bernard, physics tutor)

There is a very conscious element within staff, certainly within this department, you know, the students firstly are never wrong. Er, ... if there's anything wrong it must be the way you teach; it's all the staff's fault. *We've* got to give more time, got to give more patience, *we've* got to do ... you know ... it's never contemplated that it might just, on a few occasions, be that *they* haven't done any work or *they* don't take it seriously. They've got no scholarship, they've got no cultivated mode of study. (Ted, physics tutor)

MAINTAINING STANDARDS

Interestingly, though, the range of views on teaching responsibility and availability to students amongst our sample of tutors does not appear, from their accounts, to be reflected in the effort which they put into the teaching component of their work. Considering the strong research-focused culture which prevailed in the university in our study, we were surprised to find that the majority of them shared a concern to develop as effective teachers.

Smith's and Brown's (1995, p. 14) anecdotal evidence of tutors wanting to push teaching aside to concentrate solely on research reflects an image of a tutor fashioned by a concern to prioritize research above the teaching-related elements of the job:

> Apocryphal stories are common of advice given by old hands to newly recruited lecturers in old universities to have as little to do with the students as possible, to leave lectures promptly without allowing time for questions and to maintain a closed office or lab door so as to preserve from contamination the precious time available for research. In this way they will be able to achieve academic success and career advancement. The new universities are not immune from such thinking: a respected senior research chemist known to the editors was heard to advise a group of new lecturers on a postgraduate teaching certificate course that if they worked hard and achieved success in research, they might, like him, be able to get out of teaching completely.

Yet our findings do not corroborate this image of teaching in higher education. Whatever their other commitments and pressures, our tutors' descriptions and explanations of how they tackled the teaching component of their work conveyed a clear impression of a group of very conscientious professionals who generally set high standards for themselves in relation to planning, preparation and delivery:

> Sometimes I go through the course again and I see something I hadn't noticed, and it worries me. So, sometimes, ... you can go over it for a week ... some small point. There was one small point that came up in the course this year – one – my very first, question, I couldn't answer. And I still don't know the answer to it ... so, I've got to sort that out before next year ... Also, I spend fifteen minutes, *at least*, before I do the lecture, going through the lecture to prepare for it. (Ivan, physics tutor)

> I've always felt it important ... er ... to teach well, and to be prepared. I mean I don't have the self-confidence to walk into a group without being pretty well organized. (Beverly, law tutor)

> For every hour of teaching I probably do two hours of preparation. (Bernard, physics tutor)

Even those who identified teaching as less important to them than other aspects of their job clearly endeavoured to teach to high standards. Meryl, for example, whom we categorized earlier in the chapter as a tutor seeking to minimize the time she allocated to students, was nevertheless very conscientious about her teaching:

> I think my relationship to teaching is so difficult because I'm always so self-critical. I really am *very* critical about my own teaching, and I know ... much better than they do, what's wrong with what's going on, and I know when the seminars are getting dull ... I'm very sensitive to that. So, I'm much more agonized by that than they are. They're probably just sitting there thinking 'Oh, you know, I wish this seminar would end' or 'I wish it would pick up in some way'. But, for me, that's real agony ... you know ... I'm still very caught up in teaching. That's probably why ... I mean, I remember talking to colleagues at _____ about it, and we all said that we all felt sick before we taught a class. And I thought how interesting that was. We were all very experienced teachers, and we all said – and I *do*, I feel physically sick before ... especially a seminar group. (Meryl, English and American studies tutor)

The general conscientious approach to teaching amongst our tutors manifested itself in ways which suggest that it was underpinned by a concern to be professionally competent, rather than by a love of the activity itself. Tutors might complain, for example, about the aspects of teaching which they disliked, whilst still wanting do the job to the best of their ability:

> I'd also be very happy if I didn't have to, for example, write notes to all my students who didn't turn up for seminars. But if you're going to be conscientious about teaching, and catch up with them, and work out what's going on, and why they aren't turning up, it often involves writing a lot of notes. And if, in one week, because they've got an essay to write, a lot of people don't turn up, I find I write a lot of notes. So, I think, in some ways, I'd be very happy to get rid of those sorts of things, too, but I can't see how I *can* – I mean, that seems, to me, to be part and parcel of teaching ... if you want to be responsible, and keep in touch with your students, and have a personal relationship with them, which I *do*, you've got to do all that as well. And that, really, I find galling. (Louise, English and American studies tutor)

Similarly, recently appointed tutors spoke of their anxiety to establish themselves as competent teachers, even, in some cases, at the expense of the more highly valued research:

> Er ... in the first term I didn't even think about ... er ... doing any research – I just wanted to survive to Christmas, basically ... I find the teaching time manages to take up most of the time in here, just now. (Brian, law tutor)

> I am relatively research-focused, but I am very concerned about my lectures ... If I have a lecture I ... er ... I get nervous and I start working very hard so I can get this lecture done and I regard these lectures almost as an article I have to write, and, maybe this is just a beginner's, sort of, attitude, but I notice the same with most of the young colleagues. If they have a lecture on Tuesday they'll start working on Friday and work right through the weekend to get the lecture done. It's the major event in the week. (Otto, law tutor)

The high status enjoyed by this university means that competition for jobs may sometimes be quite intense, and staff who are appointed are considered to be, or to have the potential to be, relatively high achievers. Many have either been identified as experts in their field or displayed the potential to become successful academics. Therefore, their desire to maintain high standards in relation to their work with students can be viewed as a component of their wish to succeed in all aspects of their work – as a manifestation of perfectionist tendencies, or simply of professional pride.

TEACHING APPROACHES

Whilst there was general agreement among tutors about the importance of achieving and maintaining high standards in their teaching there was less commonality in relation to the form which it took. A fairly wide range of teaching methods seems to have been employed, including traditional, didactic methods of instruction and more student-centred approaches. These differences in approach reflected a diversity of conceptions of teaching and views about the purpose of higher education. The two opposite extremes of the range of views represented amongst our tutors are exemplified by Ted and Stephanie. Ted believed that the tutor's teaching role involved his/her being a repository of knowledge, of which students should be passive and grateful recipients:

> Really I think the students go away with an idea that we are a marketable commodity, and they must be satisfied with what they find, and if they're not, they're entitled to complain ... And the very ... it's the attitude that *underlies* it, to feel that we ... er ... we must allow them to comment – what do *they* know about the subject. They're here to learn, you know, that's why they're here, because they're not experts. *We're* the experts ... and yet, we're compromising ourselves ... by inviting this criticism and attacks on our academic integrity along these lines. It's *totally* unnecessary. (Ted, physics tutor)

In contrast, Stephanie believed strongly that students should play a more active role in their own learning and that the function of the tutor was to act as a facilitator to the development of a range of skills:

> Ideally, I would want to work with students who want to develop themselves as learners ... For example, if I'm doing work on women's autobiography ... I would want to, perhaps, take a paper I was preparing to a seminar with students, for their input, and actually ask them to contribute to the process and to use my work as a basis for going off to do their work. *Not* to be perceived as the expert, but more as someone who is further along the path and is helping them follow.

Tutors' conceptions of higher education and their views on the respective roles of students and lecturers influenced the kinds of teaching approaches which they employed. Those who veered towards Ted's opinion, predictably, favoured more traditional approaches to teaching, in particular, lecturing. Those who shared Stephanie's concern to develop more co-operative, or semi-autonomous, learning amongst students had a wider repertoire of more informal, participatory teaching styles. The majority of our sample represented less extreme stances than those of Ted and Stephanie. Many tutors, particularly those in the education, law and English and American studies departments, tended towards the general approach favoured by Stephanie, incorporating considerable participatory teaching methods. Yet the traditional lecture was still a widely adopted teaching method. In many cases it seemed to be cost-effectiveness, rather than ideology, which underpinned the widespread use of lectures, as Louise's comments suggest:

> I think lectures are very difficult in terms of pedagogy. I think they're not, to my mind, a very good teaching method. And I think the problem with lectures is, exactly that problem I highlighted about seminars; they're passive. Students sit there, they make notes, they go away, they don't necessarily look at the notes again, they don't reflect on them. They just have them there and use them for revision and I'm not happy about lectures at all.
> *Interviewer: Is that an element of the course you would change, ideally; would you get rid of the lecture programme?*
> Well we're talking about it, but it's hard to know how we could do that and not increase our workload massively. Lectures are very economic – which is why we use them. (Louise, English and American studies tutor)

These pedagogic concerns about traditional teaching methods were shared by other tutors who believed that the development of innovative teaching methods, involving increased student participation, would, in turn, lead to greater student motivation. Yet there was no escaping the problem highlighted by Louise, which, in a sense, reflects the key issue underlying the research upon which this book is based: how to meet what are becoming recognized as students' learning participation needs without imposing heavier workloads and increased pressures on tutors. The response of many tutors to this seems to have been to try to inject a student-centred dimension into lectures by encouraging their participation, or engaging their interest, in order to improve the general acceptability and the success of lectures as modes of course delivery. We include examples of such 'innovations' to lectures in the next section.

In addition to lectures, smaller-group teaching through seminars was prevalent within the English and American studies, education and law courses. Many tutors were developing student-centred teaching approaches, and these tended to feature mainly in seminars. Such approaches typically involved co-operative learning amongst groups of students, and less tutor didacticism:

> What I might often do within a seminar is get them to do certain sorts of tasks for ten minutes while I'm not in the room, and then come back. And I get one person to be a spokesperson ... To do it internally within the seminar itself, rather than expecting someone to come on their own to a seminar and give a paper ... The point is to get them to speak, to give them confidence. (Louise, English and American studies tutor)

> I will meet with the students for two hours. Usually there will be two focuses, one will be information-giving and one will be ... information sharing and discussion. It's split in two different activities within that two hours ... The week before, they're told what's going to happen, who's going to be responsible for what. So I will say, 'I'm going to talk about *this* next week and you're going to be responsible for *this* aspect of the class, with readings, or whatever, ... with a task to do.' (Beverly, law tutor)

> I suppose one rule of thumb is that, if it's an important idea – most of the teaching I do is either an important mathematical idea or an important pedagogic idea – I want the students to explore their own thinking about the idea first, in some respect or other, before there's any sense of telling them what the answer is ... Giving them a view, if you like, which is *my* view, but set in the context of other people's views. So it's very important for me, for the children, or the students, to explore the idea for themselves ... I suppose, essentially, it's constructivist in that I do believe that we all have to construct our own ideas about things. Nevertheless I am an important player in that construction process; probably the most important player in the classroom, but that's not to diminish too much the role the students' own peers have in the classroom and the resources I can provide ...
>
> There are occasions when I would get them to reflect on something on their own, but much of the time they'll be working in groups, discussing ideas, feeding back. When we started with the students at the beginning of the year I actually suggested to them explicitly that what I wanted was for our classroom to become a critical community, and I set down a few rules by what I meant by that. It's to do with respecting other people's views, but at the same time not being shy to constructively criticize other people's views. (Stan, education tutor)

Whilst the amount of responsibility which Stan gives to students may be atypical in the context of most university teaching, several tutors' comments suggested that they were keen to encourage greater interaction within seminar groups. There was a growing recognition that students have a lot to offer in terms of developing their own learning, as Avril, a law tutor, argued:

> I'm a firm believer ... that students can learn an awful lot more from each other ... than they can possibly learn from staff. They spend so much more time with each other than they ever do with us ... and, therefore, you need to get them to see that.

Indeed, Avril's department had introduced student-led seminars, involving students meeting without the presence of a tutor, and managing their own discussions on tutor-stipulated issues.

INNOVATION IN TEACHING

When we asked tutors to consider the extent to which they considered their teaching to be innovative, thirteen provided specific illustrative examples. Interestingly, though, only one tutor asked for clarification of what we meant by 'innovative' before offering her own interpretation:

> I think there are two ways of looking at whether or not one is being innovative in one's teaching. Whether one is being innovative in terms of change, so, doing something different this year compared with what I did last year. Yes, there's quite a lot of that because the demands from schools change, the student perceptions change, *my* perceptions change. So I don't feel the teaching methods are set in stone ... The other is to do with innovation in a wider way, am I doing something which is unusual in HE generally?
>
>   I wouldn't make any claims about doing that. The range of methods I use cover straight lecture, small-group sessions, large-group discussions. A range of activities. I don't think any of those things are wildly innovative. (Jenny, education tutor)

It became clear that, within a very broad consensus, criteria for innovativeness varied. One tutor's innovative approach to teaching may be considered by another to be somewhat run-of-the-mill or lacklustre, just as innovation, to one tutor, may simply involve making minor changes to a lecture programme, whereas, for another, it might require nothing less than the introduction of experiential learning. Reflecting this relativity, the examples of what tutors categorized as innovations in their own teaching were wide-ranging. Ivan, for example, spoke of the methods he employed in lectures:

> I lecture by *only* writing on the blackboard ... er ... which means that you précis, basically, the basic information ... Er ... but if you write it down fairly quickly, the students can write it down, maybe, half as fast ... which gives you a little bit of time to, sort of, talk over what you've just written on the board, and, maybe, illustrate some little bits and pieces with stories that they don't have to write down. It adds to the interest. (Ivan, physics tutor)

In contrast, Avril provided an example of a teaching approach which stands out as unusually imaginative, in the context of higher education:

> The law students have to get to grips with a fairly complicated set of legal rules, and I want them to be able to use the statute, read the statutes ... When I was on maternity leave I actually developed a board game to take them through this stuff. So, rather than

have a discussion or a lecture on it, I make them ... play a board game. It's a way of taking them through the statute ... It gets them to understand the stuff in the end ... and when I look at their exams they can handle that area ... It's also very good for group ethos. (Avril, law tutor)

It is important to take into account subject-specific relativity. In Chapter 3 we provided much evidence of the didactic nature of teaching in the physics department, and pointed out that this is in keeping with inter-institutional traditions in the physical sciences. In view of this, Ivan's deviation from what the science community would probably accept as the norm, even though his approach is greatly overshadowed as a teaching innovation by Avril's example, is, none the less, innovative by physics standards.

Moreover, both Ivan's and Avril's examples clearly represent rational approaches to teaching, rather than a concern to jump on the latest bandwagon. Entwistle (1995, p. 37) has argued that there is little to be gained from the recommendation of one particular method of teaching and that innovation does not necessarily lead to the creation of effective learning:

So far, we have argued that improvements in the quality of student learning cannot come from recommending specific methods of teaching. Encouraging student activity is important, but the form that activity takes is crucial. And the 'right' activity comes not from any single teaching method, but from a careful arrangement of the whole learning environment, including above all assessment which provides reward for deep, active ways of studying. It is by no means clear that the most effective learning environments *necessarily* involve innovative methods, but there is a strong probability that they will. It is clear that they *will* have involved the member of staff, or course team, in considerable thought about which teaching arrangements are most likely to support the type of learning required. But components of that environment could certainly involve traditional approaches carried out thoughtfully and imaginatively. (Entwistle, 1995, p. 37)

The 'traditional approaches carried out thoughtfully and imaginatively' to which Entwistle refers were also included amongst the examples of innovations which our tutors provided:

I gave a lecture last term which I *know* went down very well with the students, where I was using ... it was the first time I'd done this actually ... I played ... I was giving a lecture on *A Streetcar Named Desire*, by Tennessee Williams, and I played the video of the film silently behind me as I lectured, so they could watch it, instead of having to look at me. And they were obviously knocked out by that – it obviously worked really well. And, in fact, it was absolutely perfect because – and this was not planned – but it actually ... when I finished my lecture, Blanche Dubois was actually saying, 'Goodbye' to somebody, so I turned up the sound and she said, sort of, 'Adios, adios', and I thought, 'I couldn't have done it better if I'd planned it'. But, I like it when I do something new that's different. The second time I do that ... I'll probably do that again next year, but I'll be bored by it ... you know. (Meryl, English and American studies tutor)

There were also examples which incorporated a mixture of what may be considered 'alternative' teaching methods and traditional approaches:

We introduced a pattern whereby students read a paper and then presented their views about the paper. We split the large group into three mini-groups of eight and saw each of the three groups for one-third of the two hours. So we saw them in rotation and they had the other two-thirds of that session to prepare the paper for the following Thursday session. And we weren't very happy ... So we decided that we needed to look again at that. So this ... current academic year, for the Thursday slot, we explicitly set it up as debates – still with the mini-groups ... but we appointed two students from each of the mini-groups to speak *for* a particular motion and two to speak against it, and the others to be witnesses, to interrogate the two sides. And we gave the students the motions for debate at the beginning of the term. They chose which of the ones they wanted to speak to ... That has been highly successful and I'm quite surprised how successful it's been this year. A lot of the students have said that's been the highlight of their four years here .... That has really forced them to think critically and they've enjoyed it very much and got a lot out of it. I said jokingly, at one stage, to some of them, 'Perhaps we'd better do it on the Tuesdays as well and take out the lecture input'. They said, 'No, no ... we need the lecture input, it follows on very well from the lecture input and then forces us to take the ideas forward'. So that's, for me, an innovation in teaching. (Jenny, education tutor)

The underlying philosophy of the course is that the educational method is experiential learning rather than Socratic teaching methods or, indeed, straight lectures ... Er ... so a legal practice course is chaos to an outsider. It's people doing things and going all over the law school and then just getting together with themselves or occasionally in a large group. We have few lecture format sessions ...

We do simulated trials as the clinical element and we've increased the numbers to forty-two ... The feedback is almost universally that it's enjoyable – which is good, but worrying. We do worry about the extent to which they enjoy it and don't get the intellectual challenge they might ... The balance between the intellectual challenge and the practical enjoyment of experiencing legal issues which are new to them, I do think it's a difficult relationship. We are constantly thinking about those things and I'm not sure we've got the relationship right ... The course changes from year to year. (Ben, law tutor)

Within the sample as a whole there was a general trend towards a more student-centred approach but there was no real consensus about what constituted innovative teaching. New approaches were, however, largely the result of the work of committed tutors rather than part of any co-ordinated institutional, or even departmental, policies to improve teaching and learning.

IMPLICATIONS FOR MEETING TUTORS' NEEDS

It was clear that, since they manifested such conscientious attitudes to the planning, delivery and preparation of teaching and set themselves generally high standards of performance, our tutors' teaching-related needs were dependent upon their maintaining a level of teaching quality which satisfied their professional pride and met their self-imposed standards of competence. At the same time, the competing pressures which had prompted some tutors to marginalize teaching within their set of priorities and to apply time-saving strategies to those elements of it which did not require, or focus upon, their public performance highlight the importance of time-and-effort cost-effectiveness considerations. Many of our tutors were clearly very receptive to innovation, particularly if they considered it to improve teaching quality and, in doing so, to enhance their image of their own professional competence, but they were also adamant that any extra demands on their time were unwelcome. Indeed, there was none who would not have welcomed opportunities to save time on teaching.

The implications of this are that, in relation to teaching, meeting tutors' needs involves providing the best of both worlds: the opportunity to excel, with the minimum expenditure of time. Our suggestions for specific ways of moving towards this ideal are presented in the final chapter.

Chapter 9

Meeting Tutors' Job-fulfilment Needs: A Framework for Institutional Policy

INTRODUCTION

In Chapters 6, 7 and 8 we have examined the nature of university tutors' work and presented illustrative examples of the different ways in which academics achieve varying, and fluctuating, degrees of job fulfilment. These illustrations have conveyed something of what it is about their work that contributes towards satisfying tutors' job-related needs, and what aspects of the job are unsatisfactory and, in many cases, impede fulfilment.

The purpose of this book, however, is not simply to identify tutors' needs but to examine how the business of teaching and learning in higher education, in its widest sense, may be better adapted to serving those needs, whilst also accommodating those of students. In order to do this, it is essential to analyse and to elucidate the process whereby university tutors' job-related needs are satisfied, so that institutional policies for developing teaching and learning may incorporate consideration of, and mechanisms for facilitating the reproduction of, this process.

If it is to satisfy their needs, university teaching must provide tutors with opportunities for job fulfilment. Our research findings have illustrated the nature of such job-fulfilment opportunities, and the ways in which they present themselves, in the context of academics' working lives. Out of our analysis of these findings, and informed by occupational psychology and motivation theory and by work in the field of schoolteachers' morale and job satisfaction carried out by one of us (Evans, 1992a; 1992b; 1997a; 1997b; 1997c; 1997d; 1998), we have developed a model of the job-fulfilment process. This model may be incorporated into a framework for the development of institutional policy which aims to accommodate tutors', as well as students', needs. In this chapter we present our model and examine its implications for institutional policy.

A MODEL OF THE JOB-FULFILMENT PROCESS

The process whereby job fulfilment is achieved by individuals is represented in our model, illustrated in Figure 9.1. Eight stages are identified. According to our interpretation of job fulfilment, which is explained in Chapter 6, all eight stages are essential components of the process. These stages reflect the subjectivity of the individual experiencing job fulfilment and relate to her or his actions without necessarily reflecting general consensus and without necessarily incorporating objectivity. We explain, stage by stage, in the next sub-section the job-fulfilment process, as represented by our model. In the following, much shorter, sub-section we provide examples of the model's application to different components of tutors' work.

Explaining the process

Stage 1

The first stage is the individual's awareness of an imperfect situation in relation to his or her job. The imperfection reflects the individual's perception, which may not necessarily be shared by others. Examples of perceived imperfections amongst the sample of tutors in our study are the negative job-comfort factors to which we refer in Chapter 7. As the basic component in the job-fulfilment process, perceived imperfections may range in magnitude, from tiny to enormous, but it is likely that their perceived magnitude will, under certain circumstances, correlate with the magnitude of the job fulfilment experienced at the end of the process.

Our research findings revealed a wide-ranging array of imperfect situations in relation to their work, as perceived by our tutors. Some were clearly ranked as minor irritants, such as the organization of one of the courses on which Otto, a law tutor, taught:

> Four tutors are involved in the course, which is more difficult to organize, not only because there are more students, but because there are more staff involved, and that's difficult. For example, the simple, practical things – you cannot say in a lecture, 'Well, we'll continue next week', because, next week, there's someone else who may not know the issue. (Otto, law tutor)

Others were more emphatically considered undesirable:

> I haven't published anything in about ... two-and-a-half years ... It bothers me greatly, because I've got lots of good stuff that I *want* to publish, and get it out of the way. It's just finding ... a sufficiently long ... span of time to do it. (Ivan, physics tutor)

> I feel frustrated because of the teaching load that I have, which is *massively* too high. (Stan, education tutor)

Yet, as a basic component of the job-fulfilment process, individuals' perceived job-related imperfections need not, and, indeed, often do not, represent such obvious deficiencies. Our interpretation of an imperfect situation, in the context of its being a catalyst for the job-fulfilment process, is simply a situation in relation to which some measure of improvement, no

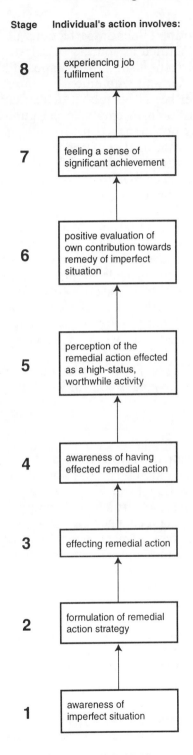

Figure 9.1 The job-fulfilment process in individuals

matter how small, is desirable. Such imperfections may be so slight that they would scarcely be identified as sources of dissatisfaction. Often they will reflect individuals' perfectionism, or self-imposed high standards. The tutor who is a prolific writer and who enjoys an international reputation may, for example, consider her or his job-related situation to be imperfect because s/he is unsuccessful in attempts to be published in a specific, prestigious journal or has not managed to procure an invitation to be a keynote speaker at an international conference. The successful researcher who has a track record of attracting external funding may consider failure to win a grant from a research council to constitute imperfection. The tutor who has earned a reputation as a dynamic and popular teacher may perceive a failure to secure 100 per cent attendance rates at seminars or lectures to be an imperfect situation. Most commonly, though, the imperfections which are the basis of the job-fulfilment process are more general and pervasive, and are taken for granted since they represent constituents of the work itself, provide its justification and determine its nature. The teaching component of tutors' work, for example, has as its rationale the 'imperfections' reflected by students' inadequate knowledge; the research component, similarly, is justified by gaps in knowledge and understanding. In this sense, all work represents a response to an unsatisfactory situation.

Imperfect situations may be within or outside the individual's control, but it is only those within the individual's control which may spark off the job-fulfilment process.

Stage 2

Stage 2 involves the individual's formulating a strategy for removing or reducing the perceived imperfection, in order to bring about an improvement in his or her job-related situation. Strategies, as we interpret the term in this context, may range in magnitude from, for example, a passing thought, which leads to an idea for a slight change to a way of working, to a carefully constructed personal career development plan. This stage does not involve putting the remedial strategy into effect; it merely involves formulating it. It is a conceptual stage. It involves nothing more than recognition of what would remove, or reduce, the imperfections in a specific job-related situation.

Beverly, one of our law tutors, spoke of the conflict that she experienced between two elements of her work: her research in the field of media law and her time-consuming administrative role, which involved considerable international travel in order to promote courses abroad. This conflict represents imperfection, yet she was aware of ways of reducing or removing it:

> It's my own fault, in terms of ... not finishing one lot of things ... before starting on a new area ... I'm vastly over-committed at the moment ... I'm supposed to be in Malaysia at the moment and ... I've had to say, 'No', because I've got to finish my book on media law.

Similarly, Bernard, a physics tutor, identified both an imperfection which he perceived in his work and a remedial strategy:

> I think we'd be hard-pushed to get an 'excellent' rating on teaching ... because there are some patently obvious deficiencies in ... some of the things we have ... particularly in our laboratories ... where they need total up-date and revision.

For Meryl, an English and American studies tutor, her lack of knowledge about music constituted one of her job-related imperfections, since it deterred her from beginning work on a book which, she felt, ought to include reference to music:

> This next book has got to draw on a lot of disciplines, some of which I know nothing about – like music. And ... er ... I'm very frightened of being ... rubbished ... you know, reviews which say, 'Well, it's clear that _____ knows nothing about music', which is true.

Yet she had formulated her remedial strategy:

> So, I have to come at music from perspectives that I *can* understand ... like, sort of, sociological-literary perspectives, really.

Remedial strategies need not reflect the individual's own, original, ideas nor represent her or his own creative input, but creativity and originality at this stage greatly influence the extent to which job fulfilment is experienced.

Stage 3

This stage involves effecting the remedial strategy, without which job fulfilment in relation to it will not occur. Returning to the example of Bernard, the physics tutor, whose remedial strategy for reducing, or removing, one of the imperfections in his job involved an overhaul of the laboratories, it becomes clear how a potentially fulfilling experience – organizing a successful revision of the laboratories – was lost to him because his strategy was not effected:

> We've been trying, for the last three years, to produce a major revision of a particular laboratory – the second-year laboratory. Staff actually agreed to this – and agreed, en masse – at a staff meeting, that each would become responsible for a specific part of that revision, and would effect the work within the year ... and nobody did – except two people ... and, of course, there's no come-back.

On the other hand, a successfully implemented remedial strategy points the individual towards the path which leads to job fulfilment. This occurred with Ken, an education tutor, who had perceived as an imperfect situation in his job his MA students' passivity in seminars. His remedial strategy of changing his teaching style was effected successfully, allowing Ken to reach an important stage in the process of experiencing job fulfilment:

> I've changed my teaching style a bit, with MA students ... I used to do a lot more straight ... 'lecturing'. I mix it up much more now, and we all try and read ... some of the course material that I provide, ahead of time, and then we discuss it. So there can be some very animated discussions and, on the whole, people have read the stuff ... but I certainly enjoy that particular course ... I very much enjoy the interaction with them.

It is important to re-emphasize, however, the taken-for-granted element in the job-fulfilment process, to which we have referred in our explanation of stage 1. The implications of this are that the formulation and the putting into effect of what we refer to as remedial action, or a remedial strategy, need not necessarily be, and often are not, anything other than what is accepted and carried out as part of the work itself. Clearly, if imperfect situations constitute the rationale, and the very need, for the work, then, by the same token, the work itself *is* the remedial action. If, for example, students' inadequate knowledge is the pervasive imperfect situation which is the underlying rationale for higher education, then the job of teaching them is, in its entirety, the remedial action strategy. Thus, every time tutors are engaged in teaching duties, they are effecting, in a taken-for-granted way, remedial action in response to a prevailing imperfect situation, and their formulation of a remedial strategy, which precedes their effecting it, is their choice of teaching methods.

Stage 4

Stage 4 is the individual's awareness of having effected remedial action. This awareness is essential to the job-fulfilment process, yet it is by no means automatic that individuals who have formulated and effected a strategy for remedying an imperfect job-related situation will be aware of having done so. Since much of this occurs in the taken-for-granted way which we have described, by tutors' simply carrying out their day-to-day work which, in itself, constitutes remedial action, it may often go unrecognized by them. As we pointed out in Chapter 4, for example, most of our tutors were unaware of the extent of their capacity for influencing students' attitudes towards and participation in their courses. We provided an example, in that chapter, of how one tutor's organization of her seminar group, which involved her asking each student in turn to speak about her or his preconceptions of the American South, encouraged the participation and, as a result, served to enhance the self-esteem of a student who reported usually being too intimidated to speak in group discussions. Yet, during our research interview with the tutor it became clear that she was unaware of the extent of her positive influence on this student. Under such circumstances job fulfilment, in relation to the remedial action in question, will not occur. One cannot experience fulfilment from something unless one is aware that it has happened.

Stage 5

This is a key stage in the process. It involves the individual's perceiving the remedial action which has been effected as a high-status, worthwhile activity. Without this perception job fulfilment, as we interpret it, will not occur. This perception is the key distinction between job fulfilment and job comfort. The extent to which a specific activity has the potential to fulfil, rather than merely to be considered satisfactory, is determined by the status and value attached to it by the individual. It is at this stage that differentiation often occurs between different components of tutors' work, and teaching and administration get left behind, although the subjectivity of the value-judgement gives rise to a diversity which is reflected in differences in individuals' sources of job fulfilment. The higher the status and value afforded by an individual to an activity, the greater will be its potential as a source of job fulfilment. Individuals will not be able to derive job fulfilment from an activity, or task, or component of their work to which they afford little value. Differentiation in relation to individuals' task-valuing was evident amongst our tutor sample:

> In *my* mind, the research is the most important aspect of a university, otherwise it becomes a museum ... you're teaching history. We've got to forge the future, and that's achieved by research. (Ted, physics tutor)

> No, I don't think research is the most important element of my work ... I think it's the teaching and research *together* ... I feel a, sort of, duty to the students. Teaching is what you have to put at the top of the list of priorities. (Christine, physics tutor)

> I think I *am* one of those people who prefers research to teaching, although I feel sad to say that ... When I came to this university I found – and, frankly, I *still* find – the students actually rather boring. I don't know *anything* about the students ... and I ... I can *tell* I'm not really interested in them because I can't remember their names ... D'you know what I mean? There's a Sophie and a Celia sitting next to each other, and I can't remember the difference between them ... And I have ... I have felt very bad about it, but I cannot remember their names. And ... er ... and so, to be honest, *I* feel these students could teach themselves. They've all got three As at A level – they're very bright ... they ... you know, with a bit of library training they could go off and read the books ... they write good essays ... and ... er ... I mean, I know that I *am* important, and I'm a good teacher, and I'm, you know ... I can see that there are ... that ... you know, in all sorts of ways, my role as a teacher is still important, but, actually, I find less satisfaction in my teaching than I ever did. And I think that's getting worse. So, yes, I think, probably, if I'm being honest, I would say that I would prefer to be quietly doing my research. (Meryl, English and American studies tutor)

> I feel actually I probably *do* put research first. (Avril, law tutor)

The reasons underlying individuals' differential, hierarchical, ranking of the values attached to the components of their work are complex. Perceptions of value may be influenced by many factors, such as professional cultural norms and attitudes, prevailing and changing trends, the views of respected colleagues, and institutional ethos and cultures. They are also influenced by individuals' experiences, which may serve to re-affirm, or to alter, preconceptions or/and long-held attitudes. Amongst our sample, for example, the higher value afforded to research than to teaching by two tutors, Maggie (education) and Ted (physics), was sustained by their experiences of having taught what they considered to be low-calibre students. Changed perceptions, however, were reported by two tutors, Avril (law) and Ivan (physics), who spoke of how they valued teaching more highly than they previously had done, or, perhaps more accurately, how they realized the full extent of the value which they afforded to teaching, during absence from teaching through sabbaticals or changes of job. Similarly, Ken, an education tutor, having reluctantly taken on a 'heavy-duty' administrative role, found it surprisingly potentially enjoyable, and the value which he afforded to the job increased accordingly.

The value accorded by individuals to specific tasks, or components of work, clearly does not remain static but is liable to fluctuate in response to changed, and changing, circumstances and situations in their lives. In this sense, the status of a particular activity or task is somewhat precarious since this relativity aspect leaves it susceptible to displacement or alteration. This is particularly likely to occur alongside individuals' professional development and career progression. The dynamism of the process of hierarchical ranking of tasks or work components is influenced by the changing perceptions and reprioritization which are an inevitable consequence of personal and professional growth and by the extent to which goals are achieved and ambitions fulfilled. Thwarted ambitions in one area may focus attention more narrowly on other areas of the work and elevate their status. Conversely, career progression may bring increased responsibilities and wider experiences, so that what was once perceived as a valued, worthwhile, activity may be relegated to the status of a routine chore. Thus, for example, sitting on a professorial board may displace the value formerly accorded to chairing the departmental research committee, and directing a research project may have the effect of reducing the perceived status of working as a research team member. Similarly, individuals' non-work lives are also influential on this dynamic process. Insights as parents may, for example, change perceptions of task values. Sikes (1997) examines the influence of parenthood on teachers in the compulsory schooling sector. So, too, may tutors not necessarily fully appreciate the value of the teaching and pastoral aspects of their work until their own children become students.

Stage 6

Stage 6 involves the individual's attributing some measure of success in remedying the imperfect situation in question to the contribution which s/he has made. Without this attribution of success job fulfilment cannot occur. It is important to emphasize that the degree of success attributed may be wide-ranging, and that job fulfilment is not necessarily dependent upon perceptions of total success. Depending upon factors such as the personal standards set by the individual – that is, the extent of her or his propensity for perfectionism – and the circumstances surrounding each case, the job-fulfilment process may be unimpeded even if only a small measure of success is recognized at this stage. In particularly challenging situations, for example, where much imperfection was acknowledged at stage 1, what is perceived as partially effective remedial action may lead to job fulfilment, particularly if the remedial action is considered to be part of a repetitive process of erosion, or as a contribution towards a larger, cohesive, team effort.

Individuals' positive evaluations of their contributions towards remedying imperfect situations may be influenced by, or based entirely upon, the views of others whom they recognize as competent assessors of their performance.

Recognition of this kind serves as an important reinforcer of positive self-assessment and several of our tutors provided specific examples of how it had played a part in their job fulfilment:

> It's illustrated in some of the evaluation comments that I've had from the final-year students ... They come in at a fairly low level but they're highly motivated. They've had a bit of general work in this area, but they're highly motivated ... You get the evaluation forms back at the end of the year, and you talk to them at the end of the year, and you get comments like, 'I've now got confidence about working with kids in this subject', 'I'm now prepared to work with kids in school' ... I feel one has not only given those students skills to deal with this area of teaching, one has also done something about changing their attitudes. That, I *do* find extremely exciting and rewarding. One feels one has made some sort of change which is consistent with one's ideals and what one is aiming for, and, therefore, it's rewarding. (Jenny, education tutor)

> Well, this term, I think, the best things have been talking to staff whom I mentor ... and, really, having a sense of being able to help them to form some sort of career plan that's given them a sense of direction and purpose. Er ... and people actually leaving the room with a sense of ... you know ... and saying, 'I know what my goals are over the next two or three years', whereas, they hadn't thought that through before, and were floundering a bit. (Ken, education tutor)

> I certainly get a lot more satisfaction from teaching women students than I do from teaching men students – I *know* that I do. And I am always really excited when I feel that I can be, in some way, a role model for my women students, and make them think about themselves in their relations to the world and get them politicized ... get them really thinking about what they can *do* in the future. So *that's* really exciting to me. So, I think, when a lecture's gone well, when a seminar's gone well, and I see them thinking, 'Yes!', or when one of them says to me, 'I think I'd like to do what *you're* doing' ... that's a good feeling. (Louise, English and American studies tutor)

> I gave one lecture which was assessed ... er ... by Avril, as a sort of dry run for the HEFCE assessment, which is a voluntary thing. We did it at a staff meeting and established ... er ... teaching circles. Colleagues ... er ... assessing other colleagues in ... er ... a constructive way, so they asked people to choose their own teaching partners, so you could choose somebody you trust, or like, so it's useful ... Well, I had intended, of course, to prepare very well for this one, but ... er ... I had been teaching a week in Poland and I came back on Sunday and I was very, very tired, so, Monday, I had to give this lecture ... So, I couldn't do it any better than I normally do, but I think it was a bit worse. Probably this was more useful than me giving this one lecture which was not representative of my normal teaching. Avril was quite happy. Er ... she is one of the HEFCE assessors herself, so that's why I picked her. I thought I may as well, and she said that the assessor would probably have rated my teaching at the top end of satisfactory. Had I used things like the OHP and some of these ... er ... teaching aids, it might have been excellent. And so I was quite pleased, I think. Er ... I'm pleased that I am at the top end of satisfactory, and if it was excellent, that would be excellent ... So, she was very constructive, and it was very useful. (Otto, law tutor)

It is, however, important to emphasize that, whilst the views of others may be influential, they are not essential to individuals' self-assessments. Consistent with the focus on individuals' subjectivity which is reflected in all stages of the job-fulfilment process outlined in our model, stage 6 represents the individual's own, subjective, positive evaluation of her or his contribution towards the remedy of what s/he perceives as an imperfect situation. Precisely how this positive evaluation is formulated is unimportant. In many cases it will reflect a consensual view, and it is likely to be strengthened if the individual knows it to be supported by others, but, essentially, it reflects the individual's view only, even if this may be generally considered to be misguided. In the job-fulfilment process, misperceptions at stage 6 are as valid as what may be considered to be more objectively accurate perceptions. The tutor who holds firm to the view that s/he has just delivered a Nobel-Prize-winning-calibre lecture remains well on track for experiencing job fulfilment even though colleagues and students consider it to have been the worst lecture they have ever sat through. Our findings revealed several examples of how tutors' self-belief was sustained in the face of contradictory or unsupportive views of others, demonstrating the significance of subjective, rather than objective, perceptions of adequacy in the job-fulfilment process:

> The background to my own promotion was that I was put forward last year, and refused ... One of the reasons that I was refused was because it was not felt that my teaching was of sufficient quality ... Er ... *that* made me quite angry, because I was employed here ... er ... specifically to teach on a course which was quite innovative ... It was a course that, frequently, every year, has at least three or four international visitors that come to watch it ... Er ... I've written about it, I've researched about it ... I've got University innovation fund money which I've spent, and developed materials on ... er ... and it was an area which, without feeling I necessarily had to put myself forward, I didn't know what was expected of me by my colleagues if I wasn't regarded as a more than adequate teacher ... The Law School was annoyed as well, at that, because ... not that I'm the *best* teacher, at all, but I think they give regard to most of us being pretty good teachers, and that I was within the realm of people whom others referred to, and I taught other colleagues to teach, so, if *I* wasn't regarded as good in that area ... then neither would anybody else. (Ben, law tutor)

> There's a lot of people that know what they're doing, that appreciate what *I* do ... so, I don't mind that. But, I'm very happy when I see something which *I'm* happy with – that's what gives *me* the best kick. (Ivan, physics tutor)

> I mean, I've tried to do my best – there'll be people here who'll think I *haven't*, and that I should've ... you know ... done lots more politics and administration earlier on ... er ... but I did do what I think was a fair share ... you know ... anything from being on Senate, to ... er ... say, running the department's research development side of things ... There are times when I've resisted it, purely – not out of lack of interest or thinking that it's not important – but, purely because, if I *hadn't* taken the decisions that I was making, then, I would not have ... got research grants in, I would not have set up projects, I would not have got books completed, and articles written ... It would not have been possible to do that. (Ken, education tutor)

Stage 7

In most cases, stage 7 is an inevitable one which occurs automatically as a result of the previous six stages having been achieved. Many of our tutors spoke of feeling a sense of achievement which clearly arose out of their considering themselves to have made an effective contribution, through an activity which they valued as being worthwhile, towards remedying an imperfect situation. Bernard, a physics tutor, provided a teaching example:

> I enjoy the *contact* type of teaching. Lab work, we're in the labs and we're walking round, talking to students ... we're sorting out their problems, we're looking at what they're involved with ... their understanding of what's going on ... all the time ... and you feel that, at the end of the day, you've achieved something – you can *see* that you've achieved something. We can also see, because we're marking their work on a regular basis, they are improving. So, that's the side of teaching which gives me *most* pleasure – the contact on a one-to-one basis. (Bernard, physics tutor)

In some cases, however, the job-fulfilment process is arrested once stage 6 has been reached, because there are circumstances which prevent the individual's feeling a sense of significant achievement, despite the awareness of having made an effective contribution in relation to a valued component of his or her job. Meryl, an English and American studies tutor, exemplified this:

> Last term I really enjoyed teaching my MA option ... it worked fine, and the students liked it ... and I questionnaired them all, and they were all very happy with it ... And, when I give a good lecture I think I enjoy seeing that that's going down well ... so, when things work well ... you know ... or when there's a good atmosphere in the class ... No ... I do get very excited, but it's ... it's, kind of, it's sort of ... frankly, it's like a good meal or an orgasm ... it's gone pretty quickly. I don't get *lasting* satisfaction from it.

One of the factors underlying individuals' failure to feel a sense of significant achievement in their work is the relativity factor (see also Evans, 1992b; Evans, 1997b) – the relative consideration which the individual affords to his/her work, or to aspects of it, alongside other, competing, priorities. In her study of morale amongst primary school teachers, one of us (Evans, 1992a) distinguishes between two teachers, Brenda and Amanda, who prioritize their job differently in relation to the rest of their lives. This relative prioritization of work is equally applicable to all jobs and professions. Meryl, our English and American studies tutor, clearly gave her work very high priority and reported being extremely conscientious and hard-working. But she also explained how it was not the main priority in her life:

> I don't get lasting satisfaction from much ... apart from my garden ... No, that's not true ... I get lasting satisfaction from lots of things, like my friendships ... my relationships with people ... and my home, and so on.

She summed up the outcome of her prioritization:

> You can see why I'm not, classically, the sort of person who's going to rise to great heights because I'm not ... I put certain kinds of limits ... there are other things that are important to me in my life.

Within the parameters of her job, Meryl was able, and sufficiently motivated, to formulate remedial action strategies for remedying imperfect situations, and to recognize when she had effected these successfully. These activities were valued by her and afforded high status in relation to other components of her work. She was, therefore, able to reach stage 6 of the job-fulfilment process, but her general, overall, relative perspective on her work precluded her, for the most part, deriving a sense of significant achievement out of all this since, in relation to other aspects of her life, her work as a whole was insufficiently significant.

In contrast, Ivan, a physics tutor, admitted to being a workaholic. His relative perspective of his work afforded it top priority in his life:

> I've never gone home at five o'clock ... I usually leave at about quarter to six ... and then come back at about quarter past eight, and then go back at about half past ten or eleven, – if I *can* – otherwise, I do go out *occasionally* ... I might go to the cinema, or play cricket ... or something like that. During the winters I come in to work at weekends, and in summer I play cricket ... If I won the pools ... it wouldn't be enough for me. I had this discussion with a friend of mine – he's a multi-millionaire, and ... er ... he offered me a job ... with a new BMW ... a smashing house ... and a yacht. And I said, 'Well, I don't actually fancy that ... 'cos, you know, why should I want a BMW, and a yacht, when, at work, I've got this £10 million-worth of equipment that I need for my research? So, you know, why should I bother with silly things like that?' So, in that sense, if I could survive ... and ... er ... if I won the pools, sort of, fifteen times over, I'd buy my *own* equipment and do my research ... Basically, if you want to know what's the motivation ... it's immortality. When I write, I want to be used in years to come. (Ivan, physics tutor)

Stage 8

Stage 8 is the final stage in the process, involving the individual's experiencing job fulfilment, as defined in Chapter 6: 'a state of mind determined by the extent of the sense of personal achievement which the individual attributes to his/her performance of those components of his/her job which s/he values'. As this definition makes clear, individuals' job fulfilment does not necessarily apply to their work in its entirety but may be specific to certain components of it, or even, within these job components, to specific activities and/or tasks. Overall job fulfilment depends upon what is effectively an unconsciously applied equation, or calculation, which balances fulfilling activities against those which are not fulfilling, at any one point of time, and which incorporates consideration of other, non-work-related, circumstances and situations, bringing in the relativity factor.

Illustrating applicability

Figure 9.2 illustrates how our model of the job-fulfilment process is applicable to the different components of tutors' work. We have chosen three examples to represent applicability: specific aspects of each of the research, teaching and administrative components of the job. These are hypothetical examples, which do not directly illustrate specific, individual cases drawn from our research but which are empirically based composites, chosen to represent different degrees of activity-related specificity. Each of the three examples of tutors' work is illustrated as a sequential representation of what we have identified as the eight stages in the job-fulfilment process. This process, as represented in Figure 9.1, is reproduced in the left-hand column of Figure 9.2. In the other three columns of Figure 9.2, each box contains an illustrative example of a manifestation of the stage in the job-fulfilment process specified in the relevant box in the left-hand column.

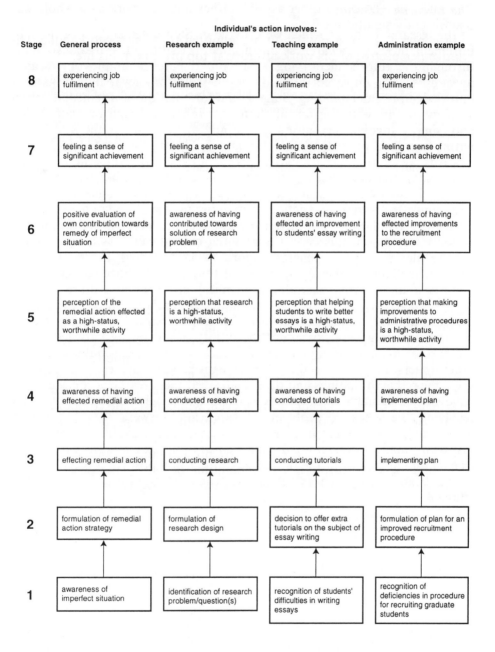

Figure 9.2 The job-fulfilment process in individuals by application to examples of tutors' work

The research example

In the research example which we provide in Figure 9.2, stage 1 of the job-fulfilment process – awareness of an imperfect situation – manifests itself through the tutor's identifying a specific research example or research question(s). The imperfect situation lies in the tutor's awareness of gaps in knowledge or understanding. Stage 2, the formulation of a remedial action strategy, occurs with the formulation of a research design or plan, which may simply involve the tutor's developing an idea about the scale, size, nature and kind of research which might yield data that would contribute towards resolving the research problem or answering the research question(s). Stage 3, effecting the remedial action which has been planned at stage 2, involves the tutor's carrying out the research. Stage 4, awareness of having effected remedial action, would, in the case of research activity, be difficult to avoid. Stage 5, which involves the tutor's perceiving the remedial action effected – in this case, the research carried out – as a high-status, worthwhile activity, is generally more likely to occur in the research component than in other components of tutors' work, since recognition of research's high status pervades academics' professional culture. Never-theless, stage 5 is by no means automatically reached, since some tutors' cynicism about the practical value of their own research, or about research in their field in general, or about the futility of advancing knowledge and increasing understanding which is ignored by policy-makers and/or practitioners, may impede the job-fulfilment process. Stage 6 is dependent upon the research findings and their analysis. If the research is considered to have yielded valuable information which makes some contribution towards resolving the research problem or supplying answers to the research question(s), this may provide the basis for the tutor's evaluation of her or his own contribution towards the remedy of the imperfect situation (recognized at stage 1 of the process) as sufficiently positive to yield a sense of significant achievement (stage 7) and, from that, to lead to job fulfilment (stage 8).

The teaching example

The teaching example which we provide is more specific than our research example. We illustrate stage 1 of the process by the tutor's recognition that her or his students are experiencing difficulties in essay writing, and stage 2, the formulation of a remedial action strategy, by the decision to incorporate into her or his course delivery extra tutorials aimed at developing students' essay-writing skills. Stage 3, effecting the remedial action, involves the tutor's conducting the tutorials, and stage 4, her or his awareness of having done so, is, in this particular example of the job-fulfilment process, clearly unavoidable. It is at stage 5 that, in the case of the teaching component of tutors' work, the job-fulfilment process is most likely to be impeded. In our example, because it is so specific, stage 5 involves more than a perception on the part of the tutor that teaching, in general, is a high-status, worthwhile activity. In order to experience job fulfilment from helping students to write better essays, s/he needs to value this specific activity. Stage 6 involves the tutor's considering him/herself to have been instrumental in bringing about an improvement to students' essay writing. As we have pointed out in our explanation of the basic job-fulfilment process, it is not essential to consider oneself to have effected widespread, or sweeping, improvements. Continuation of the process beyond stage 6 depends much upon individuals' self-imposed standards and criteria for success and upon familiarity with the activity, but many tutors will derive job fulfilment from their efforts even if only a small proportion of their student group manifests modest improvements in essay-writing skills. The key factor at stage 6 is that the tutor considers his or her own efforts to have effected sufficient improvements to give rise to a sense of significant achievement (stage 7), from which job fulfilment is experienced (stage 8).

The administration example

We have chosen what we refer to in Chapter 6 as a 'heavy-duty' administrative task to illustrate the applicability of our model to this component of tutors' work. Our example involves the tutor's recognizing, as an imperfect situation (stage 1), deficiencies in his or her department's procedure for recruiting graduate students and formulating, as a remedial action strategy (stage 2), a plan for an improved recruitment procedure. Stage 3 involves implementing the plan, of which s/he will clearly be aware (stage 4), and stage 5 requires the tutor to value the specific activity of making improvements to the department's administrative procedures. Stage 6 is dependent upon the tutor's considering his or her efforts to have yielded sufficient improvement to the department's procedure for recruiting graduate students to merit his or her feeling a sense of significant achievement (stage 7), from which s/he will derive job fulfilment (stage 8).

IMPLICATIONS FOR INSTITUTIONAL POLICY

At both institutional and departmental levels, universities may significantly influence the extent to which the job-related needs of their academic staff are met. In particular, they have the capacity to facilitate or to impede the job-fulfilment process through those of their policies and informal mechanisms which directly or indirectly relate to and impact upon tutors' working lives.

In Chapters 6 and 7 we referred to Herzberg's (1968) Motivation–Hygiene Theory of job satisfaction and, in Chapter 7, we suggested that those factors which Herzberg (1968) identifies as motivation factors – achievement, recognition (for achievement), responsibility, advancement and the work itself – may all be incorporated, as contributors or/and reinforcers, into one key motivation factor, achievement. Consistent with the definition of job fulfilment which we employ, the job-fulfilment process, as presented in the model which we have developed, involves the individual's feeling a sense of significant achievement from having made a contribution, through a valued activity, towards the remedy of a situation which is recognized as imperfect.

Universities may contribute much towards creating for their academic staff working environments which provide those factors which Herzberg (1968) categorizes as motivation factors and which we identify as contributors to or reinforcers of individuals' sense of achievement.

In Chapter 10 we suggest specific policies aimed, in part, at meeting tutors' job-related needs. Such institutional policy needs to be developed within a framework of institutional focus, culture and organization which is facilitatory to the job-fulfilment process. We suggest that such a framework needs to be underpinned by a concern for individualism.

A prerequisite of universities, taking on board a framework for policy which aims to accommodate tutors' needs is reprioritization of institutional purpose. This involves a shift from the predominantly client-focused culture which has pervaded higher education in recent years towards one which has a wider focus, incorporating not only a concern to satisfy the demands of external accountability and to meet clients' needs, but also recognition of a responsibility towards employees. Such a wider view of institutional purpose extends the parameters of service provision. It goes beyond the self-interest reflected in a concern for the institutional gains which may be accrued by cultivating a contented workforce. It is essentially altruistic in so far as it accepts the notion that one of the purposes of an institution or organization is to serve employees' needs and to promote their welfare, as far as this is possible without serious detriment to the fulfilment of other organizational purposes.

The policy framework itself, reflecting the concern for individualism which, we suggest, is a key constituent of job-related needs fulfilment, should prompt the development of, and support, a new institutional culture. This new culture should be one which values and accommodates the diversity which emanates from individualism. It should give rise to revised administrative procedures which, rather than promote and reward conformity and uniformity, celebrate and capitalize on individual differences which are congruent with institutional aims and which fall within the parameters of the institution's conception of its purpose and function.

A key feature of this administrative framework is staff development. Measures which have tended merely to support rhetoric, and procedures to which there may have been a tendency to pay only lip service, such as appraisal and mentoring systems, promotion policies and staff training programmes, need to become effective vehicles for enabling the individual to develop, personally and professionally, in the way which is most appropriate for meeting his or her needs. Universities need to embrace a wider view of staff development, accepting it as an important channel of communication about their respective needs, between the institution and the tutor, and as the most effective mechanism for realizing individual potential. The job-fulfilment process, as we have illustrated throughout this chapter, involves activities which include: the pursuit of individual interests; meeting challenges; achieving success; experimentation; innovation; evaluation; reappraisal of needs; receiving recognition; and developing awareness. In the next chapter we make suggestions for policy which aims to provide some of these features of the job-fulfilment process, but, if it is to be really effective in meeting needs, such policy needs to be developed within a framework which is based upon individualism.

Part IV

Policy Implications

Chapter 10

Compromising Policy

INTRODUCTION

Throughout this book we have presented our research findings in a way which is intended to develop a picture of teaching and learning, in its widest sense, in one university, but as reflected by two perspectives: that of students and that of tutors. The purpose of this final chapter is to consolidate these two perspectives into a composite image; to identify specific flaws in this image, by highlighting deficiencies which have been identified through our findings or which have emerged as a result of our applying wider perspectives and considerations to our analysis of the situation; and to discuss remedial policy. The chapter is a combination of prescription and analysis. It seeks to fulfil the main aim of the research upon which this book is based, which is to examine student and tutor perceptions of effectiveness in relation to teaching and learning, and to identify policy which represents a compromise in so far as it is aimed at meeting both parties' needs. In trying to incorporate this, the chapter highlights the elusiveness of compromising policy which is sufficiently well-founded to be effective, enduring and transformational.

A framework for quality in higher education has been suggested by Harvey and Green (1993, cited in Rowley, 1996b, p. 238). This framework incorporates five conceptions of quality: the *exceptional* view, which considers quality to be something special; quality as *perfection*, which perceives quality as a consistent or flawless outcome; quality as *fitness for purpose*, which views quality from the perspective of fulfilling a customer's requirements, needs or desires; quality as *value for money*, which perceives quality in terms of return on investment; and quality as *transformation*. To this list we add another conception: *quality as effectiveness through compromise*, which focuses on quality in terms of meeting all parties' needs, not just those of customers or clients. Elton (1993, p. 135) suggests that the first stage in any scheme for quality control involves 'agreement on the needs that have to be satisfied', and that 'Agreement on needs should come out of a negotiated accommodation between the needs of all the relevant "customers" and of the professionals who provide the service.' Following Elton's suggestion, then, this chapter represents an initial discussion which contributes towards developing a basis for quality control in teaching and learning in higher education. It synthesizes the evidence presented in the rest of the book about the needs of 'relevant customers and of the professionals who provide the service' and makes suggestions which might represent negotiated accommodation of those needs. It examines ways in which quality as effectiveness through compromise might be achieved.

The chapter first identifies both what needs improving in teaching and learning in higher education, as reflected in the case of the university upon which our study focused, and what needs retaining, in relation to tutors' job-related needs and students' study-related needs. From this, it moves on to consideration of what constitutes effective teaching in higher education and, in order to address this issue, consideration of the aims of higher education. Alongside this, suggestions for policy which aims to effect a compromise are examined.

UNIVERSITY TEACHING AND LEARNING: A CONTEXTUALIZED PICTURE

The picture presented by our university is generally positive, in relation to students' and tutors' perspectives of the extent to which their needs were being met. For the most part, we did not find evidence of low morale or significant dissatisfaction with their jobs amongst the academics in our sample. Certainly, there were some tutors who identified specific sources of dissatisfaction and, as we reveal in Chapter 7, these were typically administrative loads or, in the cases of two physics tutors, the repercussions of the higher-education expansion policy, the increase in external interference in the ways in which universities are run and the gradual proletarianization of the profession. Dissatisfied tutors did, however, represent a minority and, generally, dissatisfaction was outweighed, sometimes quite considerably, by satisfaction. McCann's (1996) suggestion that 'there are many dispirited academics in today's universities' was not borne out by our findings, though we accept fully that the wider picture, beyond the case of a single university, may be very much different.

Students, too, reported few sources of significant dissatisfaction and, collectively, presented a picture of a largely satisfied clientèle, corroborating the findings of a 1993 interview survey of 2,000 final-year undergraduates at forty-nine universities (Meikle, 1994). The needs which our students identified were generally much more short-term and narrowly focused than those of their tutors, and they were, for the most part, evidently being met.

There are, of course, several issues which may be drawn from this rather simplistic outline of the general picture of teaching and learning in our university. Some of these have been examined in previous chapters. One issue relates to students' satisfaction with their higher education and concerns the capacity of those who are in the process of a prolonged learning experience, to evaluate it. This issue underlies arguments against setting too much store by student course feedback. Similarly, it underlies the point made by Barrett (1996, p. 204) that it is unwise to treat higher-education students as customers, since they represent

> people who are acknowledged to lack discernment enough to understand what is a college, as distinct from a shop or a brothel, and whose understanding of the range, depth and subtlety of human needs is so limited, that they think their needs – *all* their needs – are satisfied when the service is pleasant at the burger-shop or the dry cleaner's.

Although Barrett's (1996) arguments fail to incorporate recognition of the distinction between satisfaction in the sense of its application to customers (that is, what is satisfactory or unsatisfactory to them) and satisfaction in the sense of fulfilment (that is, what is satisfying, rather than satisfactory), nevertheless, if the point which he makes about their lack of discernment is a valid one, then, as such, it is equally applicable to both positive and negative student evaluations. What this leads on to is recognition that, if acceptance of students' limited capacity for discernment and, hence, of their limited capabilities as evaluators underlies responses which afford limited value to these evaluations, then a complacent, or even self-satisfied, response to broadly positive evaluations is inappropriate. In short, if we can justify paying only lip service in reacting to students' complaints, on the grounds that we consider that they do not really know what is best for them, then, by the same token, we cannot give ourselves a pat on the back and resolve to effect only cosmetic enhancements to the status quo on the basis of high levels of student satisfaction.

In a similar way, the issue of who is best qualified to evaluate a situation may be applied to examination of the broadly positive picture of teaching and learning created by our tutors' perspective. We have already referred, in Chapter 6, to the likely influence on our tutors' work and work-related attitudes of a strong institutional culture. This influence may extend to being confirmatory and play its part in a cyclical verificatory process which perpetuates a situation by providing reciprocal validation of ideologies, norms and expectations. Thus, the tutors broadly comply with the institution's aims and cultural focus and their tacit acceptance, or even assimilation, of them strengthens and adds credence to the institutional focus and sets in motion a chain reaction of self-confidence, self-assurance and self-approval. Tutors' job-related needs, therefore, not only are, in part, determined by and relate to their institution but they are also, in part, met by it. The issue in question incorporates consideration of whether or not the broadly positive picture which emerges from this somewhat cloistered environment of reciprocal approval and self-approbation is myopically selective.

On the other hand, whilst this issue is pertinent to consideration of the appropriateness of prevailing situations which determine individuals' needs, there can be no doubt that the more immediate consideration of the precise nature of those needs, and of the extent to which they are being met, at least in the short term, lies within the capacity of those whose needs they are.

Consideration of these issues leads us to incorporate two strands into the analyses which follow: one which is based upon the perspectives of our tutors and students, as reflected in our research data, and one which extends to a more far-reaching focus on issues relating to the fundamental purpose and nature of higher education, and to the wider context and implications of our research findings.

KEY ISSUES AND POLICY IMPLICATIONS

The key issues arising out of our research findings reflect the needs of students, or tutors, or both. These issues are: group sizes, student–tutor interaction, presentation of course-related information to students, the link between teaching and research, and tutors' roles and responsibilities. In addition, there are several related key issues which feature prominently in the current debate about the future of higher education: innovative teaching approaches, tutor-independent learning and the status of teaching. We have combined all of these issues into three categories: course delivery, tutors' roles and the status of teaching in higher education. We examine each, in turn, below.

Course delivery

As we illustrated in Chapter 5, our findings revealed course-related information to be the fundamental study-related need amongst our students. More specifically, students reported a need for *clear* information. Lecture presentations involving garbled explanations which were incoherent, were pitched at too high a level, were rushed or which deviated from the main point with resulting obfuscation were identified as sources of dissatisfaction and impediments to this need being met. Student–tutor exchanges were also considered an important means of clarifying information, through discussion or questioning. One-to-one exchanges with tutors, either in individual tutorials or, as was more often the case, in small-group sessions, were generally considered by students to be the most potentially valuable learning opportunity. Group size was therefore seen as an important determinant of the extent to which the fundamental need for clear, course-related information was met. Most students evidently regarded their tutors as very knowledgeable, and their capacity to engage in confirmatory or challenging dialogue rendered them incomparable as sources of information.

Tutors tended to be much more dismissive of their significance and usefulness in this capacity. Their consensual view was that, for the most part, students could gain as much from exchanges with each other as they could from exchanges with them. A minority of tutors commented upon the constraints imposed by group sizes, but these were constraints on the types of activities which they would like to incorporate into their course delivery, which included student–student, as well as tutor–student interaction. Tutors' recognition of their own dispensability also prompted them to regret what most perceived to be students' overdependence on them, and to favour more facilitatory, rather than directive, roles as teachers, and more tutor-independent learning. Moreover, an important consideration is that, whilst, as we have shown in Chapter 7, tutors identified teaching as a source of job fulfilment, most of them would ideally like to have lighter teaching loads, and increased loads would be a significant source of dissatisfaction.

In relation to course delivery, then, policy which would meet students' and tutors' needs more effectively would create more opportunities for student–tutor interaction whilst reducing tutors' workloads and, ideally, promote more tutor-independent approaches to study. In the context of the expansion of higher education, which is not matched by increased funding, simplistic solutions, such as employing more tutors to share the workload and to reduce tutor–student teaching ratios, are entirely out of the question. By 2009 the average student–staff ratio is predicted to be thirty to one (Association of University Teachers, 1995, p. 15). The problem which is universally recognized within higher education is summed up by Smith and Brown (1995, p. 14):

> Many university lecturers are finding that they are under pressure to teach more and more students with no more resources, just at a time when they are expected to produce graduates with a range of skills and abilities attractive to employers: simultaneously lecturers are urged to adopt new, creative and student-centred teaching approaches.

Fewer students, fewer hours

A policy which emerged from analysis of our research findings, and one which offers much potential as a compromise response to the student–tutor interaction issue, is that of smaller groups which meet less frequently or for shorter periods, resulting in students receiving fewer hours' contact time. This was first suggested by a law student interviewee, in response to inquiries about the acceptability of increased group sizes, which might allow tutors to double-up groups and team-teach courses with colleagues, in order to free up time. Our interviewee's response was that any increase of group sizes would be likely to be detrimental to the quality of learning since it would inhibit discussion and restrict levels of participation. Much more preferable, the interviewee suggested, would be fortnightly, instead of weekly, seminars. We included reference to this suggestion in all subsequent interviews with students and found the consensual view to be one of approval for the basic idea of *fewer students, fewer hours* as an alternative to larger groups. Indeed, this seems a more viable solution from the tutors' perspective than a policy of doubling up groups, which could only be applied effectively to generalist courses. The law, English and American studies and physics tutors tended to teach mainly specialist courses, drawing on individuals' expertise and research interests which were seldom shared by colleagues. Moreover, it represents a response to reductions in funding and increases in student–staff ratios which is much more acceptable to academics than one alternative

152 *Teaching and Learning in Higher Education*

which has been predicted (Meikle, 1996) of twelve-hour teaching days, weekend lectures and summer courses.

There are, of course, several variations of the fewer students, fewer hours policy, and their appropriateness will be determined by course requirements. One variation, which we refer to as *intensification of teaching*, was, in the light of our research findings, applied by one of us to her own teaching on the third-year education component of the BA(QTS) degree at Warwick University during the 1995–96 academic year (see Utley, 1997d). Very large seminar groups of twenty-seven, which had previously been taught as one group for weekly two-hour sessions, were divided into three sub-groups which each met for forty minutes during the two-hour slot. Teaching during this forty-minute session was intense, focused and incorporating diverse activities, such as smaller sub-group work, whole-group discussions, student presentations, games and debates. Supplementing the intensified teaching sessions were activities, usually based on texts or videos, which students undertook in their groups, independently of the tutor. These tutor-independent activities were planned to last for approximately an hour and, to ensure that they were not neglected or regarded as superfluous time-fillers, they were always followed up at the beginning of the next seminar. It was emphasized to students that these were as important a constituent of the course as the activities undertaken during contact time.

This intensified approach did not free up time for the tutor, but it could be modified to do so. In this instance it was experimental. It was intended to test the workability, and acceptability with students, of the fewer students, fewer hours policy. It proved to be extremely successful. Student evaluation was almost entirely positive. End-of-course questionnaire responses included:

> Good to have smaller numbers as it makes it easier to discuss and gave me more confidence to speak out.

> Very good idea – helps you feel more relaxed and able to contribute.

> Good idea to have small groups for forty minutes each – very intense forty minutes – useful.

> Good. It's much better having smaller groups for forty minutes instead of a big group for two hours. Less intimidating and less boring.

> Very good. Using small groups allowed everyone to speak and to work together rather than using the whole class.

The only reservation, reflected by the comments of a minority of students, was that forty minutes was a little short, and that a full hour would have been preferable since it would have provided scope for longer discussion. This is a valid point, but, with a full group as large as twenty-seven, the alternative would still have involved sub-groups of up to fourteen, which several of the students in our research sample considered to be too large and to inhibit participation.

From the tutor's perspective, too, the intensification of teaching experiment at Warwick yielded several benefits. A better rapport between students and tutor resulted from the opportunities for more widely distributed one-to-one exchanges, from the tutor's ensuring that she spoke to every single student individually at least once in every session, and from the greater ease with which students' names were learnt. Planning and preparation time was reduced since the repetition of shorter sessions required less content to be delivered. Moreover, the repetitive feature of this teaching approach allowed for spontaneous modifications to content and delivery, in the light of the first group's responses, and, since the three sub-groups rotated the times of their meetings each week, it was not always the same group which was advantaged or disadvantaged by this opportunity.

Creative lecturing

The fewer students, fewer hours policy evidently has much to recommend it as a contribution towards meeting students' learning needs, not only by facilitating and encouraging their greater participation but for the positive effects which this will have on developing oral communication skills, building confidence and enhancing self-esteem. It has the potential for allowing students to receive more individual attention from their tutors at no additional cost, in terms of time, to the tutors. Indeed, it may incorporate a reduction of expenditure of time. Yet it involves more than simply an organizational strategy which aims to make effective use of time: its greatest benefit is that, at its best, it offers a more personalized approach to teaching and learning in higher education.

Fewer students, fewer hours does not, however, have the potential for meeting all of students' perceived main study-related needs. In addition to the need for the verification-oriented information which interaction and exchanges with tutors provided, students also expressed the need for pertinent, course-related information from sources which they recognized as expert. Our findings revealed that, whilst such information was available to students in various formats, their preferred way of receiving it was through well-delivered lectures.

Much prescriptive writing on teaching methods in higher education dismisses lectures as ineffective. Tutors are urged to undertake more participatory and innovative methods of teaching, on the grounds that lectures do not work. Our findings do not support this over-simplistic premise. As we illustrated in Chapters 3 and 4, students did indeed report examples of lectures which did not work, but there were also many references to effective lectures, and it was perhaps their experiences of these which underlay our students' general approval of lecturing as a useful and efficient mode of imparting valuable information. Whilst our study was not intended to examine the depth of student learning that occurs as a result of the teaching which they receive, our findings reveal, categorically, that lectures *can* and, indeed, that many of them *do* work to the extent of engaging students' attention and conveying relevant information.

Since lecturing clearly represents a teaching method which is extremely cost-effective in terms of tutors' time, it has much potential as a feature of compromising policy. The key to realizing this potential lies in making lecturing consistently acceptable to students. We suggest that this may be achieved by developing the notion, and promoting the practice, of *creative lecturing*.

We have adapted the term *creative lecturing* from that of *creative teaching*, introduced by Woods, as a result of his research which focused on primary school teachers (Woods, 1990; Woods, 1995). Creative teaching is not a widely recognized term in primary education, nor is it clearly defined, but Woods's interpretation of it seems to be that it is teaching which incorporates the teacher's own individual input and which represents her or his own strategic response to a situation which is, in some way, problematic. Creative teaching has the teacher's own, personal 'stamp' on it; it is a customized response which reflects his or her creative application of pedagogical knowledge and understanding and experientially acquired skills to a contextualized problem such as: why does this child fail to grasp this concept? or, how may that child be better motivated to work? It involves the teacher's thinking through, trying out, and evaluating a responsive teaching approach, rather than simply effecting a textbook response. It represents fairly widespread practice amongst primary school teachers, despite its being a largely unrecognized term.

Interpreting the term slightly differently from Woods's (1990, pp. 28–53) apparent interpretation of it, one of us has developed an undergraduate education course on creative teaching in the primary school, and recognizes her own practice during an earlier career in primary education as an example of a creative approach to teaching (Evans, 1991; Evans, 1992c). Evans's interpretation incorporates a wider view, embracing teaching which is simply more imaginative, with the intention of being more stimulating, than lacklustre, run-of-the-mill teaching. Fundamentally, however, this interpretation does not differ from that of Woods since it, too, recognizes creative teaching as remedial, in the sense of being a response to an unsatisfactory situation; namely, that, without creative teaching, not all primary school children will be motivated to learn.

In the same way, creative lecturing, as we interpret it, represents a response to an unsatisfactory situation, which is, specifically, that lecturing is not consistently effective in 'reaching' all students. Our research findings have revealed the basic key features of effective lecturing, as perceived by students, to be: structure, coherence, explication, relevance and clarity. Throughout this book we have provided illustrative examples of the various individual ways in which tutors have, either by their own accounts or by those of their students, added their own personal 'stamp' to their lecture presentations in order to render them effective. Sometimes this individuality was particularly prominent in relation to one or two of the key features identified above; sometimes it permeated the entire delivery. In either case, it constitutes injection into the lecture of the tutor's creativity. Often this creativity resulted in a particularly spectacular, imaginative, entertaining, innovative or otherwise memorable presentation which exceeded the incorporation of the five basic key characteristics of effectiveness. Yet creative lecturing, as we interpret it, need not necessarily be so excessive: it simply requires tutors to be creative in their planning and delivery of a lecture which, at the very least, incorporates the key features identified. Without necessarily being spectacular, if lecturing were to be more consistently treated as if it were a performance and perceived by tutors as both a challenge and a creative act, it would become consistently more effective and hence consistently more acceptable to students. Developing creative lecturing is, therefore, the second compromising policy which we suggest in relation to course delivery.

Innovative teaching methods

The increasing emphasis on teaching quality, which has developed out of the more general concern for quality assurance in higher education, has tended to follow the path of advocating more innovative teaching. Drawing out parallels between the post-Plowden progressive movement which took hold of the primary education sector in the late 1960s (and which has recently been under attack) and the current focus on teaching in higher education, McNamara (1997) comments:

> At the very time when educationists and political commentators line up to condemn progressive teaching methods in primary schools, those self-same methods are being actively encouraged in our universities to foster student learning ... There is a developing realisation in universities that students cannot be treated as the passive recipients of conventional bodies of knowledge taught by traditional methods; that there is considerable variation and difference among student learners; that greater use must be made of individual and distance learning methods; that learning resources, including especially those based upon information technology, must be organised within coherent teaching and learning strategies so as to support individual learners. These are all developments which echo the language and rhetoric of progressive primary education.

Anyone within the higher education academic community will be acutely aware of the push towards innovative teaching and the increasing pressure for experimentation in relation to course design, delivery and assessment. Yet we wish to emphasize that the two teaching approaches which we suggest above are not intended as a compliant response to this pressure; they are, quite simply, in keeping with the purpose and the remit of this book and of the study which it reports, suggestions for features of a course delivery policy which is intended to meet the needs of both students and tutors. Any innovative qualities which may be considered attributable to them are incidental.

Indeed, in relation to teaching, we do not support the notion of innovation for its own sake. It is essential that the innovative teaching movement presents a clear rationale for what it is advocating, supported by evidence, where appropriate. McNamara (1997) comments on the seeming irrationality of one sector of education being encouraged to adopt a form of pedagogy which is being discouraged, if not discredited, in another sector:

> Why, at a time when primary schools are being pushed into traditional teaching methods, are we encouraging university students to take responsibility for their own learning and pursue projects – now a suspect activity in the primary lexicon – arising from their interests? Why, when formal systematic testing under controlled conditions is permeating primary education, are universities questioning the traditional unseen

examination and innovating with forms of coursework and other assessment methods
which test genuine understanding and application?

Yet it is not its contrasting position with another sector of education which
requires higher education to provide a rationale for its veering towards
innovation. Even if both sectors were following parallel paths in relation to
pedagogy, each still ought to provide its rationale for doing so, not in relation to
each other but in relation to its own aims. Wall (1997) reinforces this point in
relation to the increasing promotion of autonomous learning, arguing that such
a policy should be based on a sound pedagogical rationale, rather than merely
representing economic expediency. Too often, innovation, as a general, or even a
generic, term, is equated with quality in higher-education teaching without
adequate specificity in relation to the nature of the innovation and without
adequate examination and analysis of the aims of higher education. Ramsden
(1992, pp. 2–3), for example, in a section covering less than one-and-a-half
pages, presents such an underdeveloped 'rationale for learning to teach better':

> Let us be clear about one fact: the quality of undergraduate education needs to
> improve, and it has needed to improve for a long time. No golden age of impeccable
> instruction and taken-for-granted high academic standards ever existed, except in the
> world of academic mythology. Appraisal or no appraisal, large classes or small, it is
> useless to deny that, although there is much that is and has been excellent in higher
> education teaching, there is a great deal that has always been frankly bad. And there is
> little in the world of education that is more depressing than bad university teaching ...
> it is a tragic waste of knowledge, experience, youth, time and ability. There need never
> be any excuse for it: every teacher can learn how to do better. Anyone who has seen
> really good teaching in action will not need to invoke the exigencies of performance
> appraisal and maintaining academic standards as reasons for improvement. I think
> they will begin to understand the truth of the proposition that good teaching, though
> never easy, always strenuous, and sometimes painful, is nevertheless its own reward.

Barnett (1997a), on the other hand, recognizes the need for the development
of higher education, as it moves towards the next century, to be guided by a
set of clear aims. He evidently shares our concern that, without a coherent
framework and direction, innovation seems to lack purpose and is being
encouraged for its own sake:

> there is an incoherence of underlying philosophy, which remains tacit: what educational
> aims ought to be at work? Should higher education be a vehicle for enabling the student
> to acquire the wherewithal to cope effectively with the challenges of the external
> environment, especially of the economy and work; or should it be a means of enabling
> the student to become a quasi-academic in which her mind is developed through a
> conversational initiation into one or two disciplines; or should it be a means of enabling
> the student to realise herself in some personal sense ...? (pp. 14–15)

He points out that 'an insufficient degree of educational thought is being
given to the new developments and ideas' (p. 35), and spells out the potential
dangers of incoherent, aimless, development:

> Rather than teaching being informed by a deep understanding of and insight into
> educational aims, it is liable to be reduced to strategic and operational responses to
> external manoeuvrings and gameplans. New teaching methods could easily be taken on,

dressed in the garb of educational justification but which lack a deep and firm educational purpose. (p. 17)

Our research did not address the issue of teaching and learning as a vehicle for advancing towards the fulfilment of specific aims of higher education. Its focus was more narrowly confined to the more immediate, pragmatic, concern of individuals' perceived needs and of identifying possible ways of meeting them. Within these confines, the rationale underlying the fewer students, fewer hours and the creative lecturing policies which we suggest is simply that our empirical evidence presented them as likely compromises for meeting the perceived needs of two parties. Our research evidence does not provide a rationale for promoting teaching approaches whose innovative features render them sufficiently exciting, or experimental, or noteworthy, to parallel some of the most extreme examples of progressive teaching in primary schools. The rationale for progressive primary school teaching methods is that they constitute an improvement on conventional methods by motivating young children better and by facilitating differentiation of teaching. It is questionable whether such factors are applicable to a higher-education context, though this questionability rests, in part, on assumptions about where lies the onus of responsibility for university students' learning, and about the role of university teachers. These issues are discussed more fully in the next section. Certainly, our research evidence reveals students to be generally no more impressed or motivated by exceptionally innovative teaching than by what they considered to be high-quality teaching which exemplifies our suggested policies. Indeed, we found examples of their being decidedly unimpressed by attempts at innovative teaching which failed to incorporate the features of student-approved lecturing identified above.

Yet, whilst the rationale for the compromising policy which we suggest is adequate for the purpose of our study, we acknowledge the confines of this purpose, which may be considered myopic alongside the need to develop a framework for higher education as it moves into the twenty-first century. We are also aware that these narrow confines result in reducing our suggested compromising policy ideas for course delivery to the status of what Barnett (1997a, p. 17) describes as 'strategic and operational responses to external manoeuvrings and gameplans'.

Changing students' perceptions

An alternative, or perhaps supplementary, compromising policy to what we have suggested, which is both more future-oriented and radical, is that of trying to change students' perceived needs. This would involve a process of re-educating students, in order to change their perceptions of higher education and of their and others' roles and responsibilities within it, and thus modifying their perceptions of their needs. The intensification of teaching example, above, of the fewer students, fewer hours policy incorporates this. To some extent this is a policy which is already familiar to proponents of more tutor-independent learning, who recognize that, for course design and delivery to incorporate this feature with any measure of success, students' attitudes towards it need to be positive. It is also widely accepted that, since students enter higher education with preconceptions about the value of the kind of didactic teaching approaches which they will typically have encountered throughout their schooling, dissemination of the value of alternative approaches needs to extend beyond the undergraduate student body to reach schoolteachers, pupils and, arguably, the wider public. However, in order to reap the full long-term potential benefits of changing students' perceptions and expectations of, and hence their needs in relation to, higher education, the process needs to be undertaken alongside the formulation of an agreed set of aims of higher education, and it needs to reflect these aims. Essentially, if students are to be educated, or re-educated, about what constitutes quality in higher-education teaching, then the notion of quality which is being promoted with them should be determined by a notion of the purpose of higher education which, in turn, stems from, and reflects, the aims of higher education. As Barnett (1997a) points out, this dimension has so far been lacking in the formulation of policy and, without it, all that can be hoped to be achieved are stop-gap measures and responsive strategies. A clear aim, or set of aims, for higher education will determine the purpose of higher-education institutions, which will inform decisions about course content and delivery, incorporating consideration of issues such as whether universities should simply be providers of information which students are responsible for taking on board and assimilating as knowledge, skills and understanding, or whether they ought to share responsibility for their students' learning. This would determine the university's role in the learning process: whether, for example, it should simply involve imparting, or whether it should include motivation and differentiation; and this perceived role would, in turn, be reflected in teaching methods. Changing students' perceptions of their study-related needs involves reaching consensus about these issues and disseminating more widely the consensual view, the stance which results from it, and the rationale underlying it.

This section has incorporated our research evidence and analysis of wider issues into suggestions for course delivery policy which is acceptable to the two main parties involved: students and tutors. We presented two broad suggestions. The first suggestion was course delivery which effected compromise by aiming to give both students and tutors something of what they considered themselves to need. The second suggestion was course delivery which, rather than being fashioned on students' and tutors' overlapping needs, effectively aimed to meet the wider society's needs, as reflected by the aims and purpose of higher education, and which would be made acceptable to students by changing their perceptions of their needs. There is clearly the potential, in this second suggestion, for bias in favour of the emerging policy reflecting more of tutors', than of students', fulfilment of perceived needs, since tutors will be influential and instrumental in the process, outlined above, of formulating aims, defining purpose and roles and identifying policy. Our third suggestion, therefore, is that of changing tutors' perceptions of their needs. Whilst consideration of this is pertinent to course delivery issues, its wider implications merit its incorporation into the next section's examination of how tutors' roles may better accommodate their job-related needs.

Tutors' roles

As we illustrated with our model in Chapter 9, our tutors' job-fulfilment needs were related to their feeling a sense of achievement through making a contribution towards the improvement of specific situations. A sense of personal achievement could be experienced in various job-related contexts and roles, including research, teaching, collegiality, management and administration. Impediments to the fulfilment of job-related needs were those elements of tutors' jobs which they resented having to undertake, either because they did not conform with tutors' perceptions of what their job ought to involve or because, by undertaking them, tutors had insufficient time left for carrying out, to their satisfaction, the tasks which they valued and which created opportunities for job fulfilment. Policy which is aimed at meeting tutors' needs would therefore incorporate provision for reducing or removing the impedimentary tasks and increasing opportunities for undertaking tasks which have the potential to fulfil.

Task–talents matching

The most frequently identified impedimentary tasks were low-level administrative ones, and, amongst those tutors who held them, what we refer to as 'heavy-duty' administrative responsibilities sometimes constituted an even greater impediment. The most obvious remedial policy would be to re-allocate such tasks to those whose qualifications, interests and expertise, and, in some cases, general job descriptions render them better matched to the task requirements. We refer to this as *task–talents matching*. It may be applied as widely or as narrowly as contextual circumstances allow. Extra clerical, or ancillary, staff could be employed to take on the routine and low-level administrative and preparatory tasks for which academics typically consider themselves overqualified, and the recruitment of more academic-related administrative staff could free tutors of the onerous higher-level administrative tasks for which many of them consider themselves ill-suited. In theory, provided it were sufficiently well thought-out and well executed, this would be financially viable, since the costs incurred by employing additional staff would be recouped through the readjustment of tutors' responsibilities made possible as a result of the policy. Bearing in mind that administrative tasks are generally accepted as constituting one-third of their responsibilities, if tutors were to lose a significant proportion of these, they could then be expected to undertake extra teaching duties and/or research activities, both of which have financial gain implications for the institution which would offset the expenditure on extra staff.

Other forms of task–talents matching include, through course design and allocation of teaching duties, maximizing opportunities for tutors to link their teaching with their research interests and for specialist teaching, which reflects individuals' expertise, rather than generalist teaching, which is more demanding and less fulfilling.

An alternative form of the task–talents matching policy which, on the one hand, runs counter to that of strengthening the link between teaching and research, but which, on the other hand, represents an extreme degree of specialism is the segregation of academic staff into two task-related categories: researchers and teachers. We refer to this as *mono-functionism*. This is not a new idea in higher education, although in its literal, extreme form it is not widely operated, since academics' employment contracts generally require them to undertake research and/or scholarship as well as teaching. Where it does occur, it is more likely to involve teaching only, rather than research only, and this is more likely to feature in new, rather than old, universities. A diluted version of mono-functionism has, however, long been a status-related feature of old universities, reflected by differentials of task focus and responsibility between junior and senior academics, typified by the eminent professor's total annual teaching load of half a dozen one-hour lectures and the junior lecturer's three hundred hours' teaching contact time. It is now being seriously considered, in its extreme form, as a strategic expediency measure for maximizing universities' potential to take on board, to their best overall advantage, the conflicting demands imposed by the higher-education expansion policy, quality assurance mechanisms, and the research selectivity exercise. Setting the ball rolling, the mathematics department at Warwick University recently announced an initiative to make a teaching-only appointment (Meikle, 1997). Similarly, Oxford University is reported to have veered away from the traditional policy of having academics undertake research, teaching and administration:

> Whereas most Oxford staff used to combine these activities, cash cuts meant one third were now employed for research alone and another third, who were members of colleges but held no university post, concentrated entirely on teaching. (Swain, 1997)

It is difficult to predict how successful a policy of mono-functionism might be, not only as a strategy for coping with the demands of the various forms of externally imposed accountability but as a compromise policy for meeting tutors' different needs and, indirectly, the needs of students. Our research evidence strongly suggests that, in its extreme, literal form, it would not be welcome since it would take from tutors one of their sources of job satisfaction and would sever the link between research and teaching which most of our tutor interviewees, and many of our student interviewees, considered so important. The overwhelming majority of our tutor sample said that they would not want to undertake a research-only role. Our findings did suggest, however, that, amongst research-focused and research-active tutors, a diluted form of the policy, making research the predominant constituent of the job, and reducing the teaching component, would be welcome, particularly if the teaching were to reflect research interests and specialisms. Those of our tutors who reported close proximity to their 'ideal', in job terms had jobs which incorporated such a task distribution, and others felt that such a distribution would take them closer to their 'ideal' job. Owing to what we consider to be the effects of institutional culture, as we pointed out in Chapter 6, our sample of tutors did not include any who categorized themselves as teaching-focused, with little, or no, interest in research, so our research evidence provides no indication of how welcome mono-functionism would be in such quarters. However, it is reasonable to assume that, amongst those who consider themselves to be, first and foremost, teachers rather than researchers, teaching-only roles would be welcome.

The notion of a job redefinement policy which veers towards mono-functionism has been heavily criticized by detractors who object to what they perceive as the exploitation of those who would be employed on teaching-only contracts. Such a policy would, it is argued, heighten status differentials and offer unequal opportunities, since, in old universities at least, research activity far outweighs teaching competence as a basis for promotion. Yet, the introduction of such a policy in individual universities could be accompanied by a promotion policy which recognizes and rewards teaching competence, allowing parallel career progression paths which follow either a teaching or a research route. Even without such an accompanying promotion policy, it is difficult to argue that there is an ethical problem with teaching-only posts, even if these do offer fewer and inferior promotion prospects, so long as appointees are made fully aware of these conditions from the outset and take up their appointments with their eyes open.

A mono-functionist policy clearly does not represent a straightforward means of satisfying individuals' different job-related needs. It carries with it potential problems, some of which are outlined above. Yet it should not be discounted without careful consideration. It does have much to recommend it, not least of which is its potential for enhancing the quality of academics' working lives, by increasing job satisfaction. It offers opportunities for individuals to come closer to achieving their ideal job situations, by undertaking more of those elements of their work which they enjoy and which fulfil them, and by reducing the amount of unfulfilling or unsatisfactory work. We are aware that this is a simplistic and somewhat optimistic interpretation of the impact of the policy, since it fails to acknowledge that individuals' conceptions of their ideal job are unlikely to remain static, but will be likely to change continually and thus become recurringly elusive, or that conceptions of the ideal job may be limited and distorted by a narrow range of experiences. Nevertheless, there is more potential for providing and increasing job fulfilment in a policy which allows those who love teaching to teach, and those who enjoy research to research, than in one which requires people to undertake tasks which they do not particularly enjoy, but which others would gladly take on. Moreover, as Elton (1996b, p. 138) points out, 'the efficiency increases that could be obtained through maximising the effectiveness of all by matching their tasks to individual abilities and interests within institutional plans must be considerable'. Clearly, there is a lot to be said for a certain amount of task redistribution on the basis of individuals' personal preferences, talents and qualifications. Indeed, just as there is a distinction amongst hospital doctors between physicians and surgeons, and amongst secondary school teachers between those who follow the pastoral and those who follow the subject career paths, so, too, could there be a sharper distinction between university academic-related staff who hold teaching, or research, or administrative roles. There already exists a distinction between academic and academic-related staff in universities, which is not status-related but role-related. Building on the existing typical staffing model, and extending Elton's (1995, p. 46) recommendation for 'not a level playing field, but two separate playing fields, one for those who strive for research excellence and one for those who strive for teaching excellence', it is possible to envisage a modified version, incorporating more categories of what would be called academic-related staff, enjoying parity of status and including, for example, administrators, librarians, computer professionals, teachers, researchers, teacher-researchers and researcher-teachers.

Changing tutors' perceptions

An alternative approach to implementing a policy which is directed towards meeting tutors' perceived job-related needs is, as we suggested for students, to change tutors' perceptions of their needs by changing their attitudes to their work. Our findings revealed several specific examples of attitudes which, whether or not they are justifiable, seem destined to sustain dissatisfaction since they are clearly at odds with prevailing trends and policy for the future development of higher education. The derisory attitude of one of the physics tutors in our sample towards what he perceived to be the general inadequacies of, and low standards achieved by, a lower-calibre student body is one such example. However understandable it may be, this attitude represents a futile expression of disapproval of the higher-education expansion policy. It represents 'a concern at the breakdown of elite homogeneity and cultural transmission' which, King (1992, p. 40) suggests, represents the fear that 'more inevitably means worse'. Yet railing against what he perceives as the dilution of excellence and the consequent diminution of his job fulfilment is an ineffective coping strategy for this tutor. Much more effective would be his acceptance that his role as a university teacher needs to be redefined. This would effectively replace his perception of his own need for higher-quality students with one of his need for professional development.

At a general level, though, as we have suggested in relation to changing students' perceptions, policy which aims to effect a redefinition of tutors' teaching roles, which is accepted and assimilated by tutors and which alters their perceptions of their job-related needs accordingly, ought to be underpinned by an explicit rationale which is informed by agreed aims and objectives of higher education. It needs to be decided what are the main purposes of universities, as agencies for fulfilling higher education's aims, how these purposes translate into policy on teaching and learning, and how tutors, in their teaching roles, may contribute towards putting the policy into practice. Radical, rather than cosmetic, change will be achieved only by this process and, in the UK, where the recent reforms of higher education and the quality-assurance mechanisms have been implemented without reference to clearly articulated aims, as Barnett (1997a) points out, this is an appropriate time for a rethink and a redefinition of what higher education is about and how it is to operate. Writing in 1992, Elton reviewed the progress of higher education in the UK in relation to Kurt Lewin's conception of systemic change. Elton describes the 1992 situation as higher education's being 'balanced on a knife edge' between Lewin's first stage of 'unfreezing' and his second stage of 'developing new beliefs, attitudes, values and behaviour patterns on the basis of new information obtained and cognitive redefinition' (Elton, 1992, pp. 3–4). Six years later, higher education seems only slightly further advanced towards this second stage of attitudinal change. The Dearing Report's (NCIHE, 1997) presentation of a twenty-year vision of higher education's place and role in an evolving learning society will provide yet another policy change framework, but, unless attitudes change in accordance, the knife-edge position to which Elton refers may be retained for much longer than it ought to be.

A policy of pluralism

We do not, however, necessarily consider it essential to achieve national consensus in relation to aims of higher education, purposes of universities, teaching and learning policies and tutors' roles. Here, once again, the primary school, or indeed any school parallel may be applied. Whilst fulfilling certain national requirements, schools formulate their own individual set of aims and objectives in relation to the educational experiences and opportunities which they provide, and these reflect the school's educational philosophy and ideologies, values, vision and contextual considerations. For the most part, curriculum organization, teaching styles and learning activities reflect the school's aims and objectives and the school sets itself up as a community whose purpose is to fulfil these aims and objectives. By this process it develops its own institutional culture and ethos and, alongside these, its own reputation. In primary schools in particular, there is scope for a wide range of ideologically and pedagogically determined orientations which differentiate schools according to their positions on the 'traditional–progressive' continuum. In theory, this allows parents greater choice, though, in reality, for various reasons which are not pertinent to the issues being examined in this chapter, most parents choose their child's primary school on the basis of proximity to home. Another advantage – though more a potential than an actual advantage – of this individuality is that teachers may select the schools where they work with a view to ideological compatibility, thus increasing the likelihood of their job-fulfilment, through their job-related needs being met. Similarly, schools may recruit new members of staff with the same considerations of compatibility and, in doing so, increase the likelihood of perpetuating their individual institutional culture and ethos.

There does not appear to be any reason why universities should not operate on the same basis, defining their own institutional aims and purpose and developing out of this a strong, institutional culture, on the basis of which they 'sell' themselves, through their well-defined image, perhaps even targeting a specific clientèle. Students, as clients, unlike primary schools' parental clientèle, are generally both willing and able to exercise choice in this way, and, as Scott (1997) suggests, universities should not have to conform to uniform criteria for excellence; rather, 'excellence should be defined according to universities' stated purpose and mission'. Of course, to a large extent, this product-offering and consumer-choice mechanism has long existed in higher education in the UK, where, unlike what occurs in many European countries, most students select universities not on the basis of geographical location but on the basis of institutional or departmental academic reputation and standing, or specific course content. Yet, within this, the assumption has prevailed that, for the most part, in relation to teaching styles and foci of course delivery, there is little to distinguish one university from another.

What *could* develop, however, is much greater institutional individualism, incorporating many more facets of universities' functions and moving towards Barnett's (1997b) suggestion that, in a mass system of higher education, the title 'university' can mean all kinds of things. Without diminishing the part it would play in developing a learning society, such individualism could enrich the higher-education sector as a whole by injecting into it a pluralism which facilitates individual, radical experimentation and development and which, in its entirety, offers, as a result, a more comprehensive system to accommodate a greater diversity of needs of a more expansive clientèle. The advantages of this developmental approach are recognized by Hague (1996):

> Radical innovation cannot be managed from the centre. Experimentation is needed and that means pluralism. Perhaps 10 – even 20 – universities should be encouraged to experiment to discover how to run the university of the 21st century. They should set objectives for genuinely innovative teaching and research by drawing on research in cognitive science and by using emerging technologies.

However, whilst Hague's implication is that pluralistic experimentation should constitute an initial, pioneering stage of development in higher education, we suggest that pluralism has many benefits as a more enduring feature of the system, and as a means of coping with the greater diversity imposed upon it by its expansion, by potentially offering something for everyone. On a small scale, this is beginning to occur in the United States, where several universities' promotion of themselves as teaching, rather than research, institutions has prompted what may develop into a bifurcated system (see, for example, Fram and Lau, 1996).

Universities could set out their stalls through the various publicity media which they employ for recruitment purposes, making it explicit what they stand for, how they see themselves and what this, in turn, means that they offer to students. Into this would be incorporated clear definition of tutors' roles, predominant methods of teaching and learning, and the rationale for them, and explicit reference to what, in turn, will be expected of students. Thus, even more so than is now the case, what tutors do at work would depend upon *where* they work. Where, for example, universities see their purpose as being, in part, to encourage and facilitate students' learning, motivational roles may be assimilated into tutors' conceptions of what their jobs involve and their teaching methods may be modified accordingly. Similarly, in universities which see their purpose as playing a part in developing students into independent thinkers, capable of proactive, rather than reactive, formulation of ideas, tutors' teaching roles and the methods which they employ would be modified accordingly. In this way, purpose would inform policy about teaching roles and methods.

The problem facing higher education, though, is that the process whereby aims inform decisions about purpose, which inform decisions about teaching and learning, which inform decisions about tutors' roles, is in danger of breaking down and of not being taken on board seriously, because teaching has traditionally had such a low status, in comparison to research, in the higher-education sector. The final, brief section examines how the status of teaching in higher education may be raised.

The status of teaching in higher education

The recently instigated debate on the status of teaching in higher education (Fender, 1997) reflects something of the concern surrounding this issue. Above all, the low status typically afforded teaching by academics is seen to be the greatest impediment to developing and raising its quality. There can be no doubt that teaching's low status compared with research is perpetuated by its failure to be recognized as a basis for job promotion, in old universities at least. Yet the problem is more fundamental than this: it lies with the conception of teaching, shared by many academics, that it is less of an intellectual pursuit, and therefore of less value, than research. It is to this conception of teaching that McLean and Blackwell (1997, p. 95) seem to be referring:

> many academic teachers . . . want to challenge the traditionally low status of teaching . . . The solution lies in making teaching professional. This is done, in part, by providing programmes of training and development which engage and convince academics enough to persuade them to change their habits of thought about teaching.

A specific training programme which they describe is, they suggest, successful because of 'its congruence with academic values. That is, it resonates with the way academics set about their business in the sphere of their disciplines: they pursue critical enquiry.'

An intellectual approach to teaching

No matter how much recognition of its value is afforded to teaching in higher education, by means of initiatives such as internal awards for teaching excellence, mentoring schemes, appraisal systems, external assessment of teaching quality, or promotion opportunities, it will always be under threat of being devalued by a core of academics who will consider it a second-class academic pursuit unless it becomes as intellectually challenging as high-quality research. This devaluation threatens to undermine the effectiveness of any pluralistic system of higher education by perpetuating the notion of a 'hierarchy of institutions with "first division" research institutes at its pinnacle and "third division" teaching colleges at its base' (Garnett and Holmes, 1995, p. 50). The key to effecting intellectual parity between teaching and research lies in identifying precisely what features and constituents of research activity afford it intellectual credibility, and applying these to teaching.

As we illustrated in Chapter 7, our findings show that it is their personal contribution to the resolution of an intellectual problem which is the fundamental source of personal fulfilment that academics derive from research activity. Yet, there has been and there remains, typically, little encouragement for university tutors to apply intellectual problem-solving to the process of teaching. Teaching has typically been uncomplicated and unchallenging. Moreover, staff development programmes or individual courses which aim to promote more effective or innovative teaching seldom pose real intellectual challenges. Too often they focus upon presenting practical suggestions and exchanging ideas; whilst this may be a successful means of disseminating new developments, by presenting ready-made solutions to typical teaching problems or, at best, by stimulating discussion out of which emerge practical ideas and remedial strategies, they generally make only a limited contribution towards enhancing the status of teaching.

In all sectors of education, teachers derive job fulfilment by injecting their own creativity into, and by applying their own analytical and intellectual skills to, the teaching process. The advent of the National Curriculum in the compulsory schooling sector was greeted with much concern by teachers primarily because it was perceived as a potential threat to this source of job fulfilment, though, in actual fact, since it stipulates curriculum content not methods of delivery, teachers' capacity to make their own creative contributions to children's learning remained relatively intact. Similarly, the potential for teaching in higher education to develop into a valued, intellectually challenging activity lies in allowing university teachers to seek their own solutions to the organizational and pedagogical problems posed by the post-expansion system, rather than to have solutions handed to them on a plate (see Smith and Brown, 1995, p. 188). Indeed, this view is supported by the findings of a study of seven Australian university tutors (Zuber-Skerritt, 1991, p. 338):

> the best way to learn about university teaching is *not* to be given information and advice (about how to improve teaching) by outside experts who determine what academics need to know. Rather, their theory of professional development is that academics can and should try to learn about teaching in the same way as they learn about their discipline, or particular subject areas, that is, as personal scientists ... and problem solvers, through active involvement, practical experience, and critical reflection about the experience ... An important condition is that these developmental activities must be personally initiated, self-directed, and consciously controlled by the university teachers themselves.

Staff development policy, therefore, needs to incorporate an added dimension. It needs to focus much more on the rationale, rather than ideas, for innovative teaching methods. It needs to allow tutors the opportunity for exploring and experimenting with ways of delivering courses which meet the specified aims and objectives of higher education and which are congruent with the purposes of universities. By this process there will be built up a reliable body of knowledge about how students learn, how understanding of this impacts upon tutors' roles and how the needs of both students and tutors may be better met.

References

Abbott, I. (1997) 'Why do we have to do Key Skills?' Student views about General National Vocational Qualifications, *Vocational Education and Training*, **49**(4), 617–30.

Ainley, P. (1994) *Degrees of Difference: Higher Education in the 1990s*. London: Lawrence and Wishart.

Alderman, G. (1996) Audit, assessment and academic autonomy, *Higher Education Quarterly*, **50**(3), 178–92.

Ashcroft, K. and Foreman-Peck, L. (1994) *Managing Teaching and Learning in Further and Higher Education*. London: Falmer Press.

Association of University Teachers (1995) *Higher Education Preparing for the 21st Century*. London: Association of University Teachers.

Bailey, A. (1993) Empowering students for life-long learning: Proceedings of syndicate group D, in L. Harvey (ed.), *Defining and Assessing Quality in Higher Education*. Birmingham: University of Central England.

Barnett, R. (1997a) *Towards a Higher Education for a New Century*. London: London Institute of Education.

Barnett, R. (1997b) Still breathing ... Are universities on their deathbeds?, *Times Higher Education Supplement*, 30 April, p. 10.

Barrett, R. (1996) 'Quality' and the abolition of standards: arguments against some American prescriptions for the improvement of higher education, *Quality in Higher Education*, **2**(3), 201–10.

Becher, T. (1989) *Academic Tribes and Territories*. Milton Keynes: Open University Press.

Biggs, J. B. and Telfer, R. (1987) *The Process of Learning*. Sydney: Prentice Hall.

Bligh, D. A. (1972) *What's the Use of Lectures?* Harmondsworth: Penguin.

Carvel, J. (1997) Cash 'threat' to universities, *Guardian*, 19 July, p. 4.

Chalmers, D. and Fuller, R. (1996) *Teaching and Learning at University*. London: Kogan Page.

Court, S. (1996) The use of time by academic and related staff, *Higher Education Quarterly*, **50**(4), 237–60.

Crace, J. (1993) Strain of the numbers game, *Guardian Education*, 16 November, p. 6.

Dixit, M. (1985) Effect of teaching experience on the level of job-satisfaction among secondary school teachers, *Perspectives in Psychological Researches*, **8**(1), 43–6.

Drew, S. and Bingham, R. (1997) *Student Skills*. Aldershot: Gower Publishing.

Elton, L. (1992) Quality enhancement and academic professionalism, *The New Academic*, spring, 3–5.

Elton, L. (1993) University teaching: a professional model for quality, in R. Ellis (ed.), *Quality Assurance for University Teaching*. Buckingham: The Society for Research into Higher Education & Open University Press.

Elton, L. (1995) Effect of funding council policies on teaching quality, in B. Smith and S. Brown (eds), *Research, Teaching and Learning in Higher Education*. London: Kogan Page.

Elton, L. (1996a) Strategies to enhance student motivation: a conceptual analysis, *Studies in Higher Education*, **21**(1), 57–68.

Elton, L. (1996b) Task differentiation in universities: towards a new collegiality, *Tertiary Education and Management*, **2**(2), 138–45.

Entwistle, N. (1995) The use of research on student learning in quality assessment, in G. Gibbs (ed.), *Improving Student Learning through Assessment and Evaluation*. Oxford: The Oxford Centre for Staff Development.

Evans, L. (1991) Teaching the National Curriculum in Narnia, *Education 3–13*, **9**(3), 50–5.

Evans, L. (1992a) Teacher morale: an individual perspective, *Educational Studies*, **18**(2), 161–71.

Evans, L. (1992b) *Teachers' Morale and Satisfaction: The Importance of School-specific Factors*, paper presented at the Annual Conference of the British Educational Research Association.

Evans, L. (1992c) Robbing Peter to pay Paul: teaching subtraction through role play, *Education 3–13*, **20**(1), 48–53.

Evans, L. (1997a) Addressing problems of conceptualisation and construct validity in researching teachers' job satisfaction, *Educational Research*, **39**(3), 319–31.

Evans, L. (1997b) Understanding teacher morale and job satisfaction, *Teaching and Teacher Education*, **13**(8), 831–45.

Evans, L. (1997c) A voice crying in the wilderness? The problems and constraints facing 'extended' professionals in the English primary education sector, *Teachers and Teaching: Theory and Practice*, **3**(1), 61–83.

Evans, L. (1997d) Managing to motivate: some pointers for primary headteachers, *Primary School Manager*, July/Aug., 16–18.

Evans, L. (1998) Getting the best out of teachers: morale, motivation and job satisfaction in the primary school, *Education 3–13*, **26**(1), 26–30.

Farrugia, C. (1986) Career-choice and sources of occupational satisfaction and frustration among teachers in Malta, *Comparative Education*, **22**(3), 221–31.

Fender, B. (1997) Eyes on the prize, *Guardian Higher Education*, 8 April, i.

Fram, E. H. and Lau, G. H. (1996) Research universities versus teaching universities – public perceptions and preferences, *Quality Assurance in Education*, **4**(2), 27–33.

Further Education Development Agency (1997) *GNVQs 1993–97: A National Survey Report*. London: FEDA.

Garnett, D. and Holmes, R. (1995) Research, teaching and learning: a symbiotic relationship, in B. Smith and S. Brown (eds), *Research, Teaching and Learning in Higher Education*. London: Kogan Page.

Gibbs, G. (1992a) *Lecturing to More Students*. Oxford: Oxford Centre for Staff Development.

Gibbs, G. (1992b) *Improving the Quality of Student Learning*. Bristol: Technical and Education Services.

Gibbs, G. (1995a) Research into student learning, in B. Smith and S. Brown (eds), *Research, Teaching and Learning in Higher Education*. London: Kogan Page.

Gibbs, G. (ed.) (1995b) *Improving Student Learning through Assessment and Evaluation*. Oxford: The Oxford Centre for Staff Development.

Gibbs, G. and Habeshaw, T. (1989) *Preparing to Teach*. Bristol: Technical and Educational Services.

Gibbs, G. and Harland, J. (1987) Approaches to teaching in colleges of higher education, *British Educational Research Journal*, **13**(2), 159–73.

Gibbs, G. and Jenkins, A. (eds) (1992) *Teaching Large Classes in Higher Education*. London: Kogan Page.

Griffin, A. (1997) Knowledge under attack: consumption, diversity and the need for values, in R. Barnett and A. Griffin (eds), *The End of Knowledge in Higher Education*. London: Cassell.

Guba, E. G. (1958) Morale and satisfaction: a study in past/future time perspective, *Administrative Science Quarterly*, **3**, 195–209.

Guion, R. M. (1958) Industrial morale: the problem of terminology, *Personnel Psychology*, **11**, 59–64.

Halpin, A. W. (1966) *Theory and Research in Administration*. New York: Macmillan.

Halsey, A. H. (1979) *Higher Education in Britain: A Study of University and Polytechnic Teachers* (final report to SSRC).

Halsey, A. H. (1995) *Decline of Donnish Dominion*. Oxford: Clarendon Press.

Halsey, A. H. and Trow, M. (1971) *The British Academics*. London: Faber and Faber.

Harvey, L. (1996) Editorial, *Quality in Higher Education*, **2**(3), 177–84.

Hague, D. (1996) From spires to wires, *Guardian Education*, 14 February, 2–3.

Herzberg, F. (1968) *Work and the Nature of Man*. London: Staples Press.

Higher Education Statistics Agency (1997) *HESA/USR Student Records*. Cheltenham: Higher Education Statistics Agency.

Hoyle, E. (1975) Professionality, professionalism and control in teaching, in V. Houghton *et al.* (eds), *Management in Education: The Management of Organisations and Individuals*. London: Ward Lock Educational.

Janes, D. (1997) Life of a lecturer beggars belief, *Guardian Higher Education*, 14 January, p. v.

Johnson, N. (1994) Dons in decline, *Twentieth Century British History*, **5**, 370–85.

Kalleberg, A. L. (1977) Work values and job rewards: a theory of job satisfaction, *American Sociological Review*, **42**, 124–43.

Katzell, R. A. (1964) Personal values, job satisfaction, and job behavior, in H. Borrow (ed.), *Man in a World at Work*. Boston: Houghton Mifflin.

King, R. (1992) The funding of teaching quality: a market approach, *Higher Education Quarterly*, **46**(1), 39–46.

Lawler, E. E. (1973) *Motivation in Work Organizations*. Monterey, CA: Brooks/Cole.

Locke, E. (1969) What is job satisfaction?, *Organizational Behavior and Human Performance*, **4**, 308–36.

Lortie, D. (1975) *Schoolteacher: A Sociological Study*. Chicago: University of Chicago Press.

Lowther, M. A., Gill, S. M. and Coppard, L. C. (1985) Age and the determinants of teacher job satisfaction, *Gerontologist*, **25**(5), 520–5.

Marsh, H. W. and Roche, L. (1993) The use of students' evaluations and an individually structured intervention to enhance university teaching effectiveness, *American Educational Research Journal*, **30**, 217–51.

Maslow, A. H. (1954) *Motivation and Personality*. New York: Harper and Row.

McCann, G. (1996) The view from here, *Independent Education*, 31 October, p. 3.

McLean, M. and Blackwell, R. (1997) Opportunity knocks? Professionalism and excellence in university teaching, *Teachers and Teaching: Theory and Practice*, **3**(1), 85–99.

McNamara, D. (1997) Plowden's message is alive and well – in the universities, *Times Educational Supplement*, 23 March, p. 25.

Meikle, J. (1994) All in the mind, *Guardian Education*, 15 February, p. 2.

Meikle, J. (1996) Spot the lecturer, *Guardian Higher Education*, 19 November, p. i.

Meikle, J. (1997) Bridging the gap, *Guardian Higher Education*, 22 April, p. i.

Meyer, J. H. F. and Scrivener, K. (1995) A framework for evaluating and improving the quality of student learning, in G. Gibbs (ed.), *Improving Student Learning through Assessment and Evaluation*. Oxford: The Oxford Centre for Staff Development.

National Committee of Inquiry into Higher Education (1997) *Higher Education in the Learning Society* (Dearing Report). London: HMSO.

Nias, J. (1981) Teacher satisfaction and dissatisfaction: Herzberg's 'Two Factor' hypothesis revisited, *British Journal of Sociology of Education*, **2**(3), 235–46.

Nias, J. (1989) *Primary Teachers Talking: A Study of Teaching as Work*. London: Routledge.

O'Neil, M. (1995) Towards a model of the learner in higher education: some implications for teachers, in B. Smith and S. Brown (eds), *Research, Teaching and Learning in Higher Education*. London: Kogan Page.

Oshagbemi, T. (1996) Job satisfaction of UK academics, *Educational Management and Administration*, **24**(4), 389–400.

Packwood, A. and Sinclair-Taylor, A. (1995) Learning styles and student progress, in G. Gibbs (ed.), *Improving Student Learning through Assessment and Evaluation*. Oxford: The Oxford Centre for Staff Development.

Parry, G. (1997) Patterns of participation in higher education in England: a statistical summary and commentary, *Higher Education Quarterly*, **51**(1), 6–28.

Pennington, G. (1994) Developing learning agents, in P. Nightingale and M. O'Neil (eds), *Achieving Quality Learning in Higher Education*. London: Kogan Page.

Raaheim, K., Wankowski, J. and Radford, J. (1991) *Helping Students to Learn*. Buckingham: Open University Press.

Ramsden, P. (1991) A performance indicator of teaching quality in higher education: the Course Experience Questionnaire, *Studies in Higher Education*, **16**, 129–50.

Ramsden, P. (1992) *Learning to Teach in Higher Education*. London: Routledge.

Ramsden, P. and Entwistle, N. J. (1981) Effects of academic departments on students' approaches to studying, *British Journal of Educational Psychology*, **51**, 368–83.

Redefer, F. L. (1959a) Factors that affect teacher morale, *The Nation's Schools*, **63**(2), 59–62.

Redefer, F. L. (1959b) Toward a theory of educational administration, *School and Society*, **28** (March), 19–37.

Robbins, Lord (1963) *Higher Education: Report of the Committee*. London: HMSO Cmnd 2154.

Rosen, R. A. M. and Rosen, R. A. A. (1955) A suggested modification in job satisfaction surveys, *Personnel Psychology*, **8**, 303–14.

Rothblatt, S. (1996) Inner life of don-dom, *Times Higher Education Supplement*, 22 March, p. 18.

Rowley, J. (1996a) Motivation and academic staff in higher education, *Quality Assurance in Education*, **4**(3), 11–16

Rowley, J. (1996b) Measuring quality in higher education, *Quality in Higher Education*, **2**(3), 237–55.

Saljo, R. (1984) Learning from reading, in F. Marton, D. Hounsell and N. J. Entwistle (eds), *The Experience of Learning*. Edinburgh: Scottish Academic Press.

Schaffer, R. H. (1953) Job satisfaction as related to need satisfaction in work, *Psychological Monographs: General and Applied*, **67**(14), 1–29.

Scott, M. (1997) The straitjacket of forced uniformity, *Times Higher Education Supplement*, 7 February, p. 14.

Sergiovanni, T. J. (1968) New evidence on teacher morale: a proposal for staff differentiation, *North Central Association Quarterly*, **42** (winter), 259–66.

Sikes, P. (1997) *Parents Who Teach*. London: Cassell.

Smith, B. and Brown, S. (eds) (1995) *Research, Teaching and Learning in Higher Education*. London: Kogan Page.

Smith, K. R. (1966) A proposed model for the investigation of teacher morale, *Journal of Educational Administration*, **14**(1), 87–93.

Smith, K. R. (1976) Morale: a refinement of Stogdill's model, *Journal of Educational Administration*, **14**(1), 87–93.

Stagner, R. (1958) Motivational aspects of industrial morale, *Personnel Psychology*, **11**, 64–70.

Swain, H. (1997) Oxford colleges' powers set to slip, *Times Higher Education Supplement*, 21 March, p. 4.

Tait, H., Speth, C. and Entwistle, N. (1995) Identifying and advising students with deficient study skills and strategies, in G. Gibbs (ed.), *Improving Student Learning through Assessment and Evaluation*. Oxford: The Oxford Centre for Staff Development.

Thomson, A. (1997) Research value in doubt, *Times Higher Education Supplement*, 4 April, p. 52.

Trow, M. (1997) More trouble than it's worth, *Times Higher Education Supplement*, 24 October, p. 26.

Utley, A. (1997a) Lecturers set for status boost, *Times Higher Education Supplement*, 28 February, p. 44.

Utley, A. (1997b) Sages on stage loath to change, *Times Higher Education Supplement*, 24 October, p. 8.

Utley, A. (1997c) Forty-four ideas to spread, *Times Higher Education Supplement*, 28 February, p. 6.

Utley, A. (1997d) Seminars checked on size, *Times Higher Education Supplement*, 28 March, p. 5.

Vancouver, J. B. and Schmitt, N. W. (1991) An exploratory examination of person–organisation fit: organizational goal congruence, *Personnel Psychology*, **44**(2), 333–52.

Wall, G. (1997) Teach yourself autonomy does not work, *Times Higher Education Supplement*, 31 January, p. 12.

Wankowski, J. (1991) On the vagaries of students' motivations and attitudes to teaching and learning, in K. Raaheim, J. Wankowski and J. Radford, *Helping Students to Learn*. Buckingham: The Society for Research into Higher Education.

Williams, G. (1986) *Improving School Morale*. Sheffield: Sheffield City Polytechnic/PAVIC Publications.

Williams, K. W. and Lane, T. J. (1975) Construct validation of a staff morale questionnaire, *Journal of Educational Administration*, **13**(2), 90–7.

Woods, P. (1990) *Teacher Skills and Strategies*. London: Falmer Press.

Woods, P. (1995) *Creative Teachers in Primary Schools*. Buckingham: Open University Press.

Young, I. P. and Davis, B. (1983) The applicability of Herzberg's Dual Factor Theory(ies) for public school superintendents, *Journal of Research and Development in Education*, **16**(4), 59–66.

Zuber-Skerritt, O. (1991) Eliciting personal constructs of research, teaching, and/or professional development, *Qualitative Studies in Education*, **4**(4), 333–40.

Appendix

Copy of letter sent to law students, requesting participation as research interviewees

17 January 1994

[Student's name]
Second Year Student
School of Law
_____ University

Dear _____

We are researchers and lecturers from Warwick University carrying out research on the effectiveness of the teaching methods used on four of the undergraduate courses at _____ University. One of those courses is the LLB, and we are anxious to solicit the views of several second year law students on how effective their course is in meeting their individual needs.

Your name has been selected at random from the list of registered students, and we would be very grateful if you would give approximately an hour of your time to participate in an individual research interview. We will guarantee complete confidentiality.

We are happy to conduct the interview at a place and time which is convenient to you. If you like, this could be over coffee and biscuits in the _____ and, if you do not have transport, we will arrange to pick you up from and run you back to Campus. Alternatively, we could visit you in your own home/room.

We hope that you will consider it worthwhile contributing to our research. The results will be used by the School of Law to assist them in planning courses and teaching.

It would be most helpful if you would indicate your willingness to participate as a research interviewee by completing the attached pro-forma. We also enclose a reply envelope. This may be left in a designated collection box situated in the Law Departmental Office (room _____).

If you prefer, you can send your reply directly to either of us in the _____ Department, where we have been allocated temporary rooms, via the University's internal mailing system, or you may ring us.

If there is anything you wish to discuss before agreeing to participate, please do not hesitate to ring us on one of the numbers listed below:

Ian Abbott   –   tel. _____
Linda Evans   –   tel. _____

We would like to thank you, in anticipation of your co-operation.

Yours sincerely

Linda Evans & Ian Abbott
Lecturers in Education, University of Warwick

Letter to law students: attached pro-forma

**Research on teaching effectiveness
at _____ University.**

☐   I am willing to participate as a research interviewee

☐   I do not wish to participate in your research

Name: _____

**IF YOU HAVE INDICATED A WILLINGNESS TO PARTICIPATE,
PLEASE COMPLETE THE SECTION BELOW**

Telephone No: _____

I am available for interview at the following times:

	Week 8		Week 9		Week 10	
	date	time	date	time	date	time
1st choice						
2nd choice						
3rd choice						

Where would you like to be interviewed?

_____

Please return this form to: Linda Evans/Ian Abbott

Department of _____

Name Index

Subject Index

Numbers in bold refer to tables; those in italics indicate figures.

A levels   15, 108
abolition of tenure   11
academic community   8
academic culture   81, 82
academic staff
  impact of reforms on work   13–15
  segregation into researchers and
    teachers   160–1
academic-related staff   162
accountability   7, 10, 14, 15, 17, 112
active-learning   16
administration   8, 83, 115, 159
  administrative staff   159, 162
  applicability of job-fulfilment process
    model   141
  changed perception of   133
  competing pressures   115
  complaints about constraints of   106–7,
    148
  fulfilment from   100, 102–3
  funding   159
  'heavy-duty'   85–6, 102, 103, 106, 133,
    141, 159
  and research   130
  satisfaction in   91, 102
  teaching-related   85
aims of higher education   40
analytical skills   32, 41, 46
appraisal systems   142, 165
Association of University Teachers
  (AUT)   14, 89

bought-in staff   23, **23**, 83, 84, 115, 116

central control   10, 11, 14
changing as a person   71
Colleges of Advanced Technology, granting
  of university status   9
collegiality   8, 11, 104, 159
competition   11, 14, 120
compromising policy   147–67

course delivery   150–8
  changing students' perceptions   157–8
  creative lecturing   153–5
  fewer students, fewer hours   151–3, 157
  innovative teaching methods
    155–7
  key issues and policy implications
    150–67
  status of teaching in higher
    education   165–7
  tutors' roles   159–67
    changing tutors' perceptions
    162–3
    policy of pluralism   163–5
    task–talents matching   159–62
  university teaching and learning   148–50
computer professionals   162
conditions of service   14, 89
Conservative government   9, 81
consultancy   83
contracts   8, 160
  teaching-only   161
coping strategies   36, 162
cost-effectiveness   121, 125, 153
Council of National Academic Awards
  (CNAA)   11
course delivery   150–8
  changing students' perceptions
    157–8
  creative lecturing   153–5
  fewer students, fewer hours   151–3
  innovative teaching methods   155–7
  see also lectures; one-to-one interaction;
    seminar groups; small-group teaching
course handbooks   77
course materials   77, 131
course requirements, need to fulfil   *69, 75, 76*
course teams   77
coursework
  assessment   33, 61, 62, 65, 70
  written feedback   44
curriculum   163

tutors – *continued*
children of   134
delivery style   59
dissatisfaction   106–7, 108, 148, 151, 162
education   84, 105, 108, 112, 121, 131
engaging students' interest   58–60
English and American studies   84–5, 108,
121, 131, 151
enthusiasm   58–9
goals   70, 71, 73
group management   55–8
ideal job   96, 97, 105, 109, 112, 160
interview schedule   26–7
job satisfaction, *see* job satisfaction
job-related needs   96, 97, 114, 127, 149,
158, 159, 162
knowledgeable   45
law   85, 108, 121, 130, 151
needs of   77
personalities   55, 56
physics   85, 108, 131, 151
probationary period   86, 98
professional development and
training   77
recognition   100–1, 109
recruitment   77
responsibility   109, 141
self-assessment   134, 135
seniority   86
sense of achievement   136–7, 138, 140,
141, 142, 159
students' perceptions of good tutors   45
tutor sample   22–3
what job involves   82–6
tutors' roles
changing tutors' perceptions   162–3
policy of pluralism   163–5

task–talents matching   159–62
tutors as teachers   114–26
autonomy   118
availability to students   115–18
implications for meeting tutors'
needs   125–6
innovation in teaching   123–5
maintaining standards   118–20
open-door policy   117
and promotions   117–18
teaching approaches   120–3
Two-Factor Theory (Herzberg), *see*
Motivation–Hygiene Theory
typologies   27, 89, 90

universities
autonomy   9, 11, 111
choice of   163–4
excellence   164
management   117
metropolitan   9
new   9, 11, 12, 82, 83, 119
old   11, 12, 13, 83, 160, 161, 165
Oxbridge   9, 45, 82
research rating   11–12, 13
Royal Charters   9, 111
senates   11
universities/polytechnics binary divide   7,
11
University of Hertfordshire   82
university managers   15

value for money   7, 14, 43, 147
vocational courses   9, 21

Warwick University   152, 160
working conditions   93, 94, 103, 105